DATABASES FOR SMALL BUSINESS

ESSENTIALS OF DATABASE MANAGEMENT, DATA ANALYSIS, AND STAFF TRAINING FOR ENTREPRENEURS AND PROFESSIONALS

Anna Manning

Apress®

Databases for Small Business: Essentials of Database Management, Data Analysis, and Staff Training for Entrepreneurs and Professionals

ISBN-13 (pbk): 978-1-4842-0278-4

ISBN-13 (electronic): 978-1-4842-0277-7

Managing Director: Welmoed Spahr
Acquisitions Editor: Robert Hutchinson
Developmental Editor: Douglas Pundick
Technical Reviewer: Richard Roiger
Editorial Board: Steve Anglin, Louise Corrigan, James DeWolf, Jonathan Gennick,
    Robert Hutchinson, Celestin Suresh John, Michelle Lowman, James Markham,
    Susan McDermott, Matthew Moodie, Jeffrey Pepper, Douglas Pundick, Ben Renow-Clarke,
    Gwenan Spearing
Coordinating Editor: Rita Fernando
Copy Editor: Kezia Endsley
Compositor: SPi Global
Indexer: SPi Global

Distributed to the book trade worldwide by Springer Science+Business Media New York, 233 Spring Street, 6th Floor, New York, NY 10013. Phone 1-800-SPRINGER, fax (201) 348-4505, e-mail orders-ny@springer-sbm.com, or visit www.springer.com. Apress Media, LLC is a California LLC and the sole member (owner) is Springer Science + Business Media Finance Inc (SSBM Finance Inc). SSBM Finance Inc is a **Delaware** corporation.

For information on translations, please e-mail rights@apress.com, or visit www.apress.com.

Apress and friends of ED books may be purchased in bulk for academic, corporate, or promotional use. eBook versions and licenses are also available for most titles. For more information, reference our Special Bulk Sales–eBook Licensing web page at www.apress.com/bulk-sales.

Any source code or other supplementary materials referenced by the author in this text is available to readers at www.apress.com. For detailed information about how to locate your book's source code, go to www.apress.com/source-code/.

Apress Business: The Unbiased Source of Business Information

Apress business books provide essential information and practical advice, each written for practitioners by recognized experts. Busy managers and professionals in all areas of the business world—and at all levels of technical sophistication—look to our books for the actionable ideas and tools they need to solve problems, update and enhance their professional skills, make their work lives easier, and capitalize on opportunity.

Whatever the topic on the business spectrum—entrepreneurship, finance, sales, marketing, management, regulation, information technology, among others—Apress has been praised for providing the objective information and unbiased advice you need to excel in your daily work life. Our authors have no axes to grind; they understand they have one job only—to deliver up-to-date, accurate information simply, concisely, and with deep insight that addresses the real needs of our readers.

It is increasingly hard to find information—whether in the news media, on the Internet, and now all too often in books—that is even-handed and has your best interests at heart. We therefore hope that you enjoy this book, which has been carefully crafted to meet our standards of quality and unbiased coverage.

We are always interested in your feedback or ideas for new titles. Perhaps you'd even like to write a book yourself. Whatever the case, reach out to us at editorial@apress.com and an editor will respond swiftly. Incidentally, at the back of this book, you will find a list of useful related titles. Please visit us at www.apress.com to sign up for newsletters and discounts on future purchases.

The Apress Business Team

This book is dedicated in loving memory of my wonderful parents, Peter and Pam, who could not have been more supportive of me.

Contents

About the Author

Anna Manning is a founding director of an engineering startup company, having worked for eight years as a data scientist at Manchester University. A specialist in data mining and data protection, she was one of the original designers of data mining based software for protecting confidential data now used by national statistics agencies worldwide. She has also served as a data analyst for a nonprofit organization for a number of years. Dr. Manning's papers in the field of data mining have been published in various research journals. She has a PhD in data mining and a master's degree in informatics from the University of Manchester, an honors degree in law from the University of Law, and a BA hons. in mathematics from Trinity College, Dublin. Anna enjoys cycling, debating, and going to the theater. She is a parish councilor in the village where she lives, near Chester in northwest England.

About the Technical Reviewer

Richard Roiger is a professor emeritus at Minnesota State University, Mankato, where he taught and performed research in the Computer & Information Science department for 27 years. Dr. Roiger holds a PhD in computer & information sciences from the University of Minnesota. After retirement, he continues to serve as an adjunct faculty member, teaching courses in data mining, artificial intelligence, and research methods. Richard is a textbook writer and has published several journal articles. Dr. Roiger is a board member of the Retired Education Association of Minnesota, where he serves as their financial advisor. Richard enjoys interacting with his grandchildren, traveling with his wife, writing, and pursuing his musical talents.

Acknowledgments

A huge thank you to my husband, Howard, for helping me with the content of the book and providing me with endless encouragement (and cups of tea). The wheelbarrow design in the Smart Wheelbarrows Inc. case study came from Howard. He produced the drawings at the beginning of the chapter and explained which components would be necessary to build the wheelbarrow. He proofread most of the chapters before they were submitted, providing me with invaluable feedback.

I am extremely grateful to my technical reviewer, Richard Roiger, for agreeing to be part of this project, particularly as it was with short notice. We met through a mutual colleague at a data mining conference in Houston, Texas, in 2005 and later when I was visiting Minnesota State University in 2006. His contribution has helped enormously with the quality of the work.

Thank you to Joe Monaghan for agreeing to let me base the Connecting South Side case study on his ideas. Joe does a fantastic amount of work in Liverpool in the UK to help people who are struggling.

Many thanks to my good friend Lisa Marie Allen from California who was able to help me with the American English that was used in this book. Being British, American terminology didn't always come easily to me. She also advised me on the location of the legal case study that's set in California.

Thank you to the team at Apress for everything that they have done. Thank you to Robert Hutchinson for his initial enthusiasm when I approached Apress about this book and for helping me develop the ideas into something marketable. I faced a rather tough time whilewriting the book—my father died in June 2015 after several months of illness—and I appreciated the support from Rita Fernando who was very patient during this time.

Introduction

Most people who run a small business are familiar with word processing and spreadsheets. However, relatively few are familiar with databases, even though the software is easily available and often free. I have written this book with the aim of addressing this knowledge gap.

This book is written with complete database beginners in mind, with an assumption that you have experience of spreadsheets. The book shows you how to create a database from scratch, all the way through to analyzing the data and presenting it in reports. The aim is that you can build the databases presented in the book and use them as a test suite to experiment on.

Four case studies are considered throughout the book. The aim of these case studies is to provide a good variety of small businesses. The examples are:

- A small online business selling greetings cards
- A small engineering business
- A small legal firm
- A small nonprofit

Even if your business is, for example, a legal firm, it is still worth reading the other examples as well. The important point to remember is that databases are not difficult to learn. If you are familiar with spreadsheets, it is only a small step to using databases.

Relational databases (the databases addressed in this book) have been with us for over 40 years. The fundamental criteria for their design and use have not changed enormously, despite the massive changes in technology that have occurred during this time. At present, databases are following a number of new trends—for example, moving away from the desktop and into the cloud. However, wherever your database is stored and however the instructions are given, you will need to understand the fundamentals of database design in order to be effective.

Database design is part of a process of data handling and processing. Before you can enter data into the database, the data needs to be collected and cleansed. Once it is stored, you will need to know how to take advantage of it by analyzing it and assessing whether your business is meeting its goals. You will need to be able to write clear and meaningful reports based on your analysis.

After reading this book and following the examples, you will be in the position to design a simple database of your own with tables, relationships, and simple queries over those tables. You will be able to analyze the data and write reports based on the results.

Even if you choose not to create a database yourself, after reading this book you will be an "intelligent customer." You will better understand potential database designs presented to you and will be able to decide whether they are being reasonably priced or, whether, as is often the case, they are an extremely simple design behind a fancy interface.

How Data Can Benefit Your Small Business

Collecting and analyzing data is important to your small business because it can improve efficiency and profitability. Data can provide a record of what has been going on—who your customers are, what their demographic is, and what they've bought. It can enable you to find trends—for example, your customers' favorite products. There are hidden patterns in data that are important to your business, such as groups of products that sell together. Data can provide an archive that can be searched.

When those in small businesses find out what an enormous difference their data can make to them they are generally fascinated to find out more. The fact is, for small businesses, data is collected about many aspects of their operations already. All businesses collect details about income and expenditure in order to satisfy tax requirements. Many businesses collect the names and addresses of their customers so that they can contact them.

The aim of this book is to demonstrate that the data you are collecting has benefits far beyond its initial purpose. The book will explain the value of your data and show you how to take full advantage of it. The book is designed to be an introduction to databases and a signpost to further references, should these be necessary.

As a starting point, I am assuming that you have a basic familiarity with packages such as word processing and spreadsheets, but are completely inexperienced with databases. Further, I am aware that most small businesses don't have only one person working exclusively on their data and that most of their staff has several roles in the company. I also assume that your small business is constrained by a small budget.

You may have been using your data ineffectively for some time without realizing its full potential. If this is the case you will be delighted to have the improved insights and data analysis presented in this book. And, if you are simply storing your data without using it for anything beyond what's absolutely necessary, you will be pleasantly surprised to realize that the first and most important steps of learning the techniques for processing and analyzing your data are well within your reach.

Your business could be at one of a number of stages. You could be starting out and be keen to making sure you are fully abreast of the latest technology. You may have been operating for some time and wish to encourage further growth. Or your business may be experiencing challenging times and is looking for help to move forward. Whatever your circumstances, you will find that your data can make a significant difference to the profitability of your business.

What Is Meant by Data and Databases

The following sections describe the meaning of data and spreadsheets. Databases are introduced by using spreadsheets as a starting point.

Data

Data can take many forms, including numbers, text, images, hyperlinks, and sound. Data can be about any subject at all, or be about more than one subject.

Spreadsheets

As mentioned, I am assuming that you are familiar with spreadsheets, some common examples being Microsoft Excel, LibreOffice Calc, and Google Sheets. I will use a spreadsheet as a starting point for describing databases.

Spreadsheets and databases are both used to store and manage data. A very simplistic way of expressing the difference is to regard a spreadsheet as a large sophisticated programmable calculator and a database as a highly efficient electronic filing system that makes data quickly available for look-up and analysis. The main differences between spreadsheets and databases are how they store and manipulate data and often the amount of data involved.

A spreadsheet stores data items (e.g., numbers, text, and hyperlinks) in cells, with multiple cells represented in a system of rows and columns. Values in one cell can be related to values in other cells with the relationship defined by a formula.

Two of the most serious problems with spreadsheets are as follows:

- *Storing repeated data*: The same data may be stored in multiple spreadsheets. If you need to make changes to the data, the same change is likely required in every location where the data is stored, thus increasing the risk of errors.

- *Finding data*: Finding an item of data in a spreadsheet can involve scanning across numerous columns.

HYPOTHETICAL EXAMPLE OF A SMALL BUSINESS: CARDS FOR EVERYONE INC.

This book uses three case studies for the purposes of illustration: a small engineering firm, a small law firm, and a small nonprofit. They are introduced in the next three chapters. In addition, you'll read about a hypothetical example that depicts a small online business called Cards for Everyone Inc., which sells a range of cards online.

Cards for Everyone Inc. buys cards from a range of suppliers and displays images of them on its web site for sale. The web site was designed by a contractor so that employees of the company can update it themselves. The business has three employees: Pat, Zeph, and Leona.

Pat, the manager, has a number of roles, including buying the supplies and marketing the business. Pat must keep the web site up to date as stock levels change.

Zeph and Leona are assistants who process the orders by locating cards in the stockroom and putting them into envelopes for distribution. When new stock arrives, they place it in the storeroom and pass the details on to Pat so that she can update the web site.

A database addresses both of these issues. Repeated data items are minimized by splitting the data into tables (made up of rows and columns) so that, ideally, each data item is stored only once. Very efficient data retrieval is made possible by relationships defined between the tables: they link the data together and make retrieval efficient. Chapter 6 explains the pros and cons of spreadsheets and databases in more detail.

The next section gives an example of a database used by Cards for Everyone Inc.

A Database Used by Cards for Everyone Inc.

Typical data for a given customer in Cards for Everyone Inc. is their name, address, telephone number, and e-mail address. Table 1-1 shows an example database table containing this data for three customers. Each customer is allocated a row in the table, also known as a *record*. Every record is divided into five columns, one for each part of the record (i.e., Customer ID, Name, ZIP Code, etc.). Every customer record has a unique customer identification number, called the Customer ID. No two customers can have the same Customer ID, thus avoiding duplication.

Table 1-1. Basic Customer Database Table

Customer ID	First Name	Last Name	ZIP Code	Phone	E-Mail
1	Lisa	Garcia	MI 48823	517-xxx-xxxx	Lgarcia@hotmail.com
2	John	Williams	OR 97062	503-xxx-xxxx	Jwilliams@gmail.com
3	Steve	Jones	FL 33901	239-xxx-xxxx	Sjones@aol.com

Further database tables at Cards for Everyone Inc. contain details of products, suppliers, and invoices. As with the customers, each product, each supplier, and each invoice is given a unique identification number in their respective tables. Identification numbers can appear in more than one table in order to help construct relationships. At this point, these tables are for illustration purposes only; Chapter 7 contains more detail about their meanings and construction. Table 1-2 shows a table of five products for Cards for Everyone Inc., with the Product ID in column 1. Notice that the table has a column for the identification number of the supplier in column 2.

Table 1-2. Basic Product Database Table

Product ID	Supplier ID	Product Name	Category	Price ($)	Quantity Available
11	100	Cats	Birthday	2.00	5
20	200	Roses	Thankyou	3.00	8
23	200	Boats	Birthday	2.50	10
42	300	Hearts	Valentines	4.50	9
61	300	Rabbits	New Baby	5.00	11

A list of hypothetical suppliers is given in Table 1-3.

Table 1-3. Basic Suppliers Database Table

Supplier ID	Supplier Name	ZIP Code	Telephone	E-Mail
100	Special Occasions	IA 52241	319-xxx-xxxx	admin@special occasions.com
200	Old Favorites	CA 92591	503-xxx-xxxx	office@old favorites.com
300	Handmade Cards	FL 33351	954-xxx-xxxx	enquiries@hand madecards.com

Five invoice records are shown in Table 1-4 with the corresponding Customer IDs in column 2.

Table 1-4. Basic Invoices Database Table

Invoice No.	Customer ID	Date	Amount ($)
1001	1	11/4/14	...
1002	2	11/4/14	...
1003	3	11/4/14	...
1004	2	12/14/14	...
1005	1	12/18/14	...

At present these four tables are little more than four separate spreadsheets of data, as shown in Figure 1-1.

CUSTOMERS TABLE

Customer ID	Name	...
1	Lisa Garcia	...
2	John Williams	...
3	Steve Jones	...
...	...	...

INVOICES TABLE

Invoice Number	Customer ID	Date	...
1001	1	11/04/14	...
1002	2	11/04/14	...
1003	3	11/04/14	...
...	...	...	...

PRODUCTS TABLE

Product ID	Supplier ID	Product Name	...
11	100	Cats	...
20	200	Roses	...
23	200	Boats	...
...	...	...	...

SUPPLIERS TABLE

Supplier ID	Supplier Name	...
100	Special Occasions	...
200	Old Favorites	...
300	Handmade Cards	...
...	...	...

Figure 1-1. Separate Database Tables for Cards for Everyone Inc.

A database enables these tables, and their data, to be linked together using the unique identifiers of each table, as shown in Figure 1-2. A database structure such as the one shown in Figure 1-2 prevents you from having to store data repeatedly, risking both typing and mismatch errors. Databases are excellent for pulling data together, separating the themes, and enabling efficient storage, updates, and retrieval.

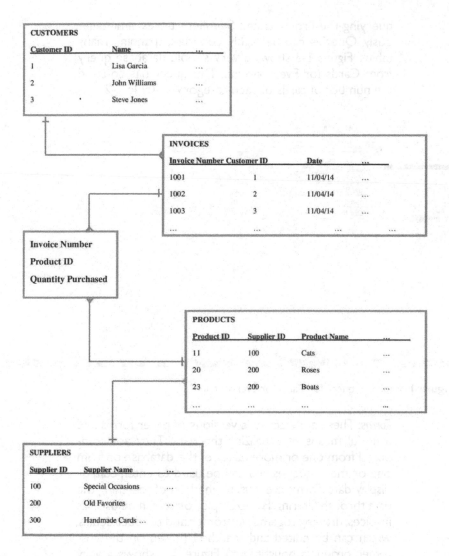

Figure 1-2. Linked database tables for Cards for Everyone Inc.

The resulting connected data structure can be viewed in three main ways:

> *Query*: This is a question asked about data in a database, from one or more tables or from other queries. Queries can be used to filter data, to perform calculations, to summarize data, and to perform management tasks. For example, when an order comes in, it would be useful to know if there are enough products in stock and, if not, where to order more from. This involves

querying the Products and Suppliers tables simultaneously. Queries can be highly complex, spanning many
tables. Figure 1-3 shows a very simple database query
from Cards for Everyone Inc. The query has counted
the number of cards of each category in Table 1-2.

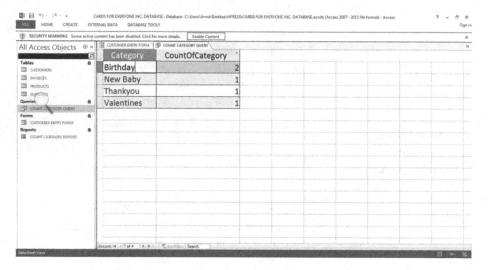

Figure 1-3. Simple query for Cards for Everyone Inc.

Forms: These are electronic versions of paper forms and
a useful means of visualizing the data. They are com-
posed from one or more tables of the database or from
one or more queries and can be used to enter, edit, or
display data. Forms are a useful method of searching the
data through filtering. For example, forms can be used as
invoices, drawing together customer and product details,
which can be edited and searched (based on the customer, products bought, etc.) Figure 1-4 shows a very
simple form for Cards for Everyone Inc., which provides
a method for viewing data in the Customers table and
a means for entering data. The form is a far more user-
friendly way than inputting data directly into the table.

Figure 1-4. Sample form for Cards for Everyone Inc.

> *Reports*: They enable a document to be designed from
> database tables or queries that can be shared easily
> in electronic form or viewed away from a computer.
> Reports can be used to summarize which products
> have been selling well and which customers have been
> buying them. Figure 1-5 shows a report of the query
> data from Figure 1-3.

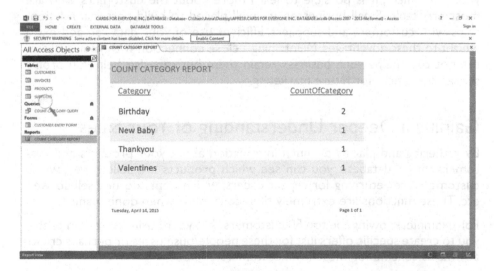

Figure 1-5. Sample report for Cards for Everyone Inc.

The relationships shown in Figure 1-2 could be handled in a spreadsheet by using master tabs, lookup formulas, cross-referenced spreadsheets, and Visual Basic programming. This will work as long as the connections are kept up to date. However, problems may arise during the introduction of a new product due to the effort needed to check the data to ensure everything matches up correctly.

■ **Note**   In this book I refer to *relational databases* by default as they are the most popular. There are other databases, such as object-oriented, hierarchical, file, and network.

The Benefits Data Can Bring to Your Small Business

There is little point in taking the trouble to create and populate a database if there is no ultimate benefit to your small business. The following sections discuss the wide range of advantages that using databases can bring.

Providing a Solid Understanding of Your Customers

Small businesses can effectively compete with large companies by targeting a niche market. Data helps you understand your customers better and identify this niche market more accurately. By storing, sorting, and filtering data about your customers, it is possible to learn more about the customers who are most profitable. Small businesses are well placed to build personal relationships with customers and suppliers. Efficient use of your data can add extra weight to these advantages. Maintaining a close connection with your customers not only helps your business retain them but can also help you profile similar customers for future marketing.

Gaining a Deeper Understanding of Your Sales

By gathering and placing as much information about your products and customers into a database, you can see which products are selling well, which customers are returning for repeat orders, which items do not sell so well, etc. These functions are extremely time-consuming when done manually.

For example, knowing the top 50 customers that your business has can enable you to create specific offers just for these people/businesses or perhaps create a rewards scheme for these loyal customers.

Efficient Stock Control

By simply glancing at your database, you can see what is nearly out of stock and where to order further supplies from. The database can also alert you when supplies are running short so you can order more before you run out of essential items.

Responding to Change

A well-organized database can help a business respond to changes and make decisions. If data covering many of the business operations is available via linked tables in a database, managers can gain a holistic understanding of the current state of the business before making decisions. This is particularly pertinent to small businesses, which can often respond more flexibly to change than their larger counterparts. This is often due to the lack of hierarchy in a small business.

Data Analysis

The querying and reporting capabilities of databases make them an invaluable resource for analyzing data and predicting future trends, as they can draw data together across the whole of your small business. For example, a report may show that sales of certain products increased after an e-mail promotion, while sales of other products increased after an in-store promotion.

Improving the Security of Your Data

Security control and authorization can be implemented in a database by moving sensitive data into a separate table with its own authorization controls. When database users log in they will only be able to access the data that they are permitted to view. For example, there could be restrictions on fields such as employees' salaries, which can be viewed only by those dealing directly with payroll.

Why Some Businesses Choose Not to Use Their Data

The reasons that small businesses neglect to put their data to beneficial use in the ways discussed in the preceding section are various and complicated. The purpose of this section is to help you understand why you have not yet found the motivation to take advantage of your data rather than to pass any judgment. The aim is also to encourage you to move away from any hesitation that you may have.

It's Too Expensive

Many small businesses have small budgets and regard databases as too expensive. They believe that they have to pay an expert to create databases. However, the software itself is not expensive and open-source versions are often available. For example, MS Access may already be available on the version of MS Office you are using. And some open-source software suites have database packages available, such as OpenOffice and LibreOffice.

Concern may also arise that new and expensive hardware is necessary. There are many options, not least of which is a database stored in the cloud, which requires minimal investment and maintenance of office hardware. Cloud computing is discussed in Chapter 18.

It's Too Disruptive

If a company is running smoothly there may be a concern that implementing a database would disrupt the status quo and cause a falloff in business. There may be apprehension that a period of time would arise when it would not be possible to take any orders.

The physical move to a database from other methods of electronic storage is not as difficult as you might think. For example, there is usually a fast method to transfer data between databases and spreadsheets and most electronic data can be quickly manipulated to the point where it can be presented on a spreadsheet.

Staff training is covered in Chapter 20. A sensible way of starting is to choose an area of your business to place onto the database so that everyone can get used to the nature of the new technology. For example, you could move a spreadsheet about your customers' contact details onto a single table in the database and allow your employees to become used to accessing and manipulating it. Once everyone is familiar with the first table, you can import more spreadsheets into additional tables.

It is worth noting that a spreadsheet and a database can be used alongside each other until all employees are comfortable. You must ensure that updates are only made to one of the files and then transferred to the other so that changes are not overwritten. The most obvious method would be to make changes to the spreadsheet and then transfer the changes to the database at regular intervals. Such a transfer can be completed with a few simple instructions known as an *update query*, which is covered in Chapter 20. In this way the spreadsheet keeps operating as normal, but employees can open the database to see how the data is stored and can become familiar with accessing it.

It Will Take Too Much Time

As in all aspects of life, only you can answer the recurrent question, "How bad do things have to get before I will make a change?" If you are using paper files and running around your office in a panic every time a customer contacts you, searching for a file, it makes sense to improve your efficiency. You do need to invest the time to learn about databases, but this is ultimately less than the time you will waste if you continue to work with out-of-date systems. You can implement the database in small steps, as described in the previous paragraph about disruption. The benefits of databases and the importance of your data to your small business was explained earlier in this chapter. The decision comes down to a balance between investment and reward, and it is up to the individual business to decide where it sits on the spectrum of possibilities.

It's Too Difficult to Learn and Implement

It may seem daunting to learn about databases when you haven't used one before. But, if you are already using word processing and spreadsheets, the step up to using a database is not as great as you might think. This book will help you set a number of small goals and make steady progress.

It's Too Low on the Priority List

Running a small business can be overwhelming, with long hours and little time to keep organized. You may have a long list of things you would like to sort out before attempting to focus on your data. It can seem like a long-term goal and, like any long-term goal, it is easy for it to become overshadowed by more short-term plans.

To improve the functioning of your business, you may be inclined to focus on what could be higher priorities, such as taking steps to improve the ways in which you manage your office, keep records, and store your products and supplies. Only then will you feel in a position to look at your data.

However, if you were to begin with your data it is likely that many of the other parts of your business would require careful organization for the process to work effectively. This is because your data often reaches all areas of your business such as your customers, your sales, and your inventory.

For example, suppose Cards for Everyone Inc. was not very efficient at handling telephone orders from customers. Customers phone in and the details are written onto pieces of paper and left in a tray on Pat's desk until she can pass the information on to Zeph and Leona to process. With a database that links products to suppliers, they can quickly check to see if there is enough of the product in stock to meet the order and, if not, who to contact for more. This provides an incentive to update the Quantity Available field of the Products table (Table 1-2) immediately and to begin an invoice for the order. The paper telephone notes can be destroyed as soon as the data has been entered onto the database, and the bottleneck of paper piling up on Pat's desk will be removed.

A Failure to Anticipate How Quickly the Business Would Grow

When a business starts it is usually possible to recognize each customer by name. Simple filing systems will suffice. However, there is a point at which customers are not instantly recognizable: generally speaking, this will occur when numbers rise above the 50 customer mark. In most instances, a small business will want to keep its service as personalized as possible.

A database can enable you to keep your service personalized even when the number of customers grows. This is because data retrieval is highly efficient. For example, important data about customers' preferences can be kept with their records so that this data can be accessed quickly when a customer contacts the company. In the case of Cards for Everyone Inc., some customers may have preferences for certain types of cards—such as cats or rabbits—and will appreciate an e-mail letting them know about the availability of new designs.

A Failure to Understand How Valuable the Data Can Be to the Business

Many small businesses do not understand the value of their data in terms of leveraging their profits. The data held by your small business has the potential to increase revenue by providing helpful information, increasing the number of customers, and improving the customer experience. Managers may be happy to make decisions on the basis of their past experiences, intuition, or comparison with other products on the market. Using data from the database allows this process to move from guesswork to precise market planning, thereby making small businesses more competitive, particularly in relation to their larger, more database-savvy counterparts.

In some cases, a small business may be operating perfectly well without a database. For example, if you own a café with regular demand for a fixed set of items that you buy fresh each day, you may well be operating from direct observation. If you notice that you are low on salt and pepper, you could easily drive down to the store for more. It is not straightforward to keep records of your customers. However, you could make records of what is selling each day, what the weather is like, and what events are going on in your town, and then use this information to improve your sales, tighten your profit margins, and introduce new products. This information is particularly important when you have competition—say, a new café opens across the street. It is never a good idea to turn a blind eye to your data.

Case Studies

Three case studies are introduced in the next three chapters and recur throughout the book: a small engineering firm in Chapter 2, a small law firm in Chapter 3, and a small nonprofit in Chapter 4. The history of each organization is described in detail in order to put the current position of each business into context. The business objectives of each case study are discussed. Business objectives are fundamental to successful database design and usage, an issue covered Chapter 5.

A Small Engineering Company: Case Study

This chapter introduces the first of three case studies that serve as examples throughout the book. Many readers will identify closely with only one of these and it is perfectly reasonable to select the case study that best fits your situation or experience. To recap, Chapter 3 covers a small law firm and Chapter 4 covers a small nonprofit.

This chapter introduces a small engineering business based on the east coast. Currently it makes and sells two versions of the same product and is looking to expand. Spreadsheets are used to store data at the present time.

Smart Wheelbarrows Inc.: Background

Smart Wheelbarrows Inc. sells foldup wheelbarrows to professionals with limited living space, such as those living in city apartments with roof-top gardens and those living in condominiums. The wheelbarrow was designed by Howard, the business's CEO, so that the frame, main container, and wheel all fold as flat as possible and can be hung on a peg. They are made of aluminum to keep them light. Figure 2-1 shows the wheelbarrow in its folded and unfolded states.

Figure 2-1. Foldup wheelbarrow, folded and unfolded

The folding mechanism of the wheelbarrow is achieved via a number of edges that divide apart, referred to as *split edges*, and a number of hinged edges.

Smart Wheelbarrows Inc. is based in Connecticut and rents a unit in a technology center. The unit is divided into a small office, a production line, and a storeroom. The company was incorporated in 2012 and started selling one size of folding wheelbarrow, the "standard" size, in four colors: red, green, black, and white.

It became clear via word of mouth that customers were using the wheelbarrows for decoration as well as gardening purposes. It was also found that some executive customers were using the wheelbarrows for things such as moving food and wine around their gardens. This led to two further colors, gold and silver.

Feedback from a customer survey indicated that there was a demand for a smaller version of the wheelbarrow for decorations, such as for holding plants. The capacity to fold up would not be necessary for this product.

The result of this information was the development of twelve products in total, six standard-sized folding wheelbarrows and six small non-folding. The standard-sized red, green, black, or white version cost $120 and the equivalent small versions cost $70. The standard gold or silver wheelbarrows cost $125 and the small gold or silver wheelbarrows cost $75. The gold or silver wheelbarrows were slightly more expensive because the paint was more expensive than the other colors and had to be ordered from a specialized company. Table 2-1 summarizes the range of wheelbarrows on offer from Smart Wheelbarrows Inc.

Table 2-1. Products Sold by Smart Wheelbarrows Inc.

Product Name	Color	Price ($)
Standard Wheelbarrow	red, green, black or white	120
Standard Wheelbarrow	silver or gold	125
Small Wheelbarrow	red, green, black and white	70
Small Wheelbarrow	silver and gold	75

Smart Wheelbarrows Inc. distributes its products via other businesses, such as florists, garden centers, and online retailers like Amazon. It also takes orders directly from consumers through a web site (designed by a contractor) and via the telephone.

The wheelbarrows are made partly on the company's premises and partly by a contractor. The manufacture of the main container is outsourced to a local firm that has the necessary equipment. The manufacture and painting of the frame is conducted in-house as Howard was unable to find anyone to make the frames, so he bought the necessary equipment and hired the staff, as described in the next section.

Employees at Smart Wheelbarrows Inc.

Smart Wheelbarrows Inc. is run by Howard, who has eight employees. Howard is an experienced mechanical engineer who used to work at a large engineering firm but felt frustrated by the lack of freedom to follow through on his own ideas. Howard asked his former colleague Sanjiv, from the same engineering firm, to join him as the Technical Production Manager.

Howard and Sanjiv recruited two people, John and Chen, to work in the office. John is responsible for taking orders and making sure the orders go out correctly. Chen is responsible for bookkeeping and payroll.

John and Chen keep the web site up to date (it was designed to be updated easily) and answer the phones. They cover for each other during sickness and vacation and work as a team.

Howard wears several hats in the company. He does a great deal of networking and marketing. He also manages the administration office, both in person and remotely. When he is in town, Howard pops his head around the door of the office a few times a week to make sure everything is running smoothly. However, much of the time Howard is out of town and checks the orders online regularly via an encrypted spreadsheet in the cloud. He also looks at the bank account online (examining the running cash flow of the business) and keeps an eye on the profit and loss account from time to time.

Howard and Sanjiv recruited four people to work on the production line, managed by Sanjiv, as follows:

- Helen, who takes tubes of aluminum and feeds them to a machine that bends them to form the shape of the frame of the wheelbarrow.

- Miguel, who takes the frames and welds on the locking hinges.

- Sam, who hangs the tubes with attached hinges and operates the paint spraying in a special booth. Each part receives two coats of paint.

- Valentina, who takes all the components, assembles the wheelbarrow (folded for the standard size), and packs it into a box ready to be shipped. One of the components is a U-clip that's bolted onto the container through holes placed there by the manufacturer and used to attach the frames. She needs to check that all the parts have been added and this is done by weighing each box to check that it is the expected weight. A small discrepancy can mean the omission of something small such as a fastener.

The storeroom manager, Steve, handles supplies coming in and finished products going out.

There is a great deal of flexibility between those managed by Sanjiv so that sickness and holidays can be covered. Sanjiv can perform all jobs, so is able to cover. He also makes sure that all four production line operators can do each other's jobs. This gives more interest to their work, increases the skills of the workforce, and provides better cover during staff shortages. Table 2-2 summarizes the staff employed by Smart Wheelbarrows Inc.

Table 2-2. Staff Working at Smart Wheelbarrows Inc.

Name	Position
Howard	CEO
Sanjiv	Technical Production Manager
John	Orders
Chen	Bookkeeping and Payroll
Helen	1st Production Line Operative: Making Frames
Miguel	2nd Production Line Operative: Welding
Sam	3rd Production Line Operative: Painting
Valentina	4th Production Line Operative: Packing
Steve	Store Room Manager

Data Stored by Smart Wheelbarrows Inc.

Data is stored in spreadsheets. The main difference in terms of data between Smart Wheelbarrows Inc. and Cards for Everyone Inc. is that Smart Wheelbarrows buys materials and components and makes something, whereas Cards for Everyone Inc. buys ready-made products and sells them without any further processing. Smart Wheelbarrows Inc. has six spreadsheets of data. The following list summarizes the spreadsheets:

- Customers
- Invoices
- Materials used in the production of the wheelbarrows
- Suppliers of the materials
- Materials (including quantities) used for the standard wheelbarrow
- Materials (including quantities) used for the small wheelbarrow

The customer spreadsheet is shown in Table 2-3 and the outgoing invoice spreadsheet for customers is shown in Table 2-4. Note how the names and ZIP codes for the customers are repeated in these two spreadsheets.

Table 2-3. Basic Customer Spreadsheet for Smart Wheelbarrows Inc.

Name	ZIP Code	Telephone	E-Mail	Category
Bright Florist	NY 11375	...	...	Business
Hilary Smith	MA 02108	...	...	Business
Bliss Garden Center	RI 02886	...	...	Consumer

Table 2-4. Invoices for Smart Wheelbarrows Inc.

Name	ZIP Code	Date	Amount ($)
Bright Florist	NY 11375	...	...
Hilary Smith	MA 02108	...	...
Bliss Garden Center	RI 02886	...	...

In addition, Smart Wheelbarrows Inc. has a materials spreadsheet for the components of the wheelbarrows (shown in Table 2-5) and a supplier spreadsheet for the suppliers of the materials (shown in Table 2-6). There is also a spreadsheet for incoming invoices from suppliers (which is not shown, but is similar to that used for customer invoices in Table 2-4). There is no spreadsheet for products, as the list is short and does not change very often.

The parts for the wheelbarrows are numbered as follows:

- For parts made in-house, the number begins with SW, which stands for Smart Wheelbarrows.

- For all other parts, the number begins with OS for Outside Supplier, so that the numbering system for these parts is consistent with numbers used by the suppliers of each part shown in the second column of Table 2-5.

- Paints are all OS07 with a suffix depending on the color.

The third column of the materials spreadsheet in Table 2-5 contains the corresponding Supplier name. Supplier details can be obtained by finding the corresponding row for the supplier in the Supplier spreadsheet in Table 2-6.

Table 2-5. Materials for Smart Wheelbarrows Inc.

SW Part No.	Supplier Part No.	Supplier Name	Product Name	Price ($)	Quantity Available
OS01	ES39	Engineering Supplies	Hinges	...	...
OS02	ES24	Engineering Supplies	Wheel	...	...
OS03	ES67	Engineering Supplies	Handle	...	...
OS04	ES09	Engineering Supplies	Fastener	...	...
OS05	AB01	Aluminum Boxes	Container	...	...
OS06	TM01	Top Materials	Aluminum tube	...	...
OS07-1	QP04	Quality Paints	Red Paint	...	...
OS07-2	QP11	Quality Paints	Green Paint	...	...
OS07-3	QP18	Quality Paints	Black Paint	...	...
OS07-4	QP19	Quality Paints	White Paint	...	...
OS07-5	LP25	Luxury Paints	Gold Paint	...	...
OS07-6	LP26	Luxury Paints	Silver Paint	...	...
OS08	ES23	Engineering Supplies	Small Wheel	...	...
OS09	ES68	Engineering Supplies	Small Handle	...	...
OS10	ES08	Engineering Supplies	Small Fastener	...	...
OS11	LP02	Aluminum Boxes	Small Container	...	...
OS12	ES69	Engineering Supplies	U-Clips	...	...

Table 2-6. Basic Suppliers Spreadsheet for Smart Wheelbarrows Inc.

Supplier Name	ZIP Code	Telephone	E-Mail
Aluminum Boxes	...	...	...
Engineering Supplies	...	...	...
Top Materials	...	...	...
Quality Paints	...	...	...
Luxury Paints	...	...	...

Smart Wheelbarrows Inc. also has what is known as a *Bill Of Materials (BOM)* for each of its products. This is a list of the raw materials and sub-components; the parts and quantities necessary to make each of the products. Table 2-7 shows the BOM for the standard wheelbarrow and Table 2-8 shows the BOM for the small wheelbarrow.

Table 2-7. Bill of Materials for the Standard Wheelbarrow

Part Number	Part Name	Quantity
SW01	RHS Frame	1
SW02	LHS Frame	2
OS01	Hinge	4
OS02	Wheel	1
OS03	Handle	2
OS04	Fasteners	4
OS05	Main Container	1
OS07	Paint	½ Liter
OS12	U-Clips	4

Notice that there is no OS06 (aluminum tube) in either BOM. This is because the aluminum tube is made into the wheelbarrow frames in-house. Four further BOMs are needed—one each for the right side frame and the left side frame of the standard wheelbarrow and one each for the right and left side frames of the small wheelbarrow. These are not shown here. (Note that the two frames of the small wheelbarrow are designed so they slot into each other through the wheel.)

Table 2-8. Bill of Materials for the Small Wheelbarrow

Part Number	Part Name	Quantity
SW03	RHS Frame	1
SW04	LHS Frame	1
OS08	Small Wheel	1
OS09	Small Handle	2
OS10	Small Fasteners	4
OS11	Small Container	1
OS07	Paint	⅓ Liter

Note that there are no hinges for the small wheelbarrow because it does not fold.

Databases

During his travels, Howard met up with his old university friend, Annette. Annette, who works as a data analyst, asked Howard whether Smart Wheelbarrows Inc. was using databases. Howard had never considered databases and, in addition, feels that the spreadsheets they use are more than sufficient. Annette is of the opinion that databases could help Howard understand his customer base better and attract new clients. A customer database would also be essential in driving an effective marketing campaign.

A database could also tighten up the stock control at Smart Wheelbarrows Inc. By linking each BOM with the Materials and Products spreadsheets, it would be possible to see whether there were enough wheelbarrows in stock to meet an order, whether more needed to be made and, if so, whether the supplies were in stock to do so. At the moment, when an order comes in, John tends to phone Steve in the storeroom and ask these questions directly, or visit the storeroom himself to check supplies if Steve is not there. This is not an efficient use of time.

Howard, encouraged by the discussion, agrees to do some reading from some online sources that Annette has suggested and get back to her.

The development of a database for Smart Wheelbarrows Inc. will be covered in future chapters.

Research Ideas

Many people have asked Howard whether the wheelbarrows could be made from recycled polymer products (that is, from recycled household plastic). He has been thinking about this and talking to people who might be able to help. There are some challenges with the use of recycled materials, which Howard would like time to investigate. The two main issues are as follows:

- The design of the frame could be more difficult. Recycled materials may be required in a larger volume in order to provide enough strength for the wheelbarrow, thus leaving the frame chunky and unattractive.

- There is also a concern that recycled polymer products can have a poor finish in the sense that they are not very smooth.

Howard needs to consider incorporating new production processes into his business. The frame would probably need to be injection-molded—that is, molten plastic pumped into a mold. He hopes that the molding would be straightforward and conducted in one molding, otherwise known as "one-shot."

Howard would like to apply for a grant for this research. Identifying a source of funding will involve searching through many potential donors. In addition, once the research is under way it will be important for Howard to keep up to date with the latest published work by finding research papers quickly. Chapter 19 covers efficient searching of online databases.

Summary

A small engineering business, Smart Wheelbarrows Inc., manufactures small wheelbarrows. The business stores its data in a number of spreadsheets that cover its customers, invoices, products, and suppliers. In addition, there are spreadsheets that describe the materials used and those that show how each product is made (called the Bill of Materials). A spreadsheet also exists for the employees of the firm. Smart Wheelbarrows Inc. will be used as a case study in many of the following chapters, showing the stages needed to convert spreadsheets into a database.

A Small Law Firm: Case Study

This chapter describes the small law firm case study. The details of its initial stages of development are outlined, together with the employment of growing numbers of staff and the adoption of new technology. Marketing plays a central role in the firm, being fundamental to its growth and success. Databases have the potential to play a key role in its marketing policy and in many other aspects of the business. However, as you'll see, many tasks of the law firm can be carried out by affordable, easy-to-use, off-the-shelf technological solutions. Marketing is one example where databases are useful for small businesses, as tailored software is prohibitively expensive.

This chapter introduces Jennings-Havard Law Offices. It is not necessary to remember everything described here. The purpose is to set the scene for later chapters. These case studies are as realistic as possible and if anything here is of interest then the best way to approach it is to take a note of it as you are reading through.

Jennings-Havard Law Offices

The following sections introduce the background history of Jennings-Havard Law Offices, the motivation for its foundation, and the nature of recent developments.

Background

Tim Jennings set up the Jennings-Havard Law Offices firm with his law school friend, Nadia Havard, five years ago. Tim owns 60 percent of the business and Nadia owns 40 percent. The firm specializes in providing estate planning, trust administration, probate services, and long-term care planning services. A brief summary of each of these is given here:

Estate planning: Decisions are made about who will be responsible for the management and administration of a client's estate should they become unable to make these decisions for themselves. This includes who will receive their property when they die and how that property will be distributed.

Trust administration: After the death of those who created a trust, the federal estate tax exclusion amount will need to be preserved and, put simply, the ownership of assets will need to change.

Probate: A process by which the estate of a person who has died is administered under the supervision of a court.

Long-term care planning: Clients need to prepare for the possibility of being unable to make their own decisions before they die. This includes protecting their assets from depletion due to medical and nursing-home costs, Medi-Cal eligibility, and Supplemental Security Income.

The work varies from basic wills to advanced estate-planning.

Tim was attracted to this area of law as he liked the fact that it meets an almost universal need, leading to the potential for a wide range of clients. Most significantly, the initial motivation came from a desire to help people avoid the hardship that dying without proper legal protection can bring. This had happened to Tim as a boy when his father died unexpectedly without having a will.

The firm has offices in downtown Palo Alto, California. This area was chosen as it was felt it would attract a diverse range of clientele from Palo Alto and its neighbor, East Palo Alto.

Tim and Nadia are now senior partners with their own caseloads. When they initially set out, they employed a personal assistant, Levana, who supported both of them. A receptionist, Janine, was also employed to look after the front desk, take phone calls, greet clients at the door, and organize the diary.

Market Research

The firm grew well and Tim was keen that this growth should be sustained. A marketing consultant was hired, at several thousand dollars, to conduct some research. The main outcome of this work was to give Tim and Nadia a profile of their existing clients so that they could attract more of the same. Most were middle income, over 50, married or cohabiting with at least one child. The consultant noticed that in the geographic area from which their clients were coming, there were a large number of people with the same profile as the firm's existing clients, with one main difference. That was that they came from families where the previous generation had not had much money. The firm's existing clients had been born into wealthier families. They concluded that the existing clients appreciated the importance of making a will, whereas the other group were less aware.

Tim believed he could attract clients from the other group by getting the message to them about the importance of making a will so that they could pass on their wealth to their children. Tim and Nadia decided that a new member of staff would be needed to tap into this market. This person would hold seminars and publicize the work of the firm to people who did not realize the importance of making a will. Tim was also aware that the growth of the firm had been putting increasing pressure on the existing staff and that they needed more support.

Although Tim had found the results of the market research useful, he wondered if it would have been possible to conduct such research in-house. After all, he had contact details for all his clients and some data about their ages. He also noted that the consultant used publicly available data from the U.S. Census Bureau. Before parting with a large sum of money again, he decided to explore how much work the firm could do itself.

Additional Employees at Jennings-Havard Law Offices

As a result of the market research, another attorney named Luciana and a second personal assistant named Dominico were hired.

About a year later Tim supervised a student, named Maneer, and took him on as a newly qualified attorney once he had passed his exams. When Maneer qualified, Tim took on a second trainee, named Christine.

Two further employees were taken on to assist with the firm's growth: Afrah, a qualified accountant, took on the accounting work, and Sophia, an administrative assistant, took on the basic administrative tasks.

Table 3-1 summarizes the staff working at Jennings-Havard Law Offices.

Table 3-1. Staff Working at Jennings-Havard Law Offices

Name	Position
Tim	Senior partner
Nadia	Senior partner
Luciana	Attorney
Maneer	Recently qualified attorney
Christine	Trainee attorney
Afrah	Accountant
Levana	Personal assistant to Tim (and covering Maneer's and Christine's work)
Dominico	Personal assistant to Nadia and Luciana
Sophia	Administrative assistant
Janine	Receptionist

Networking and Marketing

Tim has put a strong emphasis on networking and marketing from an early stage. He is always open to new ideas and welcomes input from his staff. As new staff have joined the firm, their ideas and experience have been added to the current networking and marketing activities. Jennings-Havard Law Offices' networking and marketing efforts are summarized in the following sections.

Social Gatherings

Tim and Nadia are part of a group of law school classmates who have stayed in contact. Every month or so they meet for dinner to catch up and to swap ideas and experience. Tim has found this very helpful—particularly with suggestions for marketing the firm and for adopting software to make the firm more competitive. He makes time to research any suggestions he is given and to think carefully about implementing any new ways of working into the firm. It is at these social gatherings that Tim tested his ideas about the work carried out by the marketing consultant. Some of the classmates suggested that he explore databases as a possible and cheaper way forward.

Web Site

A web site was designed by a contractor soon after the firm opened. The administrative staff can update it easily. Tim writes a blog on the site a few times a week with information he feels would be useful to current and potential clients. Tim has been told that small, regular, interesting posts about the firm that contain useful links are likely to be more effective than a few longer posts. There is also a newsletter about forthcoming events. Activity on the site is monitored by way of analytics and changes are made to attract more visitors to areas of the site where the most interest occurs.

Social Media

Maneer operates the firm's Twitter feed, sending out about half a dozen tweets a day. Their profile has accumulated several thousand followers from local law firms and community organizations. Luciana has encouraged her colleagues to use LinkedIn for tapping into professional expertise, thereby maximizing the benefits of contacts made at events and promoting the work of the firm.

Networking Events

Legal staff are encouraged to carry out careful research to identify organizations that might refer clients and make arrangements to meet representatives. Tim insists on the firm's presence at events such as those run by the bar association so that the firm is more likely to receive referrals. Tim requests that his staff market themselves in this way continuously and not just when the firm's business is sluggish. Luciana arranges her own schedule of events to attract clients to the firm who are not necessarily aware of how important their services can be.

Traditional Advertising

The firm uses adverts in local newspapers, on the Internet, and on local radio. They also circulate leaflets and business cards.

Processing a New Client

Since they opened, Jennings-Havard Law Offices has been slowly moving away from paper files with the aid of various software programs. So that you understand the workings of the office and the software they use, the procedures they use when taking on a client are explained here:

1. Each new client has 30–60 minutes of free consultation to present their case.

2. The attorney decides whether they can take the case.

   a. If Jennings-Havard can take on the case, the client is told so during the consultation.

   b. If not, the client is referred to a colleague or to a range of suitable attorneys from different practices.

3. They open a file on the client with a case number.

4. They explain the likely costs of the work.

5. After the interview, the firm sends a letter of thanks that summarizes the meeting, sets out the procedures that will be followed, specifies the costs, and explains who handles complaints.

6. Work then starts on the case. Letters may be necessary. Research may be needed, for example, to identify the latest tax laws. The amount of time spent working on any aspect of the case is recorded.

7. Some work is passed to the administration staff—for example, they send documents in connection with land registration and invoices to clients.

8. When a case is complete, the file is stored at the office.

Software Usage Within the Firm

Tim has slowly introduced software to cover individual tasks based mainly on recommendations from his law school friends. This led to a rather disjointed way of working, but the firm cannot afford a software suite that covers all of the tasks. Tim and Nadia's classmates tend to work in a similar way unless they are working for a much larger firm. The following sections summarize the main office activities and the type of software solutions they use.

E-Mail

The firm has always used e-mail to correspond between the staff and many of the clients. The postal system is used for any clients not online and for some formal documents.

Calendar

When the firm first started, Janine used a large desk diary to keep track of appointments. However, as the firm grew and took on more staff, the diary became inefficient and cumbersome. Also, if someone was out of the office the diary could not be accessed directly. As a result, the firm moved to a shared electronic calendar which they could all see and update simultaneously, regardless of where they were.

■ **Note**   Examples of the types of calendar used in these cases are Google Apps (Google Calendar), Microsoft Exchange, and web-based applications such as 30boxes.com, Zoho Calendar, and Yahoo Calendar.

Managing Client Contact Information

Names, addresses, phone numbers, and e-mail addresses are stored for each of the firm's clients. This information has become difficult to manage as the firm has grown. The firm then adopted a contact-management tool, which provided a lot of useful features for managing large numbers of contacts. For example, different groups of contacts can be created easily. They can, for example, create a group of clients choosing to receive the firm's newsletter, and then use that data to create and track mailing campaigns.

■ **Note**   Examples of contact-management tools are web-based tools such as Google Apps (Universal Contact Manager—UCM), Plaxo, and Microsoft Outlook Anywhere.

Task Management

When the firm was small, it was possible for each attorney to manage his or her workload with an informal "to-do" list and with assistance from the administrative staff. However, the firm now has approximately 400–500 ongoing cases, an average of 15–20 new cases a week coming into the practice, and 20–30 cases per week completed. Even though ongoing cases sometimes require very little day-to-day work, this can be a lot of balls for so few people to juggle. It is hard to avoid missing a deadline, keep proactive with each open case, and keep the bills paid on time. Tim paid a small monthly subscription for a web-based service that allows staff to manage tasks across the entire firm. Each member of staff can access this service, inside and outside of the office.

■ **Note** Examples of this type of task-management system are Flow, TaskMerlin, and Remember the Milk.

Case Status

The firm uses software to store information about each client. Each client has a record that includes all of their previous interactions with the firm, the status of their case(s), invoices pending, their history of cases, and so on. Tim finds that this is important in maintaining personal service for clients when the firm is growing so quickly. Details of client conversations can be noted so they can be retrieved at a later time.

■ **Note** Examples of this type of case-status software are Trello and Asana.

Time Tracking

Client invoices are calculated by determining the time spent on that particular case. Tim is aware that much of this billing is based on guesswork. He is concerned that members of the firm are underestimating the time they are spending on cases and therefore undercharging. Tim chose one of the many inexpensive software packages that combine time tracking and invoicing.

■ **Note** Examples of time-tracking software are Freckle, Paymo, and OfficeTimer.

Storing and Backing Up Documents

The firm adopted a cloud-based storage service to access their documents from any device with an Internet connection. (The cloud is described in Chapter 18.) This means there is no need to set up a physical computer server in the firm's office to store documents.

■ **Note** Examples of document-storage software are Dropbox, Google Drive, and Microsoft's OneDrive.

Note Taking

Tim has never been happy with the amount of paper notes he takes on clients as he finds them untidy and unavailable when he needs them. It is not an ideal way of working, especially if he meets a client away from the office. Classmates have recommended a cloud-based note taking and organizational tool as an alternative. This enables documents to be viewed, edited, and created electronically, both in the office and away from it. Notes can be shared with others.

■ **Note**   Examples of note-taking software are Evernote, Springpad, Google Keep, Microsoft OneNote, and Simplenote.

Document Assembly

Some documents are used repeatedly with only small changes, such as wills. Lawyers have the option to buy a document assembly package, which can be expensive and inflexible, or to create their own templates. Tim has been advised to maximize the features of his existing word processor, learning to use reusable templates. Many of the assembly plug-ins are not very expensive and, now that the functionality is familiar, he can create suitable templates with ease.

■ **Note**   Examples of document assembly plug-ins used in Microsoft Word are TheFormTool and Pathagoras. There are also web-based document assembly products, such as Rapidocs and Xi I DRAFT, that are operating-system independent.

Databases

Networking and marketing are critical to the growth of the firm, but apart from the web site and social media, Tim has not yet found a way of exploiting technology to assist him in this area. Tim's circle of classmates argue that at the very minimum a database is fundamental to taking advantage of existing, satisfied clients. The firm must make some effort to stay in touch with these clients. Tim knows that it is cheaper to sell more to your existing clients than to attract new ones.

In addition, Tim wants to understand how the marketing consultant managed to profile his clients and identify that there were potential clients of a similar profile in his catchment area. He understands that it is possible to match his data with other databases (for example, data released from the U.S. Census Bureau) to increase the amount of information he has about his clients. This process is covered in Chapter 9.

As the firm has been running for a number of years without a database, Tim is concerned about the large amount of data that would need to be processed before they could create a database. Data about clients is stored in two main places—in the contact management system and in the case status software. The contact management system allows data to be exported in a manageable form, such as MS Excel. This data can be quickly moved to a database. Case status data can often be less accessible.

However, it would be possible to categorize cases and use this information to identify demand for services. It would also be useful to look at cross-selling— for example, if it were known that a client was going to events about long-term care but not being billed for any related work, the firm could follow this up by reminding the client of its services in this area.

The starting point is to determine the main objective of the database, the process of which is discussed in Chapter 5, and to design the database accordingly, as outlined in Chapter 7. Data will need to be "cleansed"—for example, to ensure consistent spelling across the entries—and methods for achieving this are covered in Chapter 10.

Searching the Internet

A common online search that the firm makes involves the steps taken to obtain copies of a person's will and other probate court records after they have died. As probate files are public court records, it is likely that a list of the documents that have been filed will be freely available for viewing (assuming that the location where the probate estate was filed is established beforehand). Additional information should include who has been named as the executor of the estate and which attorney the executor hired. This information enables copies of any of these documents to be obtained on request from the probate clerk's office.

Part of the problem is that there might not be a will, and the attorneys in the firm need to know when this is likely to be the case. Searching online databases is covered in detail in Chapter 19.

Summary

A small law firm, Jennings-Havard Law Offices, handles cases relating to probate and long-term planning. Many of the data-related activities of the firm are handled in a rather ad-hoc manner, using web-based applications and other software.

The firm employed a marketing consultant to help them attract additional clients and sustain growth. Although useful, the advice was very expensive and the senior partners of the firm want to explore what they could do in-house using a database.

Future chapters will consider how the firm can use their existing data, and data from other sources, to conduct market research to help them retain existing clients and attract new ones.

A Small Nonprofit: Case Study

This chapter introduces a case study of a small nonprofit, called Connecting South Side. The work of the nonprofit is described in some detail so that you can understand the requirements for collecting and analyzing its data. Data is collected on a series of MS Excel spreadsheets and Word documents. The information in this chapter sets the scene for later chapters; there is no need to take notes or remember every detail.

Connecting South Side

The following sections explain why Connecting South Side was founded and describe its basic operations. You'll also be introduced to its employees.

Background

Connecting South Side is a small nonprofit located on Chicago's South Side. The aim of the organization is to improve the lives of the socially isolated people living in the community. The South Side is diverse in terms of ethnicity and standard of living. It has a reputation for high crime and poverty, although there are some affluent neighborhoods and it is home to the city's world-class Chicago University.

Social isolation occurs when someone is completely alone and has no family or friends to turn to during a personal crisis. Their interactions with other people are minimal and distant, such as during a transaction in a store. If someone is socially isolated for any period of time, it can be damaging to his or her mental and physical health.

People can become socially isolated for a number of reasons, many of which are interlinked. Health issues and disabilities, often related to the aging process, can impede the ability of people to leave their homes. The loss of a spouse can turn the other person's life upside down, leading them to become depressed and stop going out. The loss of a job can lead to depression, little income to fund social activities, and a poor self-image. If health issues and a drop in income affect the ability to drive, these problems are exacerbated.

Connecting South Side is a signposting organization that gives people an opportunity to talk through their problems, either at the premises or over the phone. Contact via e-mail or letter is also possible. The enquirers are then signposted to organizations who can help further. Enquiries are taken from those affected by social isolation, from professionals about a client, or from members of the public who are concerned about an individual.

The amount of data collected by Connecting South Side is large and its management is becoming increasingly inefficient. The data used at Connecting South Side is discussed in the next main section.

The next subsection provides a simple example of an enquiry. It should be noted that the privacy of enquirers is paramount at Connecting South Side and these issues are discussed further in Chapter 8.

An Example: Dorothy's Enquiry

Dorothy Bain was widowed shortly after she moved to Chicago's South Side and has not had a chance to get to know people locally. She has also developed a serious disability that prevents her driving or walking very far. She has little money and cannot afford taxis. Dorothy's neighbor helps with her groceries and is concerned about the recent deterioration she has noticed in Dorothy's physical and mental health. She contacts Connecting South Side and gives a brief explanation of her concerns. The Connecting South Side representative agrees to contact Dorothy directly.

The Connecting South Side representative assigns Dorothy's case a unique identification number and enters details about the enquiry into a Word file, known as a case file, with the name 255 Dorothy Bain 10 12 2015.docx, where 255 is the unique identification number of Dorothy's case and the date refers to the date of the first contact made to Connecting South Side (in Dorothy's situation, by her neighbor). The representative creates a summary of the case on an Excel spreadsheet; it includes details such as Dorothy's gender and age.

More details about how data is stored are given in the section about data later in this chapter.

After the initial enquiry, Connecting South Side contacts Dorothy directly. During a long conversation, Dorothy tells the representative about her life. She reveals that she has no equipment to help her with her walking problems and mentions that she is a practicing Catholic and would like to go to church. Further notes are added to Dorothy's case file.

The representative gets in touch with another nonprofit that aims to improve the independence of low-income disabled people in Chicago by providing mobility equipment. They arrange to assess Dorothy's needs, but there is a long waiting list so she will not be seen for a few weeks. Dorothy's enquiry continues to be tracked in her case file.

Connecting South Side contacts the nearest Catholic Church, which links Dorothy with a friendly Irish family living on the next street, Mr. and Mrs. Murphy. The Murphys are happy to give Dorothy a lift to Sunday Mass each week. The Murphys are concerned about Dorothy and ask her to dinner on a regular basis. They also put her in touch with the St. Vincent de Paul Society (SVP) at the church, which arranges visits to people who are unwell.

Connecting South Side checks on Dorothy to see how she is progressing. Dorothy is enjoying getting to church, getting to know the Murphy family, and receiving weekly visits from the SVP. She would like to stay in contact with Connecting South Side so that other activities can be arranged in the future.

Dorothy's neighbor contacts Connecting South Side to thank them for their help. She is delighted with the positive change she has witnessed in Dorothy. The representative makes a note about this feedback in Dorothy's case file.

A few months later, Dorothy contacts Connecting South Side again. She has been assessed for her equipment needs and has been given some crutches and is far more mobile.

Dorothy found out about a knitting group at a coffee shop a few miles from where she lives and would very much like to go. However, she is worried about transport. Connecting South Side contacts a charity that provides disabled people with affordable transport.

A year later, Dorothy is getting out most days with the support put in place by Connecting South Side and the follow-on support given by the church and the equipment charity. Dorothy's case is closed, although she can make contact again. The case is flagged as closed on the Excel spreadsheet record.

The Enquiry Process

In many cases, the process for handling a Connecting South Side enquiry is not straightforward. Many of the predicaments that the enquirers find themselves in are highly complex and it takes a number of lengthy discussions before they fully understand the situation. In addition, several more interactions may be required with other organizations over a substantial period of time before there's hope for any improvement. Many enquiries are more complex than Dorothy's was and involve issues such as homelessness, domestic violence, and drug/alcohol addiction. However, all enquiries follow the same basic procedure:

1. The enquirer or enquirer's representative contacts Connecting South Side by telephone, e-mail/letter, or in person.

2. The case is given a unique identification number.

3. The case representative opens a Word file, from now on referred to as the "case file", for collating notes about the case. It uses the naming convention "<Unique ID> <Enquirer Name> <Date of first contact>". For example, Dorothy Bain's file is called "255 Dorothy Bain 10 12 2015.docx".

4. The representative starts a new row on an Excel spreadsheet. The first column contains the unique ID and other columns contain relevant data, such as the enquirer's age and gender. This is discussed in more detail in the section about data that follows.

5. The enquirer (or enquirer's representative) is given time to explain the full nature of their issue. This may require a number of calls and visits if the situation has been going on a long time and/or is complex. The representative takes careful and often copious notes during this step, which they enter into the case file.

6. Connecting South Side assesses the enquirer's needs. These details are added to the case file.

7. The Connecting South Side representative conducts research to identify suitable sources of help. This can involve informal discussions with colleagues and searching data stored at Connecting South Side about local organizations, such as the nonprofit that provided the crutches in Dorothy's case. It could also involve referring to similar enquiries from the past to see how they were handled and with what results.

8. Connecting South Side identifies the most appropriate sources of help for the enquirer. These details are also added to the case file.

9. Connecting South Side contacts the potential sources of help to assess if they are suitable and/or available. The representative adds notes about these efforts to the file.

10. The enquirer is signposted to organizations that are likely to be able to help. The representative adds the names of these organizations to the case file, together with the dates of the signpostings.

11. Connecting South Side follows up to ensure that the enquirer is moving forward and getting the help they need.

12. If additional help is required, further research is conducted and the enquirer is contacted again. The case is flagged as open.

13. If no further help is required, the case is flagged as closed.

Employees of Connecting South Side

Clare is Connecting South Side's CEO and has lived in Chicago most of her life. She started work in a Community Service Center in Chicago during her college years, assisting people with welfare issues. She eventually took up a full-time post at the center after graduation. In this role she became involved with grant writing for the center and assisted in a string of successful bids. Clare was keen to set up her own organization, reaching those who were not included in mainstream society, so she applied for a grant from a local community foundation and was successful. Connecting South Side was the result of this application and the initial grant was for two years.

Six employees, in addition to Clare, were covered by the grant: five full-time helpline staff and one full-time administrator. The administrator position and one of the helpline positions are shared by two part-time staff. Table 4-1 summarizes the Connecting South Side staff.

Table 4-1. Staff Working at Connecting South Side

Name	Position
Clare	CEO
Hendrick	Helpline
Hiroko	Helpline
Frank	Helpline
Lizzie	Helpline
Jan	Helpline (part-time)
Bill	Helpline (part-time)
Ranveer	Administration (part-time)
Jim	Administration (part-time)

As part of their jobs, all staff were asked to help with publicizing the organization and with collecting information about potential sources of help for the enquirers.

Data Used at Connecting South Side

The following sections discuss the data used by Connecting South Side and the methods they use to store it.

A Case File for Each Enquiry

As mentioned in the last section, each enquirer is assigned a case file that contains a description of their enquiry. Entries have three main components:

- Date
- Initials of the Connecting South Side representative
- Description of the latest stage of the enquiry

For example, if Lizzie Shaw entered Dorothy's enquiry in the case file called 255 Dorothy Bain 10 12 15.docx, it might start as follows:

> *10.12.15 LS Call about Dorothy Bain from a neighbor, who is concerned about her mental and physical health, etc.*

> *10.12.15 LS Discussion with Dorothy about her situation. She is very isolated. She can walk only a few feet and has no equipment to help, etc.*

The case files are stored in a directory on the shared drive of the computer in the office so that everyone can access them, although it is not possible for two people to edit a file simultaneously.

A Spreadsheet Summarizing All Cases

Connecting South Side's representatives capture data about the enquirers so that they can gain an overall picture of those using their services. Some data, such as gender, can be straightforward. Other data, such as age range and ethnicity, can be more difficult. There can be many gaps in the data. It's not always appropriate to ask for a large amount of demographic data from someone who is in distress, so the helpline operators use their own discretion. Some enquirers want to remain anonymous and, in these cases, almost no data is known or collected. In general, if an enquiry takes a while to deal with, most data will become available, albeit in several stages.

An ideal enquiry file would include the following data:

- First and last name

- Gender

- Age range: 0–9, 10–19, etc.

- Neighborhood: Examples include Armour Square, Back of the Yards, Bridgeport, and Pullman.

- Ethnic origin

- Health: Covers information about the enquirer's health and disabilities.

- Source: Identifies how people found out about Connecting South Side and helps to show how well publicity campaigns are working and in which areas of the community. Possible sources include community events, word of mouth, and publicity materials.

- Number of contacts: Many enquiries consist of a number of phone calls, both in and out of Connecting South Side together with visits and research. Dorothy's example involved several phone calls and Internet searches. To estimate the level of work that Connecting South Side is doing per enquiry, a count is provided of ingoing and outgoing contacts together with the number of web pages accessed per enquiry.

- Category of call: Enquiries can cover a range of category but usually have a main focus initially. This information covers employment, immigration, housing, welfare, health-care, debt, and so on. For example, Dorothy's enquiry cat-egory is recorded as "healthcare," although her enquiry was far more complex than this.

- Type of organizations signposted to: This provides a snap-shot of the components of the signposting and includes helpline, support group, community activity, and volun-teering. Dorothy has been signposted to two support groups (the equipment nonprofit and the transport non-profit), a community group (the church), and a leisure activity (the knitting group at the coffee shop).

- Open: Each enquiry is noted as open or closed—Y=open and N=closed.

Table 4-2 shows an example of the Excel spreadsheet that Connecting South Side creates for its enquiries, one row for each. The ID numbers are shown in the first column. The row for Dorothy Bain, with ID=255, is shown. The three dots, '…', in this example indicate missing columns, rows, and values. For example, there is no space to show a column in Table 4-2 for each of the items of data listed above.

Table 4-2. Excel Spreadsheet Containing Case Summaries

ID	First Name	Surname	Gender	Age	…	Open
I	Aleksy	Budka	Male	50–59	…	Y
2	Ah Lam	Cheng	Female	50–59	…	N
3	Niamh	Brady	Female	40–49	…	N
…	…	…	…	…	…	…
255	Dorothy	Bain	Female	80–89	…	Y
256	…	…	…	…	…	…
257	…	…	…	…	…	…
258	…	…	…	…	…	…
…	…	…	…	…	…	…

Reporting

The current and future success of Connecting South Side depends on regular and accurate reports being made of its activity. It must show that it's meeting the aims and objectives of its grant. The aims and objectives of the grant obtained from the Community Federation are as follows:

Aim: To improve the lives of socially isolated people from diverse backgrounds living on the South Side of Chicago.

Objectives:

1. To make contact with a minimum of 1,000 socially isolated people living on the South Side, roughly two per day during the work week, over the two-year period.

2. To take enquiries from those of diverse age, ethnic origin, neighborhood, and health.

3. To publicize the service in all areas of the community.

4. To link the enquirers to organizations that can help them move away from social isolation.

5. To identify gaps in services.

The data collected on the spreadsheet described in the last section can be used to quantify objectives 1, 2, and 4 (objectives 3 and 5 are considered later).

Objective 1 is measured by counting the number of enquiries to Connecting South Side. If this is equal to or greater than twice the number of working days that Connecting South Side has been operating, then the organization is on target.

Objective 2 can be assessed by summarizing the data collected for each enquirer about their age, ethnic origin, neighborhood, and health status. For example, the number of enquirers from each neighborhood can be counted and comparisons can be made from month to month. More detail about data analysis is provided in Chapter 13.

Objective 4 can be quantified by counting the number of signpostings to helplines, community groups, etc.. This information is available on the spreadsheet.

Objective 3 can be quantified by listing the events that employees attended to promote the service and to give talks about their work. Details can be given about the use of advertising and social media. In addition, they can use the Source column in the spreadsheet to measure the impact of publicity campaigns to some extent. The Source column describes how enquirers found out about their service.

Connecting South Side can measure objective 5, covering gaps in services, through staff discussions and by keeping notes when a necessary service is found to be lacking. Any positive outcomes that arise after communicating information about gaps to the authorities are particularly important.

Qualitative information can be given on reports in the form of anonymized case studies that demonstrate how Connecting South Side operates. The representatives also document any positive feedback that comes back from enquiries (in an anonymized form) so that funders can see the impact the work is having. For example, Dorothy's neighbor phoned to say how pleased she was with the improvement she noticed in Dorothy. The representative added this information to Dorothy's report.

Database of Services

Connecting South Side keeps an Excel spreadsheet listing of as many relevant services as possible in the area for signposting purposes. These range from long-standing organizations such as community service centers to one-off events, such as attorneys offering free advice about issues such as housing. All employees are tasked with keeping the spreadsheet up to date. As each member of the staff lives in Chicago, they often identify new sources of support and affordable activities in the various neighborhoods. They bring in new pamphlets and circulate frequent e-mails about new services. The following data is kept about each service:

- Name
- Address
- Times/date of availability
- Description
- Category, such as legal, health, leisure, etc.
- Age of attendees

Table 4-3 shows an example spreadsheet of local services available for those living on low incomes. Each of the columns can be filtered. For example, if someone was looking for a yoga class, then column one could be filtered for yoga and the most suitable class in terms of age group and neighborhood can then be identified.

Table 4-3. Excel Spreadsheet Containing Service Summaries

Name	Address	Time/Date	Category	...
Yoga	...	...	Leisure	...
Over 75s lunch	...	...	Leisure	...
Free housing advice	...	...	Legal	...
Transport help	...	...	Transport	...
Diabetes south side	...	...	Health	...
...	...	...	...	...

Problems with the Data

Using Excel to track the enquirers and the local services worked well when the number of entries was small. However, these spreadsheets have become very large and unmanageable. Neither spreadsheet can be edited by two people at the same time as Connecting South Side is not using the latest version of Excel. This leads to delays in data being added while employees wait for the spreadsheet to become available for editing. Due to the busy nature of the office, delays can mean that information isn't available when it is needed in the case files. This causes disruption in service when follow-up calls on enquiries come in and the electronic notes haven't been updated. Sometimes several versions of the spreadsheet are in operation, which leads to confusion.

Clare is concerned about the growing problems with the data in the office. She turns to former colleagues for assistance and begins discussing the possibility of implementing a later version of Excel or using a database.

In addition to data management, it would be useful to be able to search the archive of past cases for ones that are similar to present enquiries so that work is not repeated. The search facility on File Explorer enables some searching, such as for parts of the name, file content, and date last modified. For example, a search for "Catholic" could reveal other cases, like Dorothy's, that have involved people who wanted to attend church.

However, databases provide much more sophisticated searching. For example, they could search for people who are roughly the same age as Dorothy, who live in the same area and have certain similar keywords in their case. Chapter 6 discusses choosing between a spreadsheet and a database and Chapter 12 covers database searching.

Identifying Sources of External Funding

Funding for the work of nonprofits tends to be fixed and short-term. This means that sources of new and renewed funding are always of interest. There are many government funds, grants from charitable foundations, and direct donations available, and details about these funding sources are often stored on online databases. Organizations need time to sift through the available options and identify funding opportunities that are well matched to their needs and goals. Chapter 19 covers searching online databases.

Connecting South Side keeps records of its current and potential donors on a spreadsheet. The aim is to prompt grant application deadlines and dates for final report submissions.

Summary

A small nonprofit, called Connecting South Side, aims to improve the lives of socially isolated people living on Chicago's South Side.

The nonprofit stores data in a number of MS Excel spreadsheets and Word documents, which is becoming difficult to manage as the nonprofit handles more enquiries. The design and implementation of a database for Connecting South Side is presented in future chapters.

Aligning Your Database With the Goals of Your Small Business

In order for small businesses to get the most out of a database, it must be designed with the goals, metrics, and levers of the business in mind. In summary, goals aim to move the business in a given direction, levers are variables that can be changed with the intention of bringing about such a move, and metrics measure the progress of the goals and the levers. This chapter explains these three components in detail.

A useful database is shaped by the goals of the business, with a large proportion of the data consisting of metrics. If a database is designed properly, the queries and reports produced by it will feed directly into the decision-making process of the business, enabling it to be well informed. (Queries and reports were introduced in Chapter 1 and are explained in detail in Chapters 12 and 14, respectively.)

Goals, levers, and metrics are rarely static, particularly during challenging economic times. Therefore, in order for a database to have a long life, it needs to be able to respond to new requirements quickly. This can mean adding more tables or more columns to a table. The technical aspects of database design are covered in Chapter 7 and approaches to altering existing databases are covered in Chapter 15.

The following sections lay out an example of setting goals, levers, and metrics for the Smart Wheelbarrows Inc. case study, which was introduced in Chapter 2. You'll also read about briefer examples for the Jennings-Havard Law Offices and Connecting South Side case studies, introduced in Chapters 3 and 4, respectively. Each example shows the importance of using a database for tracking the metrics and providing data about the levers and goals.

It would be highly restrictive if all database analysis was driven by business goals. Some margin for experimentation and surprise is healthy for a small business. Databases often contain hidden information that cannot be predicted in advance, but could be potentially useful. For example, Smart Wheelbarrows Inc. may discover that over half of its orders of wheelbarrows are placed on Saturday mornings. This is a fact that would be useful for stock control and is not necessarily one that could be predicted in advance. Methods for data analysis are discussed in Chapter 13.

In addition, the very nature of the structure of a database enables one table of data to operate in conjunction with other tables, irrespective of the goals, levers, and metrics of your business. This allows the stock control at Smart Wheelbarrows Inc., for example, to be tightened up by showing whether there are enough wheelbarrows in stock to meet an order, whether more need to be made and, if so, whether the supplies are in stock to do so.

Having said this, using goals, levers, and metrics is a logical starting point for database design and one that has a high chance of producing a useful database.

Setting Goals

The goals of a small business should be influenced by its mission statement, since the mission statement describes the reason the organization was founded and the principles that lie behind it. For example, Google's mission statement in 2013 was:

> *"Google's mission is to organize the world's information and make it universally accessible and useful."*

Amazon's mission statement for the last 18 years has been:

"Our vision is to be earth's most client-centric company; to build a place where people can come to find and discover anything they might want to buy online."

Goals are set with the aim of moving a business in a certain direction within the backdrop set by the mission statement. Goals should be a statement of a desired outcome; they start with a verb but give no information about how the goal will be achieved. Examples include "increase profit," "grow the client base," and "cut costs."

Goals are often separated into long-term and short-term, with long-term goals frequently running over several years. Short-term goals are there to help a company reach its long-term goals. Setting goals and reaching them is a complex procedure as many outside factors can interfere, such as access to lending from banks, changes in tax and interest rates, increasing costs (such as energy and fuel), and skill shortages. In addition, growing businesses will have more than just a few goals and these may conflict. In a very simple example, if a company has just two goals—"maintain high-quality products" and "maximize profit"—it will have to maximize profit within the constraints of maintaining the quality of its goods. Thus, it could increase profit by negotiating cheaper rates from its suppliers, but it may not be able to use cheaper and lower-quality materials for its products.

Identifying Levers

Levers alter how the goals are achieved. By identifying a lever that can be "pulled," it's possible to make improvements to a related goal. Levers are necessary, because the goals, which are set before the levers are considered, are the outcomes of a process and cannot be changed without the levers. Examples of levers include "use the sale of complementary goods to encourage larger sizes of client transactions," and "negotiate lower prices on supplies to raise profit margins".

Designing Metrics

There is little point in guessing how well levers and goals are progressing. Both need to be measurable to make sure the business is advancing toward its goals and to assess how much impact each lever is having. Such measurements, known as *metrics*, allow levers to be controlled and hopefully improved.

This section covers the design of the metrics. Metrics and databases are closely linked as the data collected as the result of a metric must be stored and analyzed. Databases are ideal for this purpose. Queries and reports are then generated within the database, which can allow decisions to be made regarding the progress of the business.

Most small businesses use some metrics, for example to measure the level of profit and loss. However, beyond what is absolutely necessary, many often operate on the basis of past experience, by intuition, or by looking at other products on the market (as explained in Chapter 1).

Examples of metrics related to sales are:

- The number of new clients over a given time period

- Income received through sales

The following factors are important when developing metrics:

- *Simplicity*: Metrics should be straightforward to use and to explain.

- *Number*: Small numbers of metrics should be implemented at a given time to avoid confusion.

- *Quality*: It should be possible to collect accurate and complete data for all metrics.

- *Collection method*: Metrics should not interfere with operations or create unreasonable overhead.

- *Impact on employees*: Metrics should not cause employees to act against the best interests of the business.

- *Appropriate scale*: Metrics should be set to reveal changes of a suitable size to enable action to be taken to improve the process.

- *Responsive*: Metrics must provide feedback quickly so that problems can be identified as soon as possible.

After the metrics have been determined, a "baseline" can be established. The baseline uses the metrics to measure the current state of performance and can be used to make comparisons with a future state.

Although it may seem obvious, it is important not to get carried away with metrics. Not everything can be measured directly. Relying to some extent on intuition may be helpful. For example, you may feel that your clients would be happier with a smarter, more comfortable waiting area and it's unlikely that metrics would inform you of this. Metrics are best used alongside common sense and gut feelings rather than as a replacement for either.

Case Studies: Outline

The use of goals, levers, and metrics for the case studies introduced in Chapters 2–4 will now follow. Each case study section presents the mission statement, which determines the motivation for everything that organization does. You'll then see how to set goals for Smart Wheelbarrows Inc. and Jennings-Havard Law Offices. For the Connecting South Side case study, the mission and goals will reflect the aims and objectives of the grant that funds the organization. For each organization, a single goal is used to demonstrate the selection of levers and metrics.

Case Study: Smart Wheelbarrows Inc.

A mission statement and potential goals will be identified for Smart Wheelbarrows Inc. We will propose potential levers for one of the goals and suggest possible metrics.

Mission Statement and Goals

The mission statement for Smart Wheelbarrows Inc. is:

> *"Our aim is to be a customer-focused company, producing and selling high-quality, innovative wheelbarrows."*

A number of goals have been put in place for Smart Wheelbarrows Inc. based on its mission statement:

- Produce high-quality, lightweight, fold-up wheelbarrows and decorative wheelbarrows

- Ensure that employees are friendly and helpful to customers

- Guarantee products unconditionally and accept returns for any reason at any time

- Provide a friendly working environment that's full of opportunities for employees

- Promote growth by giving owners and employees freedom to propose new ideas

- Increase profit

The next section considers the selection of levers for the "increase profit" goal in detail. Suitable metrics are considered for each lever: these metrics represent the link to a potential database, as it would be wise to store the data to carry out the measurements in the form of a database.

Increasing Profit

A logical method for identifying suitable levers for increasing profit is to determine the elements that make up profit.

Profit is calculated as follows:

$$Profit = Revenue - Cost\ of\ Sales - Overhead$$

Each of these components is described here:

- *Revenue* is the amount of money that Smart Wheelbarrows Inc. has coming in. In this example, we will assume this relates only to the sales of its wheelbarrows. In a more complex example, other forms of income could include interest on investments, fees from services, etc.

- *Cost of Sales* are the costs involved in producing the wheelbarrows. This includes the materials used and the direct labor costs.

- *Overhead* is the running cost of the business, including rent, fuel, and stationary items.

Each of these components is discussed in turn and suitable levers will be selected. Figure 5-1 summarizes the goal of increasing profit and the following sections refer back to it regularly. The main goal of increasing profit is shown at the top of Figure 5-1, with the subgoals of increasing revenue, reducing the cost of sales, and reducing overhead set out underneath.

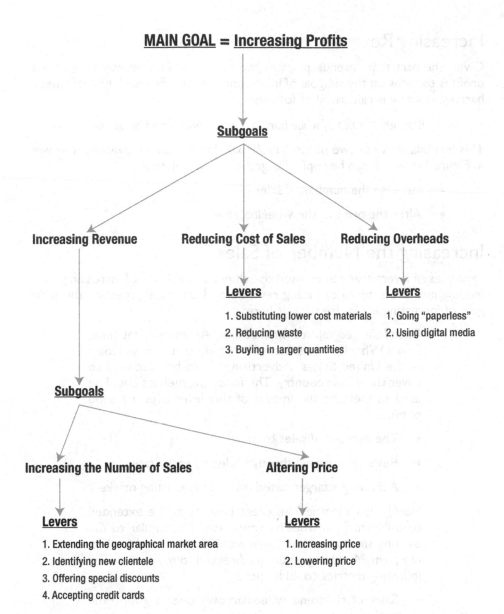

Figure 5-1. Subgoals and levers for the goal of Increasing Profits for Smart Wheelbarrows Inc.

Increasing Revenue

Given the part that revenue plays in generating profit, one way to increase profit is to focus on the subgoal of increasing revenue. For each *type* of wheelbarrow, revenue is calculated as follows:

Revenue = sales of wheelbarrow x retail price of wheelbarrow

This formula provides two potential subgoals for increasing revenue, as shown in Figure 5-1 which can be applied together or in isolation:

- Increase the number of sales

- Alter the price of the wheelbarrows

Increasing the Number of Sales

Examples of levers that can be used to achieve the subgoal of increasing sales, feeding into the subgoal of raising revenue and, ultimately, meeting the main goal of increasing profit, are set out here:

> *Extend the geographical market area:* At the present time, Smart Wheelbarrows Inc. sells mainly to the East Coast of the United States. Advertising could be extended to cover the whole country. The following metrics could be used to measure the impact of this lever over a period of time.
>
> - The number of sales by state
>
> - Revenue received through sales to each state
>
> - Achieving a target based on sales in existing markets
>
> *Identify new clientele:* The client base could be extended to children. Such wheelbarrows would be similar to the existing small ones, but there would be no need for luxury paint. Marketing would be directed to toy stores. The following metrics could be used:
>
> - Sales of children's wheelbarrows over a given time period
>
> - Proportion of total revenue generated from sales of children's wheelbarrows
>
> - Comparison of sales and revenue of children's wheelbarrows against targets

Offer special discounts: A discount for businesses buying more than one wheelbarrow may be attractive. Private and business buyers might be interested in seasonable discounts. The following metrics could be used:

- Number of discounted sales over a given time period
- Revenue obtained
- Targets reached

Accept credit cards: Credit cards are attractive to customers as they can provide greater convenience and cash flow. Fees are charged to the retailer by the credit card company but these are usually offset by a rise in sales. The following metrics could be used:

- The number of sales using a credit card
- Revenue received through sales using a credit card
- Targets reached based on existing markets

Price Alteration

The second subgoal affecting revenue is price, as shown in Figure 5-1. The price of the wheelbarrows can be raised or lowered. Higher prices mean more revenue per sale but the total number of sales may fall. The reverse is true if price is lowered.

Clients buy the wheelbarrows for different reasons; some buy because they are easy to store, others buy because they want to impress their friends. The former group would welcome price decreases but it would not make sense to apply a price reduction to the latter group as the belief that they are buying a luxury product may be diminished. In general, clients rarely react to slight price increases and often overlook them.

One suitable metric for the change in price is to compare the number of sales after a price increase with those before the increase over equal time periods.

Reducing the Cost of Sales

The second subgoal of increasing profit is reducing cost of sales, as shown in Figure 5-1. The cost of the materials used to make the wheelbarrows is one of the organization's largest sales costs. The following three levers aim to reduce material costs without impacting the quality of the wheelbarrows.

Substitute lower cost materials where possible: Mild steel, which is cheaper and heavier than aluminum, could be used for the "static" wheelbarrows, as they do not need to hang up. All the wheelbarrows are painted so the possible problem of rust brought about using mild steel is alleviated. Associated metrics:

- Income saved due to lower material costs in a given time period

- Reduction in cost of sales due to reduction in cost of materials

Reduce waste: The cost of the aluminum or mild steel is high and so the amount discarded during production is important, particularly as it accumulates over time. The tube is bought at a fixed length directly from the manufacturer. It may be possible to negotiate shorter lengths that still cover the amount required, but at a lower price. Associated metrics:

- Income saved due to less waste in a given time period

- Reduction in cost of sales due to reduction in cost of materials

Buy in larger quantities: It may be possible to take advantage of discounts when buying materials in bulk. This is often worth negotiating with suppliers. Related metrics could be:

- Income saved due by buying in larger quantities over a given time period

- Reduction in cost of sales due to buying supplies in larger quantities

Reducing Overhead

The third component of the equation for profit is overhead, which, like cost of sales, needs to fall in order to precipitate a rise in profit. Decreasing overhead forms the third subgoal of increasing profit, as shown in Figure 5-1.

The following three levers have the potential to reduce overhead for Smart Wheelbarrows Inc.:

Reduce office expenses by going "paperless": Smart Wheelbarrows Inc. could avoid printing unless absolutely necessary. They could produce and send invoices and bills electronically when possible and could file all important paperwork on the computer or in the cloud. Associated metrics could be:

- Expenses saved on office supplies over a given time period

- Proportion of overhead saved due to cut in office expenses

- Proportion of office expenses saved due to cut in office expenses

Reduce advertising expenses by using digital media: Smart Wheelbarrows Inc. could open business Facebook and Twitter accounts free of charge and cut expenditure on more traditional forms of advertising. Associated metrics could be:

- Amount saved on advertising after digital media is introduced

- Proportion of overhead saved due to use of digital advertising

- Proportion of advertising saved due to use of digital advertising

Storing Appropriate Data to Cover the Metrics

In order to demonstrate the link between goals, levers, and metrics, the following table gives an example of the data that could be captured and stored for the metrics introduced in the previous section. It is not intended to be comprehensive. In Chapter 7, you'll learn that it's not recommended to design a database with *derived* data—for example, with a column that contains total sales. With this in mind, Table 5-1 does not include derived data.

Table 5-1. Sample Data Corresponding to the Metrics Used by Smart Wheelbarrows Inc.

Subgoal	Metric
Revenue	Quantity sold of each product per transaction
	Date of each transaction
	Price of each product
	Address of customer
	Sales involving a discount
	Sales involving a credit card
Cost of Sales	Quantity bought depending on each type, length, and supplier of material
	Date of each transaction
	Price paid depending on each type, length, and supplier of material
Overhead	Quantity bought of each type of office stationary
	Date of each transaction
	Price of each type of office stationary
	Cost of each type of advertising venture, broken down as low as possible
	Date of each advertising venture

Case Study: Jennings-Havard Law Offices

The following sections identify potential goals for Jennings-Havard Law Offices. These sections will also suggest potential levers for one of the goals and will propose suitable metrics.

Mission Statement and Goals

The mission statement for Jennings-Havard Law Offices is:

> *"Jennings-Havard Law Offices aim to provide affordable, high-quality, client-focused estate planning, trust administration, probate, and long-term care planning services to a diverse range of people."*

The following goals have been set in place for Jennings-Havard Law Offices based on this mission statement:

- Keep costs low so that hourly rates are competitive
- Treat clients with attentiveness, respect, and patience at all times
- Improve client retention
- Attract new clients

- Encourage all partners and employees to suggest new ideas

- Increase growth

- Provide a pleasant and productive working environment

The next section considers the selection of levers for the "improve client retention" goal.

Improving Client Retention

It costs far less to keep clients than it does to acquire them. Client retention is therefore an important goal for Jennings-Manning Law Offices. Examples of three levers that could be used to improve client retention are as follows:

- *Maximize client interaction:* The more interaction the firm has with its clients, the less likely they are to leave. For example, clients could be encouraged to sign up for the firm's newsletter, to comment on the firm's blog, and to follow the firm on Twitter.

   Metrics: The number of new clients receiving the newsletter/commenting on the blog/following on Twitter

- *Ensure that clients are happy with the service they are receiving:* Clients could be asked for regular feedback. In the worst-case scenario, the firm could make sure that the staff understands what to do if they learn that a client is leaving. For example, they could arrange a meeting to discuss what went wrong, and deduct a small percentage from the bill.

   Metrics: Proportion of clients providing feedback, good and bad

- *Keep up with client requirements over time:* Clients often stop using a service because they believe they no longer need it. It's important to understand how client requirements progress and to market services to them. For example, estate planning may move on to a need for long-term care planning.

   Metrics: Number of repeat clients, number of clients referred by existing clients

Case Study: Connecting South Side

Chapter 4 described the case study of Connecting South Side, a nonprofit funded by a grant. The aim stated on the grant can be viewed as its mission statement with the objectives forming its goals:

Aim: To improve the lives of socially isolated people from diverse backgrounds living on the South Side of Chicago.

Objectives:

1. To make contact with a minimum of 1,000 socially isolated people living on Chicago's South Side, roughly two per day during the work week, over the two-year period.

2. To take enquiries from those of diverse age, ethnic origin, neighborhood, and health.

3. To publicize the service in all areas of the community.

4. To link the enquirers to organizations that can help them move away from social isolation.

5. To identify gaps in services.

The following levers can be applied to goal 1:

- Presence at relevant community events

- Encouraging referrals from other nonprofits

- Advertising in public places, such as libraries, churches, local stores, and coffee shops

Metrics: The number of enquiries to Connecting South Side. If this is equal to or greater than twice the number of work days that Connecting South Side has been operating, then the organization is on target.

■ **Note**   The previous metric (number of enquiries) could encourage employees to act against the best interests of the organization. The number of enquiries does not reflect the amount of effort put into each enquiry and may inadvertently encourage staff to rush through enquiries. To mitigate this problem, the organization might also gather metrics that cover the number of calls per enquiry.

Summary

For a database to be useful, it needs to be linked to the business' goals. This means working directly from the goals to develop the content of the database. Goals are affected by levers, which are "pulled" to generate change in a given direction. Metrics measure changes to goals and levers. Data collected for the metrics is stored in a database.

Further Reading

Marketing Metrics: The Definitive Guide to Measuring Marketing Performance, by Paul W. Farris, Neil T. Bendle, Phillip E. Pfeifer, and David J. Reibstein. Pearson FT Press; 2nd edition, 2010, ISBN-13: 978-0137058297.

Measuring Marketing: 110+ Key Metrics Every Marketer Needs, by John A. Davis. John Wiley & Sons; 2nd edition, 2013, ISBN-13: 978-1118153741.

Choosing Between Spreadsheets and Databases

Small businesses frequently use spreadsheets when a database would be more appropriate. This is often due to widespread familiarity with spreadsheets and the short learning curve required to begin using them productively. Time and again there is a lack of in-house knowledge about databases and their potential benefits.

This chapter aims to help you decide whether a database would benefit your small business by explaining the limitations of spreadsheets, how they can lead to difficulties, and how databases can overcome some of these problems. It aims to bring these issues to your attention and warn you about how they could worsen as your data increases in volume and complexity. There are situations when spreadsheets are more than adequate for data handling and it is not my intention to mislead you. Rather, I would like to warn you of the pitfalls of using spreadsheets as databases so that you do not end up in a crisis that you could have avoided.

Overview

This book assumes that you are familiar with spreadsheets. As you have seen from earlier chapters, spreadsheets and databases have many similarities. Given this, you may wonder why you should consider using databases at all. The choice between a spreadsheet and a database is not a matter of providing a list of criteria that enables you to make a quick decision. Such a decision can depend on multiple factors.

You don't have to make the decision to move to a database or not immediately. If, after reading this chapter, you decide to move your data operations to a database, you can start by taking small steps to prepare your data for a transition at a later stage. You can learn how to organize your data efficiently in a spreadsheet, following the suggestions in this chapter, which will save you work when you have acquired a greater volume of data.

Moving your data to a database does not mean you can't still use spreadsheets. Most databases allow for data to be moved easily back and forth from a database to a spreadsheet. So, if you're comfortable working in the spreadsheet format, you won't have to leave it behind. In fact, many businesses choose to use databases and spreadsheets simultaneously in order to take advantage of the benefits of both.

The goals of your business may help you decide whether a spreadsheet or a database is more appropriate. If your goal is reasonably straightforward and will be reflected in a one-dimensional growth in data—for example, the only data item that changes is the number of customers—the complexity of your data is unlikely to change very much. However, if the goal is to introduce new products, start new publicity campaigns, and follow new metrics, your data is likely to become significantly more complex. A spreadsheet could become less efficient at handling your data and it may be more appropriate to move to a database.

Databases are not the only alternative to spreadsheets in terms of software. For example, in Chapter 3 a number of web-based software solutions were presented for the legal firm case study, including those for task management, case status, and time tracking. By demonstrating the power of databases, this chapter enables you to compare their benefits with software other than spreadsheets. The focus is on spreadsheets, however.

As spreadsheet packages have developed over time, it has become possible to run a database-type structure within a spreadsheet package. For example, Excel 2013 can handle many database characteristics, such as linked tables. Thus, the choice is not necessarily between a database package and a spreadsheet package, but more between the concept of a database and the concept of a spreadsheet.

The following sections cover issues that you need to consider when you're making the decision to use a database rather than a spreadsheet. Data complexity gets the most attention, as it is the most pertinent issue and has stood the test of time, regardless of improved technology.

Data Complexity

Indications that it might be a good idea to move your data from a spreadsheet to a database start to appear as your data becomes more complex. This does not necessary concern the actual amount of data but the number of different "subjects" or "themes" captured within it. For example, four themes are contained in the database for Cards for Everyone Inc. that was introduced in Chapter 1—Customers, Invoices, Products, and Suppliers.

A Simple List

As mentioned, a spreadsheet is likely to be sufficient for a simple, isolated list. One example is a list of customers. Even if the list were to get very long—as many as several thousand rows—a spreadsheet would be adequate. For example, MS Excel spreadsheets from MS Excel 2007 onward can handle over a million rows.

However, if you have data in multiple columns with relationships between those columns, a spreadsheet can get complicated and cumbersome very quickly, as demonstrated in the next section.

Repeated Data

The chances of repeated data or *data redundancy* become greater as the number of columns contained in a spreadsheet rises. A very simple example of data redundancy occurs in the spreadsheets used by Smart Wheelbarrows Inc. in Chapter 2 where the ZIP code is repeated in Tables 2-3 and 2-4. To illustrate this issue, these tables are shown again here as Tables 6-1 and 6-2.

Table 6-1. Basic Customer Spreadsheet from Smart Wheelbarrows Inc.

Name	ZIP Code	Telephone	E-Mail	Category
Bright Florist	NY 11375	...	...	Business
Hilary Smith	MA 02108	...	...	Business
Bliss Garden Center	RI 02886	...	...	Consumer

Table 6-2. Basic Invoices Spreadsheet from Smart Wheelbarrows Inc.

Name	ZIP Code	Date	Amount ($)
Bright Florist	NY 11375	...	...
Hilary Smith	MA 02108	...	...
Bliss Garden Center	RI 02886	...	...

Clearly, if the data is stored in more than one place, any changes need to be made more than once. If Hilary Smith's ZIP code were to change, for example, identical edits would need to be made in Tables 6-1 and 6-2. Consequently, edits are likely to be made less reliably than if data is stored in one location. In addition, redundant data also takes up unnecessary disk space, although this is not a priority consideration today.

In this example, the problem of the repeated ZIP code can be solved easily by removing the column for ZIP code from either the Customers spreadsheet or the Invoices spreadsheet. However, many data redundancy problems on spreadsheets cannot be solved in such a straightforward manner. Suppose the data from Cards for Everyone Inc. for Customers and Invoices is stored in a single spreadsheet, as shown for the first three invoices in Table 6-3. A reason for this layout could be to keep customer data and invoice data closely linked and visible when looking at the spreadsheet.

Table 6-3. Combined Customer and Invoice Spreadsheet

Customer Name	ZIP Code	E-Mail	Date	Amount ($)
Lisa Garcia	MI 48823	Lgarcia@...	11/4/14	17.00
John Williams	OR 97062	Jwilliams@...	11/4/14	2.50
Steve Jones	FL 33901	Sjones@...	11/4/14	14.00

When John Williams places his second order there are two main alternatives for inserting this data into the spreadsheet in Table 6-3.

First, a new row can be inserted for John Williams' second order, as shown in the spreadsheet in Table 6-4.

Table 6-4. Combined Customer and Invoices Spreadsheet with Extra Row for John Williams

Customer Name	ZIP Code	E-Mail	Date	Amount ($)
Lisa Garcia	MI 48823	Lgarcia@...	11/4/14	17.00
John Williams	OR 97062	Jwilliams@..	11/4/14	2.50
Steve Jones	FL 33901	Sjones@..	11/4/14	14.00
John Williams	OR 97062	Jwilliams@..	12/14/14	5.00

However, this row creates redundant data about John Williams' ZIP code and e-mail address. Although repetitions of this nature do not pose too much of a problem if you have a small number of orders, after several orders it could become an issue. This is because any changes to John Williams' ZIP code and/or e-mail address would need to be made in several places, thus wasting time and risking errors. If several other customers also placed multiple orders, the problem would be exacerbated.

Secondly, new columns could be placed alongside John Williams' record to capture the data about his second order, as shown in the spreadsheet in Table 6-5. This would avoid the potential need for redundant data about ZIP codes and e-mail addresses. However, such an approach could become very messy very quickly. If, say, John Williams were to place a total of 20 orders over a period of a year, the spreadsheet as it stands would have 40 extra columns for dates and amounts. Searching for a particular order for a particular date would involve scanning across many columns or entering a formula into an automated search facility.

Table 6-5. Combined Customer and Invoices Spreadsheet with Extra Columns for John Williams

Customer Name	ZIP Code	E-Mail	Date	Amount ($)	Date2	Amount2 ($)
Lisa Garcia	MI 48823	Lgarcia@...	11/4/14	17.00		
John Williams	OR 97062	Jwilliams@..	11/4/14	2.50	12/14/14	5.00
Steve Jones	FL 33901	Sjones@..	11/4/14	14.00		

These problems arise because there is data relating to more than one *theme* in the same spreadsheet. The spreadsheet is about invoices, but it also contains data about customers.

Database design aims to organize data so as to minimize redundancy: more details are given in Chapter 7. A separate table is created for each *theme* and the aim is that data only takes up the space that it needs. This way, it is possible to find an invoice, check the corresponding customer unique identifier, and then find the customer's details in the Customers table: a database makes these links automatically without any need for the user to get involved with the detail. Likewise, a customer can be identified by his customer unique identifier in the Customers table and all the invoice records with that customer unique identifier can be extracted from the Invoices table. Although there are two tables, each customer and each invoice has only one entry in the system. This leads to more efficient updates, data storage, and data retrieval.

In the database for Cards for Everyone Inc., data about invoices and customers was split and linked in a database, which eliminated the problems of redundancy previously discussed. Tables 6-6 and 6-7 demonstrate how John Williams' order would be added to the Cards for Everyone Inc. database with no redundant data and no additional columns. Everything in each table relates to a single theme.

Table 6-6. Basic Customer Database Table

Customer ID	Name	ZIP Code	E-Mail
I	Lisa Garcia	MI 48823	Lgarcia@hotmail.com
2	John Williams	OR 97062	Jwilliams@gmail.com
3	Steve Jones	FL 33901	Sjones@aol.com

Table 6-7. Basic Invoice Table

Invoice No.	Customer ID	Date	Amount ($)
1001	I	11/4/14	17.00
1002	2	11/4/14	2.50
1003	3	11/4/14	14.00
1004	2	12/14/14	5.00

Maintaining Relationships Between Spreadsheets

Even if redundancy is removed from spreadsheets, there is still the problem of maintaining accurate relationships between them. This problem is addressed in a database via the use of a number of logical steps in data organization that enable data to be updated and deleted automatically across multiple tables. This is explained in detail in Chapter 7. In a spreadsheet, manual operations are generally required.

For example, suppose Cards for Everyone Inc. is working with separate spreadsheets for Products and Suppliers—see Tables 6-8 and 6-9.

Table 6-8. Basic Product Spreadsheet for Cards for Everyone Inc.

Product Name	Supplier Name	Category	Price ($)	Quantity Available
Cats	Special Occasions	Birthday	2.00	5
Roses	Old Favorites	Thank You	3.00	8
Boats	Old Favorites	Birthday	2.50	10
Hearts	Handmade Cards	Valentines	4.50	9
Rabbits	Handmade Cards	New Baby	5.00	11

Table 6-9. Basic Supplier Spreadsheet for Cards for Everyone Inc.

Supplier Name	ZIP Code	Telephone	E-Mail
Special Occasions	IA 52241	319-xxx-xxxx	admin@specialoccasions.com
Old Favorites	CA 92591	503-xxx-xxxx	office@oldfavorites.com
Handmade Cards	FL 33351	954-xxx-xxxx	enquiries@handmadecards.com

If one of the suppliers ceased trading, you would want to remove them from the Supplier spreadsheet. You would also want to remove any cards that they were supplying so that you didn't waste time trying to order them or, worse, advertise them to customers. For example, if "handmade cards" ceased trading, you would need to remove "Hearts" and "Rabbits" from Table 6-8.

Manually removing entries from spreadsheets that contain connected data can become time consuming and lead to errors. And, if there are other spreadsheets where Cards for Everyone Inc. uses that supplier, these entries would have to be deleted from those spreadsheets as well.

If a group of spreadsheets is being maintained by just one person, the chances are that such modifications can be carried out reliably, even if they are laborious. However, if more than one person is responsible for updating the spreadsheets, or if there is a change in personnel, then the possibility of the data becoming mismatched are much higher.

In a database, certain rules can be specified about table updates. With such rules in place updates in one table cannot occur without updates in related tables; data cannot be deleted from one table without corresponding deletions in other tables. Such specifications help you avoid data inconsistencies. For example, Cards for Everyone Inc. would not want to miss sending an invoice to a new customer because an invoice had been added to the Invoices table but no corresponding customer had been added to the Customers table. If they used a database, this could be avoided.

Summary of Data Complexity

If you find that your business spends a significant amount of time entering the same data into multiple spreadsheets, you are ready for a database. Databases cut down on the amount of data entry that is necessary and, in doing so, reduce potential typing errors.

A database makes it easy to store data in one place and reference it in multiple places. For instance, customer data may be stored in a table containing the name, address, phone number, e-mail, etc. It can then be referenced in other places, such as within queries, forms, and reports.

■ **Note**   Queries, forms, and reports were introduced in Chapter 1. Queries are discussed in more detail in Chapter 12, forms in Chapter 10, and reports in Chapter 14. The Appendix at the end of the book describes how to set up a simple query, form, and report.

If the customer's data changes, you only need to change that information in one place when using a database. That new data will be automatically visible from all the queries, forms, and reports that reference it.

As a final comment, if changes to your spreadsheet do not happen very often, these arguments lose their weight. The decision is one of balance that only you can make.

The Time Period the Data Will Be Used

The next decision point involves the amount of time you will be spending with your data. For the occasional short data analysis, a spreadsheet is more than adequate—it would be excessive to learn database techniques for a brief project. It does not take long to become productive with a spreadsheet and they are highly flexible. There are few people these days who cannot use spreadsheets at the basic level.

However, if you need to analyze the same data over time and if that data is complex, a database may be beneficial. Once you need to search the data, the built-in spreadsheet functions are unlikely to be enough. You'll need programming skills to enable searching and very few spreadsheet users will possess these.

The Number of Users

Another important decision point concerns the number of people who will need to access the data at any given time. If there is only one person accessing the data at a time, it is possible, although challenging in some cases, to continue with a spreadsheet. Clear notes about how the spreadsheet system works are necessary in case the responsibility of maintaining the spreadsheet is passed on at a future date.

If there are a number of people using the same spreadsheet, avoiding errors can be difficult. In past years the options for sharing documents were either via e-mail attachments or by placing a copy on the office's shared drive. Tracking versions and edits from several users could be difficult and time-consuming. These days, spreadsheets can exist in the cloud and be used by several users, for example, through using the Excel Web App. The cloud is discussed in detail in Chapter 18.

Whatever approach is used to store the spreadsheet, the risk of errors is high, particularly from those who are inexperienced. For example, sorting a single column in a spreadsheet without expanding across other columns can ruin a spreadsheet and lead to reversion to previous versions and wasted work. This is a common error made by those who do not use spreadsheets frequently.

In general, it is best to keep the number of users of a spreadsheet low and to train them thoroughly. With a database, users can access data simultaneously and it is easier to design methods of viewing the data that do not lead to changes to the data itself—for example, via forms.

■ **Note**   Forms were introduced in Chapter 1. The Appendix describes how to create a simple form.

Just having several users using the same spreadsheet would not be enough to justify the use of a database alone. For example, having several users modifying a spreadsheet that contained a simple list of customers is acceptable as it is not difficult to manage. But having several users accessing a more complex spreadsheet could lead to serious complications. A database is likely to be more efficient in such a situation.

The Requirement for Reports

If you need to generate reports regularly, it is likely that you will need a database. When working with spreadsheets, the spreadsheet and the report are not independent. When you're building a spreadsheet, the data is formatted and arranged in order to get the desired report. With a database, the data and reporting features are unconnected, which enables you to generate multiple reports with the same data, providing flexibility and efficiency.

For example, you may wish to generate the following three reports:

- Overall sales by quarter

- Annual sales by region

- Monthly sales by product type

Each of these reports involves the use of sales data. Instead of maintaining three spreadsheets with repeated data, a database allows you to use queries to generate all three reports from one data source, with no copying and pasting necessary.

■ **Note**   Queries were introduced in Chapter 1. The Appendix describes how to set up a simple query.

This approach saves time and is less prone to errors since the reports are generated directly from the database, which is the only point at which changes are made to the data. It comes back to the problem of redundant data discussed earlier: if you have several copies of the same data, you cannot guarantee that they are all updated at any one time unless you are highly vigilant.

The Best of Both Worlds

As mentioned at the beginning of the chapter, the choice to move your data to a database does not mean you no longer have the option of using a spreadsheet. In many cases, a combination of the two is the best approach. You can store your data in a database and therefore run advanced reports and queries. In turn, those reports and queries can be moved to spreadsheets for deeper analysis. The strength of spreadsheets lies in their ability to conduct individual complex calculations using advanced formulae.

Summary

Deciding to use a spreadsheet versus a database is an ever-changing process. Technology does not stand still. For example, as you have seen, the volume of data is not as important a consideration as it used to be. The functionality of multiuser access is becoming less of a problem for spreadsheets with the use of the cloud. However, spreadsheets do not handle multiple-themed data efficiently, leading to the need to store data in several places. This is inefficient and can lead to typing and mismatch errors. Databases are excellent for pulling data together, separating the themes, linking tables together, enabling efficient data storage, and updating and retrieving data. You can also create reports quickly and accurately from a database.

If you have data that contains a number of themes that you will be storing over time and that change regularly, it makes sense to adopt a database.

If you have reached the end of this chapter and have made the decision that you want to move to a database, rest assured that you do not need to do this now or in one fell swoop. You can take small steps that will help you make a more efficient move later. For example, you could think about the themes contained in your data and the amount of redundant data you have. You could think about separating some of your spreadsheets into single themes. Such steps will enable you to reduce the amount of work when you come to make the switch. Regardless, as Chapter 15 shows, it is unrealistic to expect that all the decisions about your database design will be made in advance. Some changes will occur as the business evolves. A database is rarely static.

Designing Your Small Business Database

A well-designed database will be easy to use, straightforward to adjust, and provide reliable outputs. A poor design, on the other hand, may still work initially but is likely to deteriorate with time. Problems may arise, such as erroneous or missing data and, eventually, the database is likely to be dropped by the business altogether.

There are set guidelines to help avoid problems when designing a database, but these do not cover all criteria. For example, much of what influences the database design comes from the goals and levers of the business discussed in Chapter 5. These help you find the starting point and the direction in which to focus. Thus, beyond satisfying a set of rules, your database design is flexible.

This chapter walks you through the design steps of your database, starting from the point at which no database exists and moving to the position where a structure of linked tables is in place.

The Database Design Process

The design process consists of the following steps:

1. Familiarizing yourself with the purpose of your database.

2. Identifying and organizing the required data.

3. Dividing the data into tables made up of columns.

4. Refining your design by adding a few rows of sample data to test that you obtain the desired results.

5. Defining and setting up the relationships between the tables.

6. Applying "rules" to ensure that the tables have been structured efficiently.

7. Developing queries and reports.

8. Documenting your database design for future users.

Determining the Purpose of Your Database

It is important to be clear on the goals, levers, and metrics of your small business before starting to design your database. If you do not take the time to map out the project's requirements and determine how the database is going to meet them, it is likely that the whole project will lose direction and will be far less useful than it could have been, thus wasting time and money.

Start by writing a mission statement for your database. For example, the Cards for Everyone Inc. statement could be

"This database will be used to track invoices from customers and coordinate supplies of cards."

Such a statement will help you make decisions more easily during the design process.

If more than one person will be using the database, it would be helpful to describe their roles—when and how each person will interact with the database. In the case of Cards for Everyone Inc., each of the three employees (Pat, Zeph, and Leona) will interact with the database. Their roles could be summarized as follows:

- Pat, the manager, will keep the details of the database up to date, entering details of new customers, invoices, and supplies.

- Zeph and Leona, the assistants, will use the database to check how much of required items there are in stock.

Further, you must define the database requirements, such as "must be able to produce monthly sales reports." Drafting the sample input forms, queries, and reports can also be beneficial. Clearly, it is impossible to predict every need that your database will have to meet and every issue that is likely to come up, but it is important to guard against potential omissions as much as possible.

Identifying the Data to Go into the Database

Once you have determined the purpose of the database, the next step is to gather the data you need to store. A good place to start is with your existing data.

If you are using spreadsheets, you could start by making a list of the column headings. Alternatively, if you have been using paper records, each type of data used could be placed in a list (for example, each box that you fill in on a form).

Another option is to start making your list from scratch using the database's mission statement as a guideline. Once you're finished, you can check that you have covered all the existing data.

In all cases, as you prepare this list, write down each item that comes to mind. Do not worry about structuring the list at this stage as you can tidy it up later. If others will be using the database, ask them for their ideas too.

Next, consider the types of queries, forms, reports, or mailings you'll want to produce from the database. For example, you might want to report sales by region, or show product levels in stock. Imagine what the report would look like and the data that would be included. List each data item that would appear on each report that you anticipate creating that's not already on your list.

Suppose you give customers the opportunity to receive an e-mailed newsletter and you want to extract a list of all those who have opted to receive it. To capture this data, you could add a "Newsletter" column to the database. For each customer, you can set the value of the column to Yes or No, depending on whether they want to be on the list.

Three complete database design examples are illustrated at the end of this chapter, one for each of the case studies covered in Chapters 2–4.

After gathering this data, you are ready for the next step.

Creating Tables

Databases are made up of linked tables. The following sections describe how to create and populate your tables.

The Content of a Table

As shown in Chapter 1, tables are made up of rows and columns. The rows and columns can be inserted in any order. Tables are used to represent *theme*, that is, objects in the real world. An example of a real-world object from Cards for Everyone Inc. is a customer, an invoice, a supplier, or a product.

Rarely is it the case that a small business's data is so simple that it can be represented in one table alone and, in general, a database is made up of tables that are linked together. A database enables data that's stored in tables to be put back together using queries, forms, and reports.

Databases are based on the guideline that every table represents one *theme*. Once you have chosen the *theme* that is represented by a table, the next step is to choose the columns in that table that will store the data about the *theme*. For example, the Products table in Cards for Everyone Inc. should store data about products only. As an example, although the supplier's address relates to the product, it is a fact about the supplier and not a fact about the product. It belongs in the Suppliers table.

To determine the columns in a table, decide on the data that you want to store about the *theme* represented by the table. For example, in the case of the Customers table in Cards for Everyone Inc. the columns are FirstName, LastName, ZIP code, Telephone, and E-Mail. Customer ID will be covered later.

Each row in the table contains the same set of columns so the same type of data can be stored for each customer.

Once you have determined the initial set of columns for each table, you can further refine the columns. For example, it often makes sense to divide each piece of data down into its smallest useful parts, as it is much easier to gather data items together than it is to split them apart. In the case of a name, to make each component of the name readily available, you can break the name into three parts: Title, First Name, and Last Name. The result is a much more flexible database because, for example, a report can be sorted by last name or you could create letters addressed to Mr. Jones and Mrs. Smith, which is often more appropriate than Mr. John Williams and Miss. Lisa Garcia. Similarly, the address consists of several separate components: for example, address line 1, address line 2, city, state, postal code, and country/region. If you want to manipulate the data, such as sorting by one component of the address (e.g. ZIP code), you will need ZIP Code to be stored in a separate column.

Naming Your Columns and Tables

The names that you give to your columns and tables are very important. Clear names allow current and future users of the database to understand the intended use of the column or table and the nature of the data it stores. An example of a poor alternative for FirstName in the Customers table might be FName or even FN. These names are not recognizable immediately and will slow down progress.

Avoid using spaces in column names, such as Product ID. Although I'm not proposing you do any programming in this book, column names with spaces present a problem for programmers so it is good practice to avoid them. There are many possible alternatives, such as Product_ID, productID, and ProductID. In addition, it is best to steer clear of placing quotation marks or brackets around names, examples being "Product ID" and [Product ID].

You need to choose an appropriate data type for your columns. Common data types include whole numbers, text, date/time, and yes/no.

Unique Identifiers

Each row in a table should be unique so that it can be used to link tables together or identified in a search without confusion. Uniqueness is guaranteed for a table by designating a column (or more than one column) that contains unique values for each row in the table. A naturally existing column is preferable for the unique identifier.

■ **Note**   The unique identifier is referred to formally as a *primary key,* but will be referred to as a unique identifier for the purposes of this book.

Unique identifiers should have the following properties:

- They should be as static as possible. The customer's phone number would not be a good choice as it may change.

- It is generally best to use a number (e.g. Product ID) as a unique identifier rather than a text column, as this avoids the problem of spelling mistakes and name changes.

- No unique identifier should contain missing data. This is important because you cannot identify or reference a row in a table directly if the unique identifier is missing. Some database packages, such as MS Access, automatically ensure that each unique identifier has a value.

■ **Note**   Some of the database tables in Cards for Everyone Inc. include unique identifiers from other tables. For example, the Products table contains a column with the Supplier ID in it. Such unique identifiers are referred to as *foreign keys* in database literature. Using unique identifiers in this way links tables together and is covered in the table relationships section later in this chapter.

Testing Your Database: Phase 1

To test your initial database design, it would be helpful to start becoming familiar with a database package. As mentioned in Chapter 1, if you are using MS Office, MS Access may already be available to you. And some open source software suites include database packages, such as LibreOffice and OpenOffice.

As an illustration, Figure 7-1 shows the initial steps you would take to create the Customers table from Cards for Everyone Inc. In a similar way, choose one of your own tables, giving it a name and creating its columns.

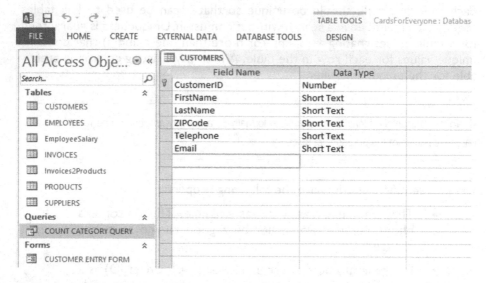

Figure 7-1. Creating a new table in MS Access 2013

■ **Note** The appendix at the end of this book provides more detailed instructions about creating a database and a table from scratch. Both MS Access 2013 and LibreOffice 5 Base are used as examples.

Then, assign each column a type. Repeat these steps for each of your tables.

■ **Note** The process for creating tables will vary according to the database package that you are using. There will be instructions available with your database package, either through an internal help facility and/or online. A straightforward search on Google will also help.

I have written this chapter with the aim of cutting out database jargon where I can as I think it can get in the way of understanding. However, when you're using database packages you may come across unfamiliar terms. For example, in Figure 7-1 there is a *primary key* icon at the top-left side that refers to the table's unique identifier. In general, try not to be put off by terms that you don't recognize.

Once you have created your draft tables, enter the data into each row. Figure 7-2 shows the data for the rows in the Customers table for Cards for Everyone Inc. These tables should feel familiar as they are very much like spreadsheets.

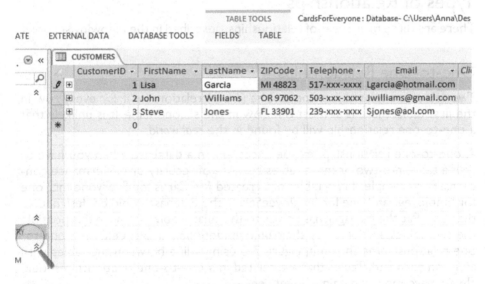

Figure 7-2. Adding data to a new table in MS Access 2013

■ **Note** It is possible to load data directly into a database from a spreadsheet. This step is quicker and helps prevent typing errors. For example, you can load data directly from MS Excel spreadsheets into MS Access. This involves an *import* step and is covered in the External Data section of the Appendix at the end of this book.

Creating your database in this way effectively begins the design-testing process. Flaws in your design may become apparent as you enter your data. As an indication of this, if you find yourself repeating the same data in more than one place, consider placing that data in a single place or starting a new table. For example, there is no need to put customer names in both the Customer table and the Invoices table: the best place for this data is in the Customers table, as it contains data about customers.

Creating the Table Relationships

A database made up of unconnected tables serves little purpose. You may as well use spreadsheets instead. A key part of designing a database is to identify the relationships between tables.

Types of Relationships

There are three main types of relationships, described in the following sections.

One-to-One Relationships

Two tables are related in a one-to-one (1—1) relationship if, for every row in the first table, there is at most one row in the second table. It is unlikely that a one-to-one relationship will be found in the *real world*.

A one-to-one relationship may be necessary in a database when you have to split a table into two or more tables because of security or performance concerns. For example, if two tables are created for Cards for Everyone Inc., one for Employees and one for EmployeeSalary, the database could be designed so that only Pat, the manager, has access to the salary table. To make this possible the two tables are joined by their unique identifier, EmployeeID, in a one-to-one relationship, as shown in Figure 7-3 using a line between the tables with a "1" on each end. Tables that are related in a one-to-one relationship should always have the same unique identifier.

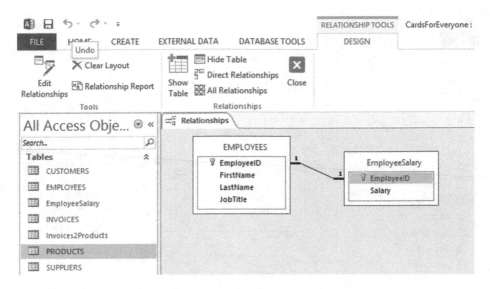

Figure 7-3. One-to-one relationship

One-to-Many Relationships

One-to-many (1—M) relationships are the most common. Two tables are related in a one-to-many relationship if:

- For every row in the first table, there can be zero, one, or many rows in the second table

- For every row in the second table, there is exactly one row in the first table

For example, each customer of Cards for Everyone Inc. can have a number of invoices, but each invoice can refer to only one customer. This relationship is illustrated in Figure 7-4 by the line with a "1" next to the Customers table and an infinity symbol next to the Invoices table. A further example is that a supplier can supply a number of products, but each product can only be supplied by one supplier. The one-to-many relationship is also referred to as a parent-child or master-detail relationship.

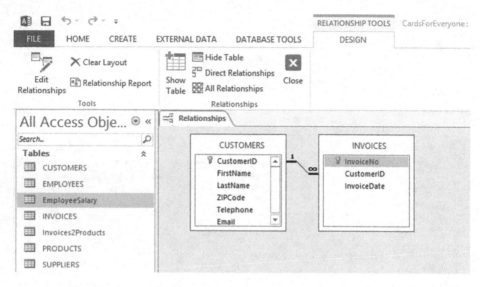

Figure 7-4. One-to-many relationship

Many-to-Many Relationships

Two tables are related in a many-to-many (M—M) relationship when, for every row in the first table, there can be many rows in the second table, and for every row in the second table, there can be many rows in the first table. Many-to-many relationships must be broken into two one-to-many relationships. For example, in Cards for Everyone Inc., an invoice may contain several products and a given product can exist on multiple invoices. Thus, as shown in Figure 7-5, the Invoices table is related to the Products table via a third, linking table, which contains a row for each occurrence of the relationship between the products and invoices by containing the unique identifier from each table.

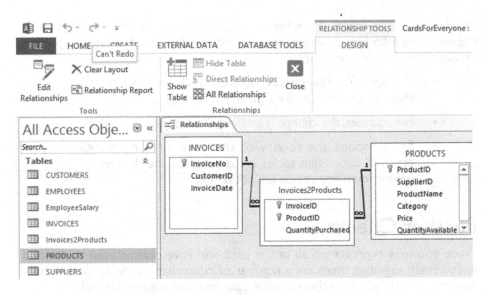

Figure 7-5. A many-to-many relationship changed into two one-to-many relationships

Relationships Between Your Tables

The next step is to determine the relationships between your tables. First, decide whether there is a relationship between two given tables. If there is, work out whether it is one-to-one, one-to-many, or many-to-many. The three case studies at the end of this chapter give further examples. If you have a many-to-many relationship, you need to insert a linking table, as demonstrated in Figure 7-5.

As mentioned in an earlier section, some tables are designed with unique identifiers from other tables: for example, the Invoices table for Cards for Everyone Inc. contains a column of customer IDs. Each of these unique identifiers must match a value in the target table. Therefore, in the Invoices table, all customer IDs must match a customer ID in the Customers table.

■ **Note**   When adding a new relationship between tables you can instruct your database to ensure that each unique identifier of one table matches a unique identifier of a target table. This process is known as *enforcing referential integrity*.

In addition, if the unique identifier in a table changes (or the entire row is deleted), the following strategies must be adopted to avoid creating *orphaned* unique identifiers in other tables:

- Disallow. The change is completely disallowed (a function that can be imposed by a database package).

- For updates, the change is applied to all dependent tables.

- For deletions, the rows with the same unique identifiers in all dependent tables are deleted or the dependent unique identifier values are set to Null.

Further Checks

Once you have represented all of the data and have drafted your tables and linked them together, there are a number of rules that can be applied to help you ensure that you have divided your data into the appropriate tables.

■ **Note** These rules are generally referred to as *normalization* in the database literature.

Recall that each table should represent one *theme* with its columns fully describing this one *theme*. As explained in Chapter 6, any redundant data should be separated and placed into related tables. Each table must contain a unique identifier.

At every row and column intersection in a given table, there should be a single value and never a list of values. For example, Table 7-1 shows a combined table for Customers and Invoices from Chapter 6 with data about John Williams' two invoices combined into the same row/column intersections.

Table 7-1. Combined Customer and Invoices Spreadsheet with Additional Data Items for John Williams

CustomerID	FirstName	LastName	ZIP Code	E-Mail	Dates	Amounts ($)
1	Lisa	Garcia	MI 48823	Lgarcia@...	11/4/14	17.00
2	John	Williams	OR 97062	Jwilliams@...	(11/4/14, 12/4/14)	(2.50, 5.00)
3	Steve	Jones	FL 33901	Sjones@...	11/4/14	14.00

You would have a difficult time retrieving data from this table, because too much data is being stored in a single column. For example, it would be very difficult to create a report that summarized the amount spent on a daily basis.

Avoid having repeating groups, even when they are stored in several columns. For example, Table 7-1 might be improved by replacing the single Dates column and the single Amounts column with repeating columns such as Date1, Date2, Amount1, and Amount2, as shown in Table 7-2.

Table 7-2. Combined Customer and Invoices Spreadsheet with Two Date and Two Amount Columns

CustomerID	FirstName	...	Date1	Amount1 ($)	Date2	Amount2 ($)
1	Lisa	...	11/4/14	17.00		
2	John	...	11/4/14	2.50	12/14/14	5.00
3	Steve	...	11/4/14	14.00		

While the data has been divided into multiple columns, it still presents problems. Any query aimed at calculating the amount spent on a daily basis would have to search both date columns and both amount columns. Clearly, as the number of invoices rises, the number of columns would need to rise to accommodate the data. If the maximum number of invoices per customer per year was 50, this would mean that you would be using 100 columns to store the date and amount data per customer, even for customers who had only one or two invoices. This is a waste of space and does not create any clear boundaries.

The fundamental problem with Tables 7-1 and 7-2 is that the columns do not refer to (or describe) the table's unique identifier—any columns that don't should be moved to another table. Tables 7-1 and 7-2 are about customers, but the columns about dates of invoices and amounts of invoices refer to invoices and not customers. They should therefore be placed in another table. Tables 7-3 and 7-4 show how to deconstruct Table 7-2 into a Customers table and an Invoices table, respectively. These tables are joined by a one-to-many relationship using CustomerID, as illustrated in Figure 7-4. All repeating data items in columns have been removed and all repeating columns have been removed. Each column in a table refers to the unique identifier of that table. It is now straightforward to run a query that calculates the amount spent on any given date.

Table 7-3. Basic Customer Database Table

CustomerID	FirstName	LastName	ZIP Code	Telephone	E-Mail
1	Lisa	Garcia	MI 48823	517-xxx-xxxx	Lgarcia@hotmail.com
2	John	Williams	OR 97062	503-xxx-xxxx	Jwilliams@gmail.com
3	Steve	Jones	FL 33901	239-xxx-xxxx	Sjones@aol.com

Table 7-4. Basic Invoices Database Table

Invoice No.	Customer ID	Date	Amount ($)
1001	1	11/4/14	17.00
1002	2	11/4/14	2.50
1003	3	11/4/14	14.00
1004	2	12/4/14	5.00

In addition, any column that describes a column other than the unique identifier must be moved to another table. For example, if there are any computed columns, then these should be removed, as database software can be used to perform the calculations when the results are required—the data is redundant. For example, suppose Cards for Everyone Inc. wants to create a report that shows the number of cards available for each category, such as the number of birthday or Valentine's Day cards. This scenario was presented in Chapter 1, as shown in Figure 7-6.

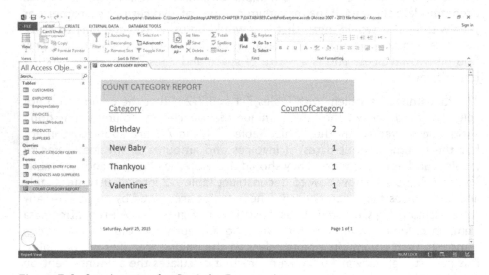

Figure 7-6. Sample report for Cards for Everyone Inc.

Table 7-5 shows a CountOfCategory column added to the Products table of Cards for Everyone Inc. However, it is not necessary to store this column in the database, because the report in Figure 7-6 can be produced directly from the Category column of the Products table.

Table 7-5. Basic Product Database Table with a calculated column

ProductID	SupplierID	ProductName	Category	...	CountOfCategory
11	100	Cats	Birthday	...	2
20	200	Roses	Thankyou	...	1
23	200	Boats	Birthday	...	2
42	300	Hearts	Valentines	...	1
61	300	Rabbits	New Baby	...	1

In general, it should be possible to change the value in each column of a table without affecting any other column. The columns should be independent of each other. In Table 7-5, you can see that the value of CountOfCategory is dependent on Category. For example, if another card with the category Birthday was added to Table 7-5, the value of CountOfCategory for each occurrence of Category='Birthday' would rise to 3.

▓ **Note** The Amount column in the Invoices table (Table 7-4) is a calculated column. Once an invoice has been sent, its amount remains static in most cases. Therefore, it would not be unreasonable to have this column.

Testing Your Database: Phase 2

Testing your database is an ongoing process and should never be regarded as complete. Chapters 12, 13, and 14 cover the use of forms, queries, and reports and discuss the analysis of your data. When carrying out these steps, you may identify problems with your design that you want to correct.

However, there is no reason why you shouldn't begin this process now. See if you can use the database to get the answers you want. Create rough drafts of your forms and reports and see if they show the data you expect. Look for unnecessary data duplication and, when you find any, alter your design to eliminate it.

If you find that you have forgotten a column try to calculate it via a query from existing columns. If the data can't be calculated from other columns, it is likely that you need a new column for it. You need to determine whether you need to create another table.

Bring the users back in and ask them to evaluate your forms and reports. If their needs are not met, refine the design.

Database Documentation

If you carefully name your tables and columns, it will be very clear what your database represents. In addition, your documentation should contain definitions of the tables, columns, and relationships. Default settings are also covered in the documentation so that it is clear how they are to be used. Examples are helpful. You should also document details of forms, queries, and reports if they are used on a long-term basis. More details about each of these is given in later chapters.

Your goal should be to provide enough information so that when you pass the database to others, they can understand its workings and make changes if they want to.

Case Studies

This section presents database designs for the case studies in chapters 2–4. You should think of these designs as one possible solution rather than the only solution.

Try to follow each design through from the data described for each of the case studies in their respective chapters. The designs are quite simple even though some have many tables. If the designs become overwhelming, take a small part, such as two tables, and do your best to understand how they are linked. Then build up slowly.

Case Study: Database Design for Smart Wheelbarrows Inc.

A possible mission statement for Smart Wheelbarrows Inc.'s database could be:

> *"This database will be used to store customer details, to make sure enough materials are in stock to meet orders, and to provide prompts to make orders of new supplies. Metrics will be stored that enable the business to monitor its levers and goals."*

The data used by Smart Wheelbarrows Inc. was presented in Chapter 2. In addition, data in the form of metrics was collected and presented in Chapter 5. That data is reproduced in Table 7-6.

Table 7-6. Sample Data for the Levers and Metrics Used by Smart Wheelbarrows Inc.

Lever	Metric
Revenue	Quantity sold of each product per transaction
	Date of each transaction
	Price of each product
	Address of customer
	Sales involving a discount
	Sales involving a credit card
Cost of sales	Quantity bought depending on each type, length, and supplier of material
	Date of each transaction
	Price paid depending on each type, length, and supplier of material
Overheads	Quantity bought of each type of office stationary
	Date of each transaction
	Price of each type of office stationary
	Cost of each type of advertising venture, broken down as low as possible
	Date of each advertising venture

To keep things manageable, only two of these metrics are added:

- Sales involving a discount
- Sales involving a credit card

Many of the tables reflect the spreadsheets presented in Chapter 2 and are considered in turn. The database design, which is the most complex of the three case studies, can be broken into three sections:

- Customers
- Color and type of product
- Materials

Figure 7-7 shows an overview of the database design.

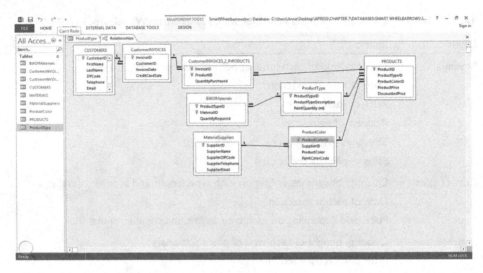

Figure 7-7. Overview of the complete database design for Smart Wheelbarrows Inc.

■ **Note** A database design is often referred to as a *schema*.

Each of these tables is discussed in the following three sections and close-ups of the design will be presented.

The Customers Table

The Customers table closely resembles the corresponding spreadsheet you saw in Chapter 2 (Table 2-3). A unique identifier has been added in the first column and the Name column has been split into FirstName and LastName. Figure 7-8 shows the data types that have been allocated to each column and Figure 7-9 shows the populated Customers table.

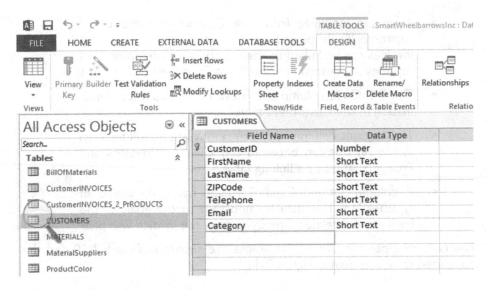

Figure 7-8. Customers table for Smart Wheelbarrows Inc.

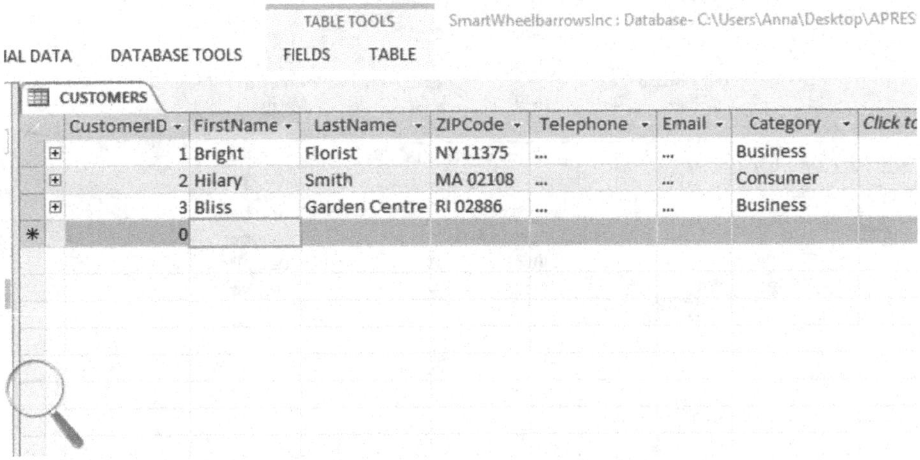

Figure 7-9. Populated Customers table for Smart Wheelbarrows Inc.

A database table, called CustomerInvoices, corresponds to the Invoices spreadsheet shown in Table 2-4. The following adjustments have been made.

- As with Cards for Everyone Inc., there is a one-to-many relationship between the Customers table and the CustomerInvoices table, because each customer can have many invoices, but each invoice applies to only one customer.

- A unique identifier from the Customers table, called CustomerID, is placed next to each invoice so that invoices can be linked to their associated customer. This replaces the customer name from Table 2-4 in Chapter 2.

- The ZIP Code column is removed as it duplicates information in the Customers table.

- The Amount column has been removed but will be seen in the relationship between the CustomerInvoices and Products tables by a linking table.

- A column entitled CreditCardSale has been added of type Yes/No. This data is important to the goals of the business and relates directly to how the invoice was paid.

The column types for CustomerInvoices are shown in Figure 7-10 and the populated table is shown in Figure 7-11.

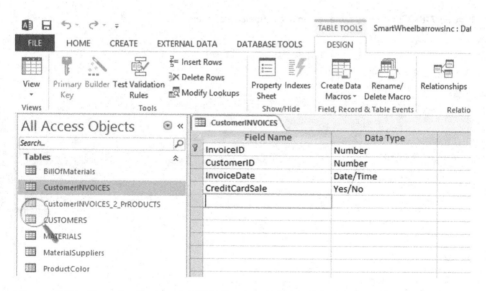

Figure 7-10. CustomerInvoices table for Smart Wheelbarrows Inc.

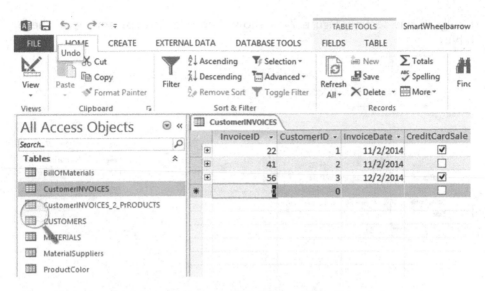

Figure 7-11. Populated CustomerInvoices table for Smart Wheelbarrows Inc.

As with Cards for Everyone Inc., there is a many-to-many link between the CustomerInvoices and Products tables. This is achieved using a linking table called CustomerInvoices_2_Products. The populated table is shown in Figure 7-12. Details about ProductID are provided in the next section.

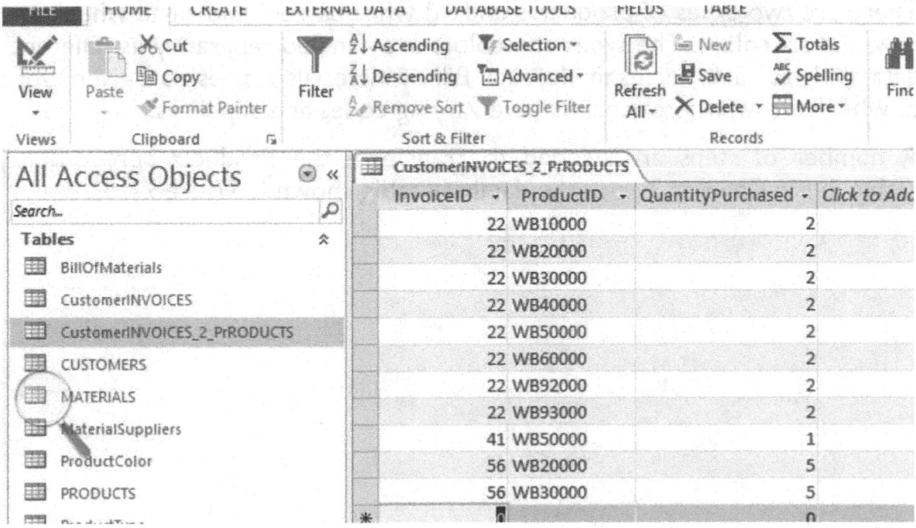

Figure 7-12. Populated CustomerInvoices_2_Products table for Smart Wheelbarrows Inc.

Finally in this section, Figure 7-13 shows the relationships among all these tables.

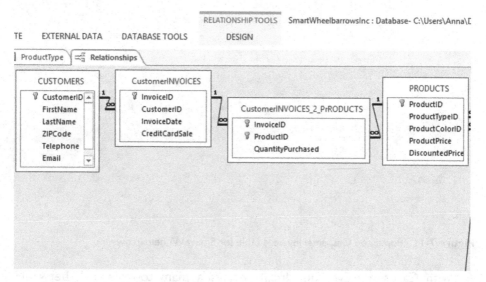

Figure 7-13. The Customers, CustomerInvoices, and Products tables, linked together

Color and Type of Product

There are two types of product, standard wheelbarrow and small wheelbarrow, and six colors. The types and colors are handled separately as different data apply to each. For example, each Bill of Materials applies to a given type of wheelbarrow, whereas paints have varying codes and suppliers.

A number of steps are needed to transform the Products spreadsheet (Table 2-1 in Chapter 2) into the database table shown in Figure 7-14.

	²⁄ₐ Remove Sort	▼ Toggle Filter	All ▾	✕ Delete	▾	▦ More ▾		⌕ Select ▾	**B** *I* <u>U</u> 🅰 ▾ ≛ ▾

Sort & Filter	Records	Find	Text F

PRODUCTS

ProductID ▾	ProductTypeID ▾	ProductColorID ▾	ProductPrice ▾	DiscountedPrice ▾	Clic
⊞ WB10000	SD	10	$120.00	☐	
⊞ WB20000	SD	20	$120.00	☐	
⊞ WB30000	SD	30	$120.00	☐	
⊞ WB40000	SD	40	$120.00	☐	
⊞ WB50000	SD	50	$125.00	☑	
⊞ WB60000	SD	60	$125.00	☑	
⊞ WB70000	SM	10	$70.00	☐	
⊞ WB80000	SM	20	$70.00	☐	
⊞ WB90000	SM	30	$70.00	☐	
⊞ WB91000	SM	40	$70.00	☐	
⊞ WB92000	SM	50	$75.00	☐	
WB93000	SM	60	$75.00	☐	
*		0	$0.00	☐	

Figure 7-14. Populated Products table for Smart Wheelbarrows Inc.

First, the column containing a list of colors for each wheelbarrow type has been split, because no row and column intersection should contain more than one item. Each product is given a separate row with a unique product code based on its type and color. This product code will act as its unique identifier, as shown in Figure 7-14.

Second, the types of wheelbarrow have been divided into SD for standard and SM for small. These types are linked to a ProductType table using a one-to-many relationship. Each product can have only one type, whereas a given type can apply to more than one product. The ProductType table contains a description of each product type, together with the amount of paint required (as this depends on the type of product). The ProductType table is shown in Figure 7-15.

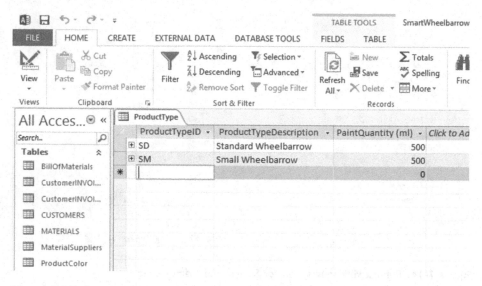

Figure 7-15. Populated ProductType table for Smart Wheelbarrows Inc.

Third, the product colors have been allocated unique identifiers and linked to a table of data about colors, called ProductColor, using a one-to-many relationship. Each product can have only one color, but each color can apply to more than one product. In this table, data is contained about the available colors and the corresponding paint codes and SupplierID. This table draws on data from spreadsheets shown in Tables 2-5 and 2-6 presented in Chapter 2 and is shown in Figure 7-16.

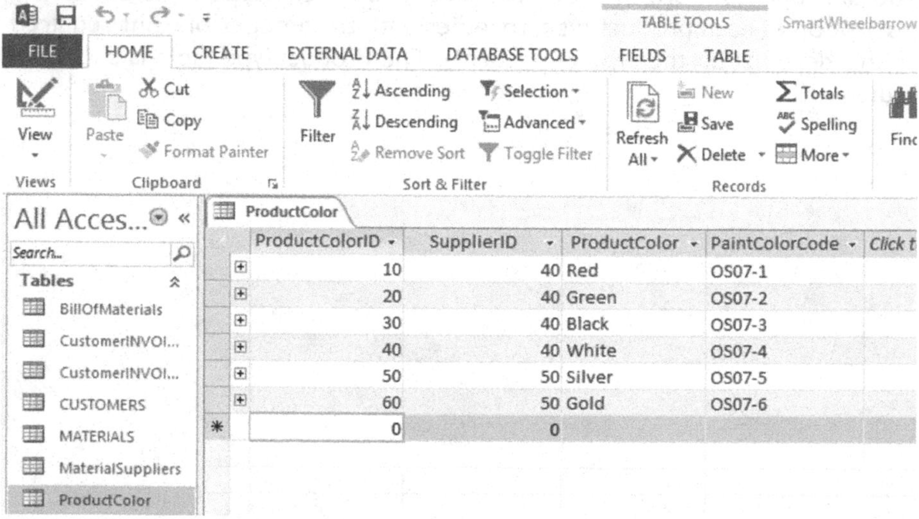

Figure 7-16. Populated ProductColor table for Smart Wheelbarrows Inc.

Fourth, the two final columns of the Products table relate to price, which is dependent on the ProductID. The discounted price uses a Yes or No column and is used for marketing purposes to gauge whether discounts have an impact on sales and from which customers.

■ **Note** The price of paint needs to be included in the database design. As the price of paint is dependent on the color of the paint the most logical place for it would be in the ProductColor table of 7-16 above.

The relationships among these four tables are shown in Figure 7-17.

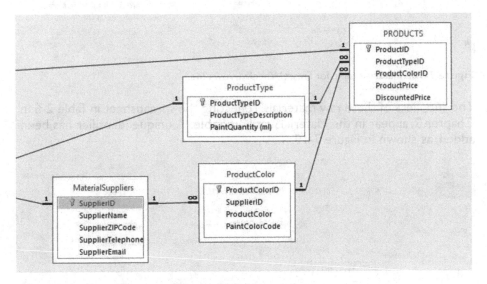

Figure 7-17. Relationships among the Products, ProductType, ProductColor, and MaterialSuppliers tables for Smart Wheelbarrows Inc.

The Materials Table

The Materials table reflects the materials spreadsheet you saw in Table 2-5 in Chapter 2. A unique identifier has been added for each material. The SupplierName column has been removed (as it is not dependent on the unique identifier for the Materials table) and has been replaced by SupplierID. Figure 7-18 shows the first few columns of the Materials table.

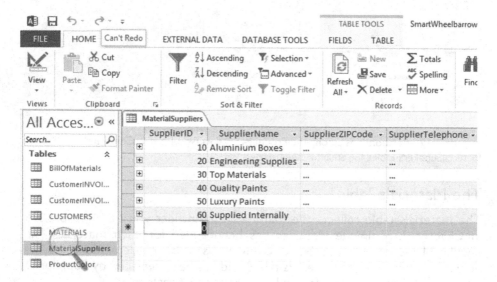

	MaterialID ⏷	SupplierID ⏷	SWMaterialNo ⏷	SupplierMaterialNo ⏷	MaterialName ⏷	Pr
⊞	1	10	OS01	ES39	Hinges	
⊞	2	10	OS02	ES24	Wheel	
⊞	3	10	OS03	ES67	Handle	
⊞	5	10	OS04	ES09	Fastener	
⊞	7	20	OS05	AB01	Container	
⊞	37	10	OS08	ES23	Small Wheel	
⊞	41	10	OS09	ES68	Small Handle	
⊞	43	10	OS10	ES08	Small Fastener	
⊞	47	20	OS11	LP02	Small Container	
⊞	53	10	OS12	ES69	U-Clips	
⊞	59	60	SW01	SW01	Standard right hand side frame	
⊞	61	60	SW02	SW02	Standard left hand side frame	
⊞	67	60	SW03	SW03	Small right hand side frame	
⊞	71	60	SW04	SW04	Small left hand side frame	
*		0	0			

Figure 7-18. Materials table for Smart Wheelbarrows Inc.

The suppliers of these raw materials, reflecting the spreadsheet in Table 2-6 in Chapter 2, appear in the MaterialSuppliers table. A unique identifier has been added, as shown in Figure 7-19.

Figure 7-19. MaterialSuppliers table for Smart Wheelbarrows Inc.

Each type of product has its own Bill of Materials spreadsheet, as shown in Tables 2-7 and 2-8 from Chapter 2. A BillOfMaterials database table is presented in Figure 7-20 and includes a QuantityRequired column for each type of product. The MaterialID and ProductTypeID form the unique identifier for the BillOfMaterials table. That is, they act as a unique identifier together rather than individually. The following relationships exist among the Products, ProductType, Materials, and BillOfMaterials tables:

- A one-to-one relationship exists between ProductTypeID in the Products table and ProductTypeID in the BillOfMaterials table. Each ProductTypeID has one BillOfMaterials and each BillOfMaterials applies to just one ProductType.
- A one-to-many relationship exists between MaterialID in the BillOfMaterials table and MaterialID in the Materials table. Each BillOfMaterials includes just one occurrence of each material, but each material can be listed on more than one BillOfMaterials.

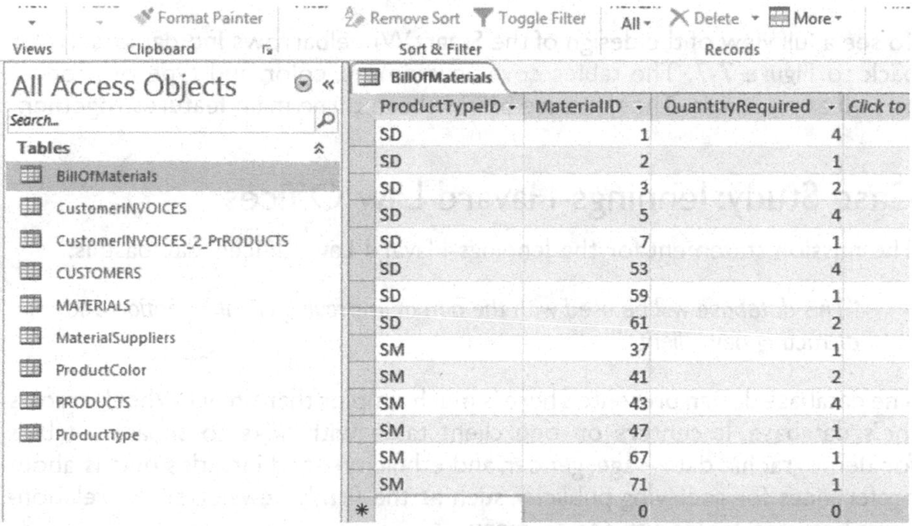

ProductTypeID	MaterialID	QuantityRequired
SD	1	4
SD	2	1
SD	3	2
SD	5	4
SD	7	1
SD	53	4
SD	59	1
SD	61	2
SM	37	1
SM	41	2
SM	43	4
SM	47	1
SM	67	1
SM	71	1
*	0	0

Figure 7-20. BillOfMaterials table for Smart Wheelbarrows Inc.

Figure 7-21 shows the relationships among the ProductType, BillOfMaterials, Materials, and MaterialSuppliers tables.

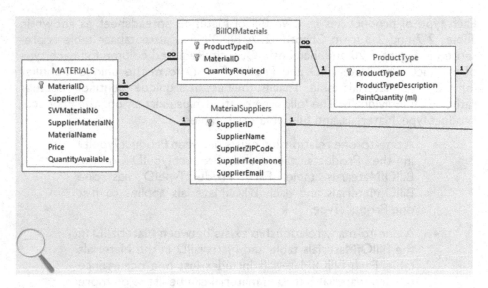

Figure 7-21. Relationships among ProductType, BillOfMaterials, Materials, and MaterialSuppliers tables

To see a full view of the design of the Smart Wheelbarrows Inc. database, refer back to Figure 7-7. The tables cover customers, color, and type of product as well as materials. The database brings these three main features together.

Case Study: Jennings-Havard Law Offices

The mission statement for the Jennings-Havard Law Offices' database is:

> *"This database will be used with the aim of improving client retention and attracting new clients."*

The database design presented here is much simpler than Smart Wheelbarrows Inc.'s database. It centers on one client table with links to separate tables for demographic data—age, gender, and ethnicity—and includes details about preferences for receiving publicity, such as the firm's newsletter. All relationships between tables are one-to-many.

Two metrics that were introduced in Chapter 5 will also be added:

- Whether a client is new
- How the client found out about the firm

These two metrics will be combined into one column, ClientSource. More detail will be given later in this chapter.

Three fictitious clients have been created to populate the database:

- Zhu Chin, aged 45, female. She has two ongoing cases with Jennings-Havard Law Offices: estate planning for herself and her husband, and long-term care planning for her elderly parents. She found out about the firm from a talk given at her local Chinese Community Center and would like to receive the firm's newsletter via e-mail. Mrs. Zhu is Chinese.

- Paul Bergen, aged 67, male. He is an only child and his father died recently. Jennings-Howard Law Offices are processing his father's will. Paul found out about the firm from a newspaper advertisement and contacted them by phone. He has opted to receive the firm's newsletter by mail. Mr. Bergen is white.

- Jane Smith, aged 53, female. She has an ongoing case of estate planning with the firm. She found about them through a friend and would like to receive their e-mail newsletter. She made initial contact by dropping into the office in person. Miss Smith is white.

Figure 7-22 shows an overview of the database design for Jennings-Havard Law Offices. The tables are presented in more detail later in this chapter.

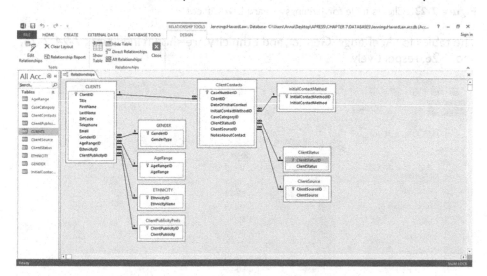

Figure 7-22. Overview of the database design for Jennings-Havard Law Offices

The Clients table resides in the center of the design since clients form the center of the mission of the database. There are columns for Title, FirstName, and Surname, together with columns for contact data. There are three columns for demographic data: AgeRange, Gender, and Ethnicity. Each of these columns has a unique identifier that links to a separate table. Figure 7-23 shows the first few columns of the populated Clients table.

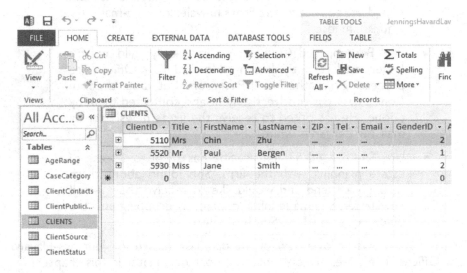

Figure 7-23. Clients table for Jennings-Havard Law Offices

The tables for AgeRange, Gender, and Ethnicity are shown in Figures 7-24, 7-25, and 7-26, respectively.

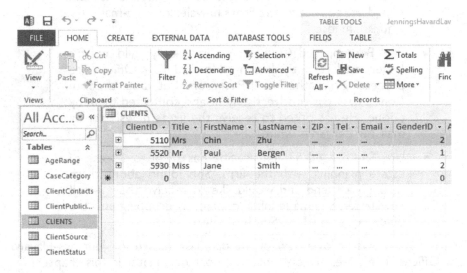

Figure 7-24. AgeRange table for Jennings-Havard Law Offices

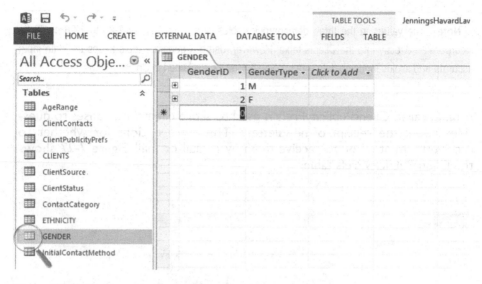

Figure 7-25. Gender table for Jennings-Havard Law Offices

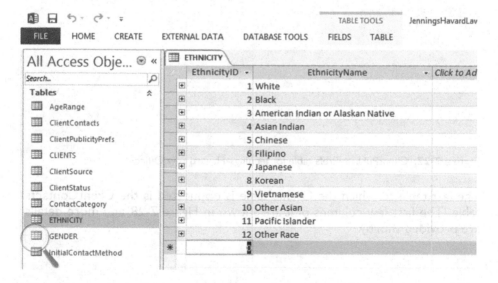

Figure 7-26. Ethnicity table for Jennings-Havard Law Offices

■ **Note** The values in the three demographic tables shown in Figures 7-24 to 7-26 could be incorporated directly into the Clients table. However, using a separate table keeps the data input accurate and avoids inputting data with spelling errors, as explained in Chapter 10.

A table called ClientPublicityPrefs is used to store clients' responses to questions about the receipt of newsletters. There are options for whether to receive them at all or to receive them by e-mail or mail. Figure 7-27 shows the ClientPublicityPrefs table.

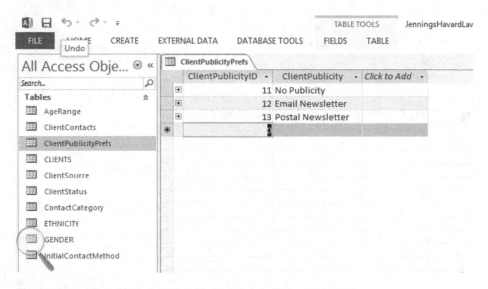

Figure 7-27. ClientPublicityPrefs table for Jennings-Havard Law Offices

The last table to which the Clients table is connected is the ClientContacts table. The first few columns of it are shown in Figure 7-28, and more details are provided shortly.

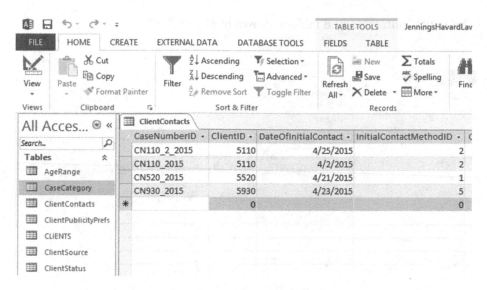

Figure 7-28. ClientContacts table for Jennings-Havard Law Offices

This ClientContacts table lists each case the firm is handling by case number. Some clients, such as Zhu Chin, will have more than one case. As shown in the ClientContact table in Figure 7-28, the date of the initial contact is provided, together with the contact method (phone, e-mail, etc.).

Figure 7-29 provides a summary of the relationships between the Clients table and its linked tables.

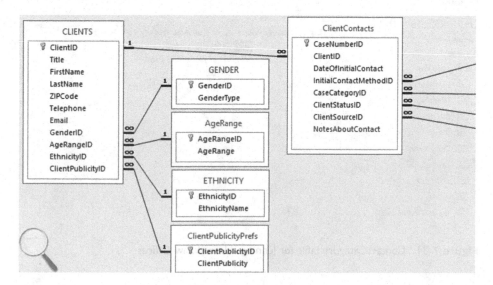

Figure 7-29. The Clients table and its linked tables

The InitialContactMethod table is shown in Figure 7-30.

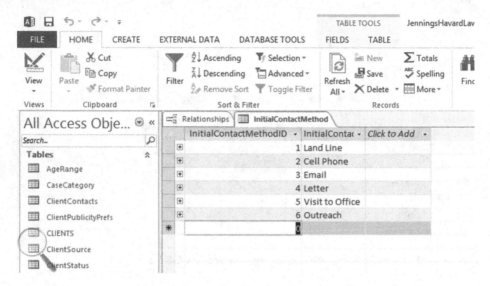

Figure 7-30. InitialContactMethod table for Jennings-Havard Law Offices

The contact category reflects the four types of work carried out by the firm, as shown in Figure 7-31.

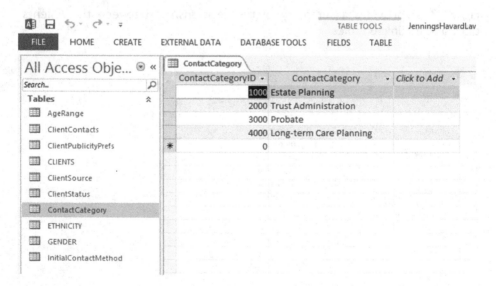

Figure 7-31. ContactCategory table for Jennings-Havard Law Offices

ClientStatus refers to the position of the client—whether they are calling for themselves, on behalf of a family member, as a professional on behalf of a service user, etc. Figure 7-32 shows the values for ClientStatus.

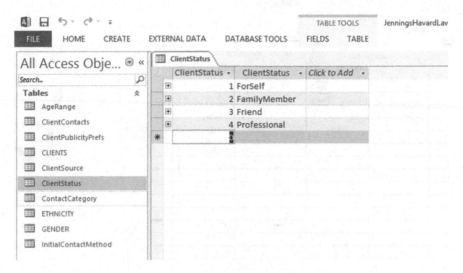

Figure 7-32. ClientStatus table for Jennings-Havard Law Offices

ClientSource refers to the source of information about the firm. Many clients have used the firm before. However, new clients will find out about the firm via advertisements, social media, and recommendations from friends. Figure 7-33 lists the possibilities considered by Jennings-Havard Law Offices.

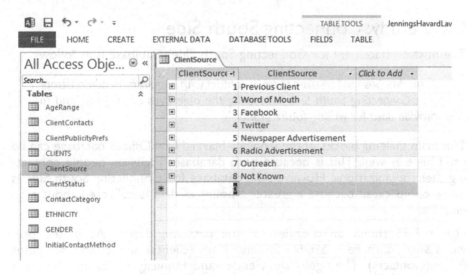

Figure 7-33. ClientSource table for Jennings-Havard Law Offices

The relationship among ClientContact and its linked tables is shown in Figure 7-34.

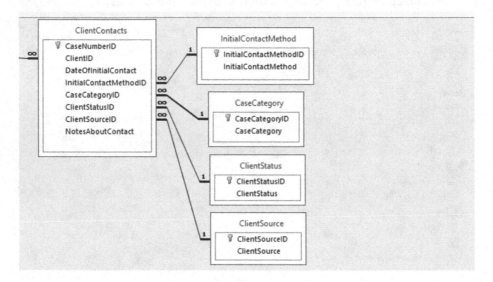

Figure 7-34. ClientContacts and its linked tables

The Jennings-Havard Law Offices database's tables and relationships are summarized in Figure 7-22. The firm has many clients, each of which can have more than one case. The database design enables demographic data and case-relation data to be captured.

Case Study: Connecting South Side

The mission statement for Connecting South Side's database is as follows:

> *"This database will be used to track contact with enquirers, to demonstrate that Connecting South Side is meeting the objectives of its grant, and to provide data for writing future grants."*

The main building blocks of the Jennings-Havard Law Offices database can be used here as well. This is because both databases focus on people contacting their organizations. However, the database for Connecting South Side is more complicated because a greater amount of data is collected about each enquirer.

Figure 7-35 shows an overview of the database design. As in the previous section, there is a table for enquirers (clients) and a table for cases (ClientContacts). The AgeRange, Gender, and Ethnicity tables are the same for both case studies. Also, publicity is the same.

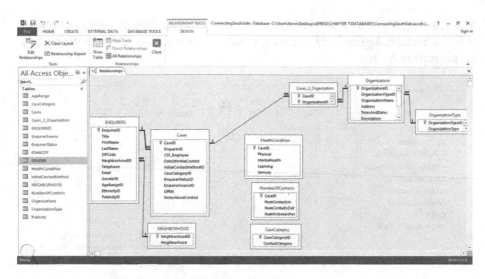

Figure 7-35. Database design for Connecting South Side

A new table, Neighborhood, is used to collect data about which of Chicago's neighborhoods the enquirers are coming from. The South Side has over 200 neighborhoods and these are added to the table when they are needed. Figure 7-36 shows the Neighborhood table.

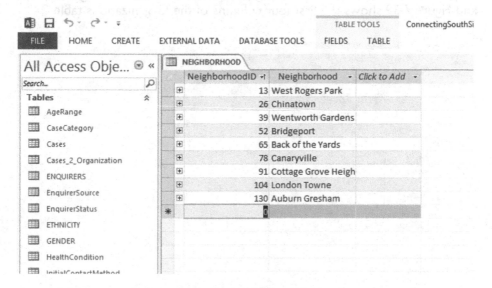

Figure 7-36. Neighborhood table for Connecting South Side

The Cases table adds a few additional columns to the ClientContacts table in the last section. Figure 7-37 shows the links among Cases, Organizations, and OrganizationType.

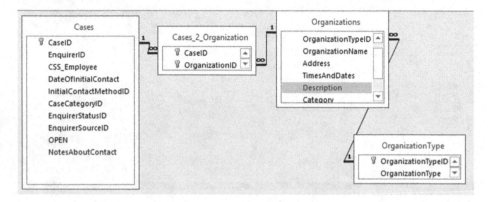

Figure 7-37. The Cases and Organizations tables

Each case is linked to the organizations the enquirer has been referred to. This is a many-to-many relationship, because each enquirer can be referred to more than one organization and each organization can apply to more than one enquirer. Figure 7-38 shows the linking table between Cases and Organizations and Figure 7-39 shows the first four columns of the Organizations table.

All Access ...⊚ «	Cases_2_Organization		
Search.. 🔎	CaseID ⬝┤	OrganizationID ▾	Click to Add ▾
Tables ☆	1_AB_6_18_2015	152	
AgeRange	2_ALC_6_18_2015	24	
CaseCategory	2_ALC_7_9_2015	93	
Cases	255_DB_10_12_2015	51	
Cases_2_Organizati...	255_DB_10_12_2015	111	
ENQUIRERS	255_DB_10_12_2015	130	
EnquirerSource	3_NB_6_19_2015	177	
EnquirerStatus	*	0	
ETHNICITY			
GENDER			
HealthCondition			
InitialContactMeth...			
NEIGHBORHOOD			
NumberOfContacts			
Organizations			
OrganizationType			

Figure 7-38. Cases_2_Organization table for Connecting South Side

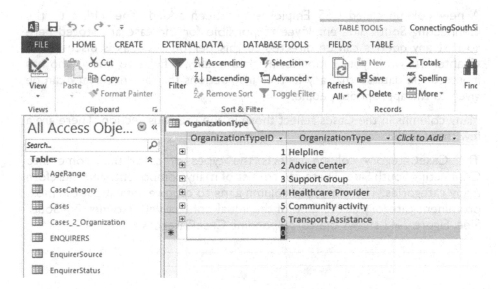

TABLE TOOLS ConnectingSouthSide: Database- C:\Users\Anna\Desktop\APRESS

JAL DATA DATABASE TOOLS FIELDS TABLE

Organizations

OrganizationID	OrganizationTypeID	OrganizationName	Address	TimesAndDates	Descriptic
7	5	Yoga Center	...	...	...
24	5	Lunch for Chinese Elder	...	...	...
42	1	Housing Advice Line	...	...	...
51	6	Transport Assist	...	...	...
72	3	Diabetes Southside	...	...	...
93	2	Debt Assistance Center	...	...	...
106	5	Happy Knitting Club	...	...	...
111	4	Equipment for Indepen	...	...	...
130	5	St Patrick's RC Church	...	...	...
152	3	Russion Connection	...	...	...
177	1	Employment Bureau			
	0				

Figure 7-39. Organizations table for Connecting South Side

Each of the organizations is allocated a type—such as helpline or support group—to make reporting easier. Figure 7-40 shows the OrganizationType table.

TABLE TOOLS ConnectingSouthSi

FILE HOME CREATE EXTERNAL DATA DATABASE TOOLS FIELDS TABLE

View Paste Cut Copy Format Painter | Filter Ascending Descending Remove Sort | Selection Advanced Toggle Filter | Refresh All New Save Delete | Totals Spelling More | Find

Views Clipboard Sort & Filter Records

All Access Obje... «

Search...

Tables

AgeRange

CaseCategory

Cases

Cases_2_Organization

ENQUIRERS

EnquirerSource

EnquirerStatus

OrganizationType

OrganizationTypeID	OrganizationType	Click to Add
1	Helpline	
2	Advice Center	
3	Support Group	
4	Healthcare Provider	
5	Community activity	
6	Transport Assistance	
0		

Figure 7-40. OrganizationType table for Connecting South Side

Figure 7-41 is a close-up look at the Cases table and its remaining linked tables.

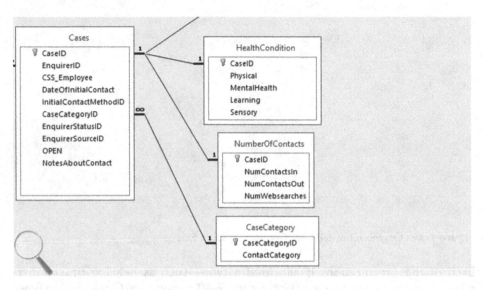

Figure 7-41. The Cases table and its remaining linked tables

A new column called CSS_Employee has been added. The initials to the Connecting South Side employee responsible for the case are stored here so that any queries can be directed to this person. Also, as is discussed in Chapter 10, when you're monitoring data quality, it helps to know who has inputted the data so that any further instructions that are necessary can be given to the appropriate people.

Many columns in the Cases reflect those in the previous section. There are a few that are different.

The CaseCategory column reflects the types of cases that come into Connecting South Side. These can consist of many components and therefore many categories. Therefore, this column aims to capture data about the most prominent category at the time of the initial contact with Connecting South Side. Figure 7-42 shows the corresponding CaseCategory table.

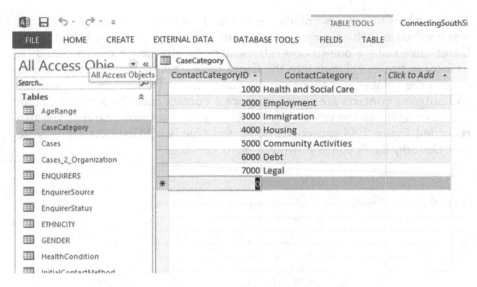

Figure 7-42. CaseCategory table for Connecting South Side

The Cases table is linked to a HealthCondition table using a one-to-one relationship. The HealthCondition table covers any disabilities or other health
conditions that enquirers have. Health conditions may change from case
to case for the same enquirer over time and therefore depend on the case
rather than on the enquirer themselves. Apart from the unique identifier, each
column is of type Yes/No. One enquirer can have more than one disability.
Figure 7-43 shows the populated HealthCondition table. Note that Dorothy
Bain from Chapter 4 has a physical disability and a mental health condition.

CaseID	PhysicalDisability	MentalHealthCondition	LearningDisability	SensoryDisability
1_AB_6_18_201	☐	☑	☐	☐
2_ALC_6_18_2C	☐	☐	☐	☐
2_ALC_7_9_201	☐	☐	☐	☐
255_DB_10_12_	☑	☑	☐	☐
3_NB_6_19_20:	☐	☐	☐	☐
	☐	☐	☐	☐

Figure 7-43. HealthCondition table for Connecting South Side

The NumberOfContacts column serves as an indicator of how much work was involved in each enquiry. Like the HealthCondition table, it is linked to the Cases table using a one-to-one relationship. An alternative design would be to incorporate its columns into the Cases table—two tables are used here to reduce the number of columns in the Cases table. The number of incoming and outgoing contacts are counted where a contact could be a phone call, an e-mail, or a visit to the office. The number of separate web searches are also recorded. Figure 7-44 shows the populated NumberOfContacts table. Note that Dorothy Bain's enquiry involved many contacts.

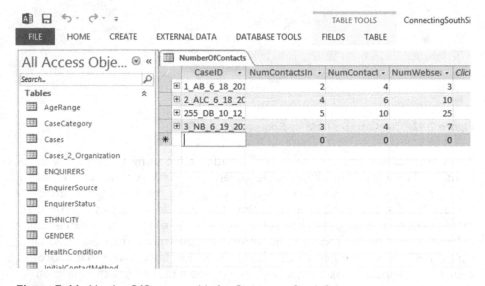

Figure 7-44. NumberOfContacts table for Connecting South Side

The Open column of the Cases table is of data type Yes/No and it identifies whether a case is ongoing or closed.

The last column, NotesAboutContact, reflects the documentation kept for each case described in Chapter 4. The case file notes are placed here.

Figure 7-35 above shows an overview of Connecting South Side's database design. Like the design for Jennings-Havard Law Offices, the database enables data about a number of clients/enquirers to be captured and is structured around the fact that one enquirer may have more than one case. With Connecting South Side, the additional relationship between cases and organizations they were referred to is included in the design.

Summary

This chapter covered the steps you need to follow to create a simple and stable database design. The process began by considering the data you are currently (or will be) working with, dividing it into tables, and determining appropriate relationships between those tables. You can apply further checks to your tables to make sure that retrieving and analyzing your data is as efficient as possible. Testing your database thoroughly and providing comprehensive documentation are essential.

Data Protection, Security, and Privacy Policy

Most businesses hold some personal data, for example, personal information about customers or employees. If this data relates to someone who can be identified, you are likely to have important legal responsibilities. The financial consequences and the impact on your reputation if that data is breached can be significant; the exact nature of the penalties depends on the jurisdiction that applies to your business. As with any law, it is important to know how it affects your business, how to comply, and how to incorporate any require-ments into your business policies. In addition, data breaches can result in other expenses, such as reimbursement to customers and data recovery costs.

The time you spend protecting your data is generally much less than the time it takes to recover your losses after something goes wrong. New threats are always present and businesses must be vigilant. Data protection and security is achieved through a combination of employee education, efficient business processes, and clear business policies. The strategy must be holistic and inte-grated into all aspects of the business. Small businesses can be more vulner-able than large companies due to their inability to afford the most effective data security.

If a breach happens, businesses need to ensure that they can handle it as quickly as possible, avoiding serious consequences. Customer trust is difficult to regain after a breach.

Data Protection Legislation

Personal data has been at risk from electronic and physical theft for a long time, but the use of mobile devices and the cloud in recent years means that there are more opportunities for criminals or simply human error to lead to breaches. There is a growing maze of applicable data protection legislation. The United States has about 20 national privacy or data security laws, as well as hundreds of such laws among individual states. For example, California has more than 25 state privacy and data security laws. These laws address particular problems or industries and it is not practical to provide a full summary here. The aim is to provide some guidance.

Some U.S. businesses have agreed to follow the first seven principles of the 1998 UK Data Protection Act in relation to their data handling. If you follow these principles, regardless of the jurisdiction that applies to your business, you are likely to be in good legal standing. These seven principles, outlined in the following sections, are a useful starting point for your data protection considerations even though they may not be the law where you are based. They are particularly useful for putting together business policies for storing, processing, and retaining your data.

The UK Data Protection Act applies to paper records as well as those held in electronic form and gives individuals certain rights. It also imposes obligations on businesses that record and use personal data to be open about how that data is used. The term "individual" means a customer, client, enquirer, or whatever term is most appropriate for your small business.

Data Should Be Processed Fairly and Lawfully

You must provide individuals with the name of your business and the purpose for which their personal data will be used. Give clear instructions about how individuals can access and correct the data that you hold about them. You should obtain personal data only from people who are legally authorized to supply it; in most cases this will be the individual themselves, unless they are minors.

You must explain to the individuals if their personal data will be used in any way that is not immediately obvious. You cannot be deceptive as to the purpose for which their personal data is held or used. For example, you must tell individuals if their personal information will be passed on to credit reference agencies.

In summary, businesses holding personal data should define, perhaps in a publicly available privacy policy, the following:

- What data will be held

- The purposes for which the data will be held

- Whether any of the data will be disclosed to any third parties, and if so, which ones

- Any non-obvious consequences of the processing

- Any personal data for which the individual may withdraw consent for the business to hold or use

- How individuals can check or amend the data held by the business or request the deletion of that data

Data Must Be Processed for Specified Lawful Purposes

You must have a specified, lawful reason for collecting data; you cannot simply collect it speculatively. Furthermore, you cannot use the data collected for another unconnected or unlawful purpose. For example, data collected by a small business for the purpose of gauging customer satisfaction should not be used for direct marketing without prior consent from the individuals.

Data Must Be Adequate, Relevant, and Not Excessive

The level of personal data held should only be to the extent to which those details are relevant and required to fulfill the stated purpose or purposes. Holding personal data because it might be useful at a later stage is not acceptable.

Sensitive personal data must be held only when it's absolutely necessary. For example, if you do not need to know a person's ethnicity, collecting such data would be excessive. However, if the ethnicity is key to the project, collecting it is deemed relevant. In the case study of Connecting South Side, the grant awarded to the organization specifically stated that one of the aims of the service is for it to be available to people of diverse ethnicity. In order to demonstrate that the organization has satisfied this particular aim of the grant, data about the ethnicity of its enquirers has to be collected.

In general, it would be useful for your business to keep a record of the reasons why any personal data is required.

Data Must Be Accurate and Up to Date

Any data you hold must be factually accurate and updated when necessary. Depending on the nature of your business, you may need to develop procedures that allow individuals to update their details quickly.

It is possible to keep your database up to date by ensuring that you check client details regularly and update your records as soon as you become aware of changes. Details could change at any time. An individual can also request that their details be changed at any time.

Keeping data accurate (or cleansed) is covered in Chapter 10 and keeping data up to date (or maintained) is covered in Chapter 11.

Data Must Not Be Kept for Any Longer Than Is Necessary

If the purpose for which you collected the data is time sensitive, you must ensure that the data is not retained once it is no longer needed. When applicable, you should tell individuals how long the data will be kept.

It is very likely that your database contains data that you no longer need and it would be useful to conduct a yearly audit of your data. However, if you are required to hold onto such data by tax and other authorities, it makes sense to place it in an archive.

You should create a data retention policy that sets out which data needs to be archived, for how long, and why.

Data Must Be Processed in Accordance with the Rights of Individuals

The Act sets out the rights of individuals, as well as the responsibilities of those holding the data. It's important to make sure that you understand these rights and operate in accordance with them.

1. Individuals have the right to access copies of personal data held about them, either on computer or in a structured manual filing system.

2. Individuals have the right to ask in writing that the business not process data where it is likely to cause them damage or distress.

3. Individuals have the right to ask the business in writing to cease processing their personal data for direct marketing purposes.

4. Individuals have the right to object to a business in writing to decisions affecting them where they are made by automated processes and can request that decisions are made with human involvement.

5. Individuals have the right to compensation through the courts for any damage and distress suffered as a result of any breaches of the Data Protection Act committed by a business.

6. Individuals have the right to rectification of data that's inaccurate or contains expressions of opinion based on inaccurate information.

Data Must Be Secure

Your business must take all appropriate measures to keep personal data secure, regardless of its format (paper or electronic). Make sure procedures are in place to prevent unlawful and or unauthorized processing and to guarantee that the data is protected against accidental loss and destruction or damage. This obligation covers staff working remotely. You may need to develop technical and organizational processes to deal with this obligation. The following sections provide guidance about keeping your data secure.

Educate Yourself

Avoid clicking on unknown links and pop-ups when working online or opening any email attachments when you can't verify the source. It may be wise for devices holding confidential data not be used to search the Internet or view social media sites. Lock your phone and tablet devices.

Password-breaking software is easily available online, so it is essential that passwords are created carefully.

- Use strong passwords with eight characters or more and with a combination of letters, numbers, and symbols
- Use different passwords on different sites
- Change passwords regularly
- Never share passwords with anyone or write passwords down

Unmanaged administrator privileges can pose a security threat, so make sure you create appropriate access limitations for non-admin employees, especially when those workers are using their own devices.

All of these precautions are pointless if someone can get at your computer physically. Even login passwords can be bypassed trivially if someone has access to your computer. The common scenario is a laptop or USB drive being lost or stolen during travel. Storing confidential data in the cloud can help with such problems, which is discussed in Chapter 18.

Most public Wi-Fi areas, such as hotel-provided Internet and Internet cafes, do not encrypt data. This means your unencrypted data can be interrupted. You must either use encryption software or only use public Wi-Fi for data that you are happy to make public.

Keep paper files to a minimum and locked in filing cabinets. These should be scanned so there is always a digital backup. If the paper doesn't have to be kept, it is best shredded.

Educate Your Employees

If a computer on your network is compromised, your whole business is at risk. Employees must be educated about Internet safety, security, and the latest threats, as well as what to do if they misplace data or suspect that malicious software (malware) has infected their machine.

Be sure to train all employees on how to manage sensitive data. Confidential information is often unintentionally disclosed by an employee who wasn't properly trained. You can incorporate training through specific teaching sessions and printed materials, or by using an employee manual. Training should include everything from

- How to construct a strong password
- The type of data that it is safe to give over the phone or in an e-mail
- Restrictions in terms of the use of company computers, smartphones, and other devices
- Care when opening attachments or when clicking links embedded in spam
- Relevant business policies

Chapter 20 gives further guidance on staff training.

Security Policies

A system that keeps data secure while enabling employees to work as freely as possible is key to ensuring that security policies are followed. All security policies should be agreed upon and clearly written and shared throughout your business before employees begin using their own devices.

A formal business computer policy should outline the acceptable and pro-hibited online activities for employees. For example, the policy could make it clear to employees that business devices should not be used for personal e-mail or social media. Guidance could be given on the use of laptops and other devices both within and outside the office.

Data should be backed up and, when appropriate, archived. Backing up data is covered in detail in Chapter 11 and Chapter 17 covers data archiving. For data that's currently being used, it is useful to have a plan for data recovery as well as a post-disaster plan. If you are ever in the unfortunate position of having to use either of these plans, you will be under stress and most likely will not have access to company resources. Provide clear, detailed instructions and include all phone numbers and web sites to execute your plan. Keep a copy of the plan in several onsite and off-site locations.

Data protection should be an ongoing priority in your office. Each quarter, set time aside to review your security policies and make adjustments. For example, you may have added new technology that needs securing.

Use Software to Protect Your Data

Make sure you are using efficient anti-virus software and are keeping it updated. Also, when possible, make sure that you are using the latest versions of operating systems with all updates in place. When possible, encrypt your data using the latest techniques. Chapter 11 covers these issues in more detail.

Principle Eight

Principle eight of the UK Data Protection Act 1998 does not relate to the United States, as it states that no country should transfer data to a county outside of the European Economic Area. However, it serves as a useful warn-ing, because you must be wary when conducting business across borders. Many countries do not have legislation in place to deal with data breaches, and if your data is compromised overseas, you may not have any recourse.

Summary

A small business holding data relating to individuals in the course of their work must consider:

- Whether the data they hold is subject to the points outlined in the Data Protection Act and described in this chapter

- Whether the arrangements they have in place satisfy the Act's requirements in relation to the security of the data they hold

- What procedures are in place to promptly respond to requests of personal data from individuals

Even if these particular data protection laws do not apply where you live, abiding by these points is prudent and good practice. The principles are outlined in Table 8-1 for easy reference.

Table 8-1. First Seven Principles of the 1998 Data Protection Act

Principle	Title
1	Data should be processed fairly and lawfully
2	Data should be processed for specified lawful purposes
3	Data should be adequate, relevant, and not excessive
4	Data should be accurate and up to date
5	Data should not be kept for any longer than is necessary
6	Data should be processed in accordance with the rights of individuals
7	Data should be secure

Collecting Your Data

Clear goals are essential for efficient data collection. The best any technology can do for your small business is help it move toward its goals cheaply and quickly. Chapter 5 covered setting business goals, levers, and metrics. Chapter 7 addressed database design, with business goals very much in mind. This chapter introduces data collection and explains a number of methods for doing it.

Overview

In all likelihood, you are already collecting data. For example, if you are accepting money from customers, you are probably invoicing them and keeping records. Such data can be placed into your database directly. However, collecting data this way does not help you understand why people behave the way they do. Therefore, further data collection techniques are required to help answer specific questions and to help your business move toward its specific goals. If you want to improve and grow your business, you probably want to move beyond the bounds of the data you are collecting for necessity. Data that may be beneficial includes:

- The demographics of your customers
- Feedback from customers about the product/service you are providing
- Attitudes of your customers toward a specific change

It is essential that small businesses collect data describing their current customers. Demographic data about gender, age, and ethnicity is important, although data protection and privacy must also be considered: Chapter 8 sets out guidelines about data protection. Data collection can be as simple as asking people how likely they are to recommend your company to friends and colleagues, or it can involve detailed questionnaires about satisfaction with all aspects of the customers' experiences.

You should collect data at intervals sufficiently frequent for your end goal. For example, inventory data may have to be collected continuously, whereas feedback about new product launches can be collected when it is required.

Small businesses should focus on the accuracy of data collection as much, if not more, than larger businesses. For example, a large business may be able to lose a few invoices a month but the impact on a smaller business could be far greater. Adequate training and supervision are essential to make sure your data is collected and inputted accurately. Staff training is covered in Chapter 20.

Data collection should be consistent so you can track trends over time. For example, when collecting data about customer invoices, make sure you do it exactly the same way each time. Data should be stored securely (see Chapter 8) and data collection procedures should be as simple as possible.

Data-Collection Methods

There are a number of methods for collecting data, as set out in the following sections and you will learn about the advantages and disadvantages of each. The methods most useful to the three case studies introduced in Chapters 2–4 are also addressed.

All the methods considered here involve the participants actively taking part. However, in many cases with such collection methods, participation rates can be very low. Luckily, it is also possible to collect data passively. Examples include collecting data about the web-browsing habits of individuals when they are viewing your business' web pages. A tool such as Google Analytics can help with this, as it enables you to determine, for example, the most popular pages on your site, the types of keywords your visitors used to reach your site, and the countries your visitors come from.

In addition, it is possible to obtain data that is not specific to your business but could be useful if its trends are compared to your collected data. An example is data from the U.S. Census Bureau, available from census.gov, which covers all manner of demographic characteristics across geographic areas of the United States. Information provided from such data is useful, as it can inform you about local demographic trends and help you put the data you've collected and analyzed from your business into perspective.

Online Survey Tools

Online survey tools are a very straightforward means of obtaining data from your customers. Online surveys—or *e-surveys*—have become the preferred way to conduct customer satisfaction surveys, as well as product and service feedback evaluations.

■ **Note** Examples of survey collection tools are AskNicely, Survey Monkey, SurveyGizmo, Qualtrics, Woofu, and Google Forms.

There are many reasons for choosing online surveys over other data-collection methods, including cost savings, time savings, and improved data accuracy levels through automatic response gathering.

It is important to give yourself the best chance of attracting responses to your survey. The factor that most influences the response rate of any survey is the interest that respondents have in the subject. For example, a survey of existing customers is likely to have a higher response rate than one of non-customers, because the respondents are being drawn from a group of people who have a relationship with your business.

Nevertheless, there are other factors that can improve the response rate, as follows:

- The target audience must use computers and the Internet regularly.

- The title of the survey should be short and relevant.

- It should be clear how to start the survey and how to complete it.

- Questions should be specific and easy to understand such as, "How satisfied on a scale of 1 to 5 were you with our customer service?".

- One objective should be used for the survey in order to keep it simple.

- Text should be kept to a minimum: one page with three to four questions is more than sufficient. Customers will not appreciate filling out detailed questionnaires when their intention is to purchase something.

You can use various styles of questions, such as multiple choice, check boxes, yes/no, and so on. Open-ended questions are difficult to manage. An example of an open-ended question is, "Describe how useful our service was". Specific choices that are broad enough to capture real responses provide data that is much easier to use. Nevertheless, it is helpful to add an optional text box so that participants can expand on their responses if they wish to. Participants should be able to complete the whole questionnaire in less than 10 minutes.

The following criteria will help improve your response rate:

- Explain how the data will be used and address data protection issues if relevant (Chapter 8 covers data protection in detail)

- Give your customers something to benefit from in return for providing their data, such as entry into a prize draw

- Avoid asking for "identifying" data such as name, address, or date of birth—data such as geographical area can be captured at the state level instead and age ranges (such as 20-29, 30-39, and so on) can be used to encapsulate age

- Make it voluntary to provide contact information such as e-mail addresses

Online surveys are straightforward to distribute. You can use e-mail to send a link to your target audience asking them to complete the survey. However, make sure your e-mail addresses are accurate and that your list is up to date. You can place a link to the survey on your business web site or blog. You can also use social media such as Facebook, Twitter, or LinkedIn to promote your survey and to ask for responses. Finally, you can provide details about the survey via paper correspondence if appropriate.

Good survey questions are hard to write and they can take considerable time to develop. For this reason, it is important to test the questionnaires thoroughly, perhaps using your staff.

Be aware that surveys require respondents to fill out the questionnaire and will often require a reasonable level of literacy. If multiple languages are common in your line of business, be sure to prepare the questionnaires using all major languages of your target groups. Many online survey platforms cater to multiple languages.

Online surveys have a number of advantages over other data collection methods:

- Compared with postal surveys, they are cheaper to administer and can cover a wider geographical area

- Compared with methods such as interviews over the telephone or face to face, the chance of evaluator bias is less because the same questions are asked of all respondents directly and there is no interviewer involved

- Some people feel more comfortable responding to a survey than participating in an interview

- Tabulating closed-ended responses is an easy and straightforward process

However, there are a few issues that you should consider before choosing an online survey:

- Beyond language barriers (which can be mitigated to some extent), questions may not have the same meaning to all respondents. This can lead to inaccurate results that do not properly reflect opinions. In an interview, these types of misunderstandings can more easily be identified and remedied.

- Given the lack of contact with the respondent, you never know who really completed the survey.

- You are not in a position to probe for additional details.

Postal Surveys

You can hand out or send printed questionnaires by mail and later collect them or have them returned by stamped addressed envelopes.

To facilitate filling out forms and data entry in a structured format, the form should be machine-readable, or at least be laid out with clearly identifiable data fields and pre-coded responses. Beyond these aspects, you design printed questionnaires in much the same way you do online surveys.

Self-completion surveys depend on suitable databases containing the correct names and postal addresses of respondents. Response rates will be low if your lists are out of date, contain misspellings, contain duplicates, or are made up of unsuitable participants.

Face-to-Face Interviewing: Using Paper Forms

Face-to-face interviews can be structured or open. Structured interviews are performed by using survey forms similar to those used for online surveys, although there is scope for making them longer. Open interviews involve taking notes during the interview, which are later structured. Mobile devices are a useful way to collect data in a face-to-face interview and are discussed later in this section.

Face-to-face interviews have the following advantages:

- They enable you to ask questions of greater complexity than with an online survey

- You can validate data as it is collected, thereby improving data quality

- You can gain a deeper understanding of the validity of a response

- Interaction with the interviewee is possible; for example, you can show them samples

- It is easier to maintain the interest of respondents for a longer period of time

- Interviewees are less likely to refuse to answer a question

- You can more readily address any concerns about confidentiality, as queries can be handled directly

- Face-to-face interviews are particularly useful for gathering quotes and stories

There are also a number of disadvantages to face-to-face interviews:

- They can be expensive to organize, particularly if they take place over a wide geographical area

- The interviewer is often working in isolation and the quality of the work depends greatly on his or her conscientiousness

- They are often time consuming because of the travel time between respondents

- They are susceptible to interview bias

- They may seem intrusive to the respondent

As in the case of preparing an online survey, it is important to test forms designed for the interviews thoroughly before the interviews take place.

Telephone Interviews

Telephone interviews can balance the advantages and disadvantages of (online and postal) surveys and face-to-face interviews. Unlike online and postal surveys, telephone interviews enable interviewers to interact directly with their respondents, thus leading to a more in-depth and possibly more accurate interview. However, the time and expense is usually much higher.

When telephone interviews are compared with face-to-face interviews, they are likely to save time and money. A telephone interview usually lasts longer that an online or postal survey; 20 minutes is a reasonable length. In addition, there is no time and money spent on travel. Face-to-face interviews do have the advantage of using visuals effectively, although with the prevalence of online technology such as Skype, this is becoming less of an issue. Lack of personal contact during a telephone interview can also impede the evaluator's judgment as to what lies behind responses. Again, technology such as Skype can help mitigate this.

Collecting Data Using Mobile Technology by an Interviewer

Another method for combining the advantages of (online and postal) surveys and face-to-face interviews is to collect data over the phone or in a face-to-face interview using mobile technology. You can use smartphones and tablets to collect data. Mobile technology has the following advantages:

- You save time collecting and delivering the data, as it's entered directly into your mobile device: data doesn't have to be transcribed from a paper questionnaire to electronic storage.

- Data quality is better. Entering data directly into mobile technology avoids the need to decipher poor handwriting.

- It may also be possible for any errors to be identified as the data is entered, thus correcting such problems through communication with the interviewer before they become widespread.

- Given the extensive use of smartphones and tablets, it is possible that interviewers may need very little training in using the technology.

- Depending on the technology being used, it is possible to combine text with data in other formats such as photographic images.

There are also potential problems when using mobile technologies:

- Your company might need to purchase the tablets and smartphones and pay for the associated contracts for use.

- The data stored on devices and transferred between them may be vulnerable. Using encryption at both the device level and during transmission can help; such issues are covered in more detail in Chapter 11.

- Data collection on mobile devices will change as the technology changes, so you have to plan carefully for the long-term.

Case Studies as Part of a Data-Collection Exercise

Case studies give a fully rounded view of people's experience of a service. They represent depth of data rather than breadth and, for this reason, they are best used alongside the other methods described in this chapter. It is usually quite time consuming to collect data for a case study, organize it, and analyze it. The data would normally be collected using an interview, preferably one that is face-to-face. However, the organization might have enough data to put together case studies without conducting extensive data collection. If this is the case, you must be sure to retain the anonymity of those involved.

Group Event/Focus Groups

Each of the previous methods pertained to data at the individual level. However, it can be useful to collect data at the group level as well. People in a group sometimes bounce ideas off each other, creating more feedback than would be obtained if they were contacted individually.

The data is not necessarily representative of other groups and a random sample may be a solution. In some cases, a *focus group* may be appropriate, especially when it's made up of people whose lifestyles are pertinent to a planned product launch.

Organizing such an event takes time and resources and people need a strong incentive to attend. Group events can be prone to interviewer bias. Also, if the interviewer does not have efficient control of the group, a few participants can end up dominating the discussion.

Case Study: Data Collection for Smart Wheelbarrows Inc.

Much of Smart Wheelbarrows Inc.'s data is collected as part of the daily running of the business. Customer details are added as new customers place orders and the details of existing customers are updated when necessary. Similarly, data is stored about invoices, products, suppliers, and materials as part of business operations.

Chapter 5 explored the goals, levers, and metrics of Smart Wheelbarrows Inc. Recall that one of the goals was to increase profits. The chapter considered various levers for raising profits. Of these levers, two lend themselves well to the data-collection methods described in this chapter—extending the client base and accepting credit cards.

Extending the Client Base

The first is the idea that the client base could be extended to children. It would be sensible to carry out some market research to see if there is any interest in small wheelbarrows for children. The company could design an online survey with a few questions aimed at gathering useful data about potential interest. They could place the survey, for example, on their web site. An example questionnaire is shown in Figure 9-1.

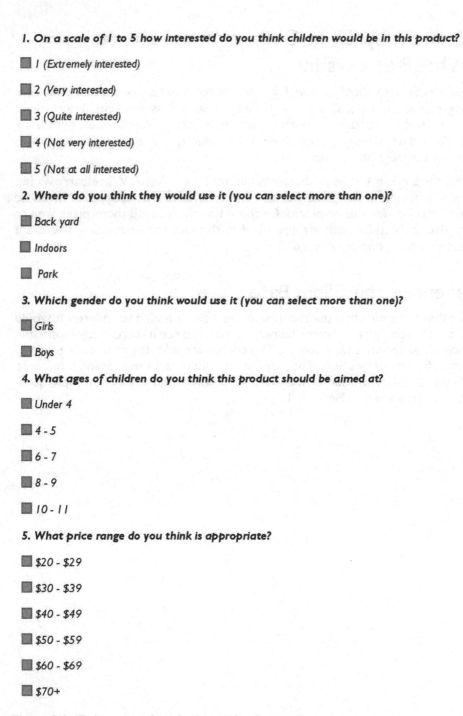

1. On a scale of 1 to 5 how interested do you think children would be in this product?

▨ *1 (Extremely interested)*

▨ *2 (Very interested)*

▨ *3 (Quite interested)*

▨ *4 (Not very interested)*

▨ *5 (Not at all interested)*

2. Where do you think they would use it (you can select more than one)?

▨ *Back yard*

▨ *Indoors*

▨ *Park*

3. Which gender do you think would use it (you can select more than one)?

▨ *Girls*

▨ *Boys*

4. What ages of children do you think this product should be aimed at?

▨ *Under 4*

▨ *4 - 5*

▨ *6 - 7*

▨ *8 - 9*

▨ *10 - 11*

5. What price range do you think is appropriate?

▨ *$20 - $29*

▨ *$30 - $39*

▨ *$40 - $49*

▨ *$50 - $59*

▨ *$60 - $69*

▨ *$70+*

Figure 9-1. Online survey form for Smart Wheelbarrows Inc.

The survey would end by asking if the respondent would like to enter a prize draw for a garden center voucher worth $100. If so, they would need to leave their e-mail address. Otherwise, they can submit their questionnaire without leaving any contact details.

Accepting Credit Cards

Another potential way for Smart Wheelbarrows Inc. to increase profits was to introduce the use of credit cards. They could conduct market research to establish how useful customers would find this service. They would want to be able to justify the fees that they would incur for using credit cards and could design the questionnaire with this in mind.

Case Study: Jennings-Havard Law Offices

The goal of the Jennings-Havard Law Offices firm was to improve client retention. One of the levers they identified is ideal for the data-collection methods described in this chapter—determining whether clients are happy with the service they are receiving. The other two levers, maximizing client interaction and keeping up with client requirements over time, are catered to by data that is already collected by the business.

Determining Whether Clients Are Happy with the Service They Are Receiving

A firm such as Jennings-Havard Law Offices is likely to have some clients who use the Internet and some who do not. Therefore, a combination of online and paper surveys would be appropriate. The survey should be very short, but provide enough data to give the firm clear direction about where improvements are needed. An example is shown in Figure 9-2.

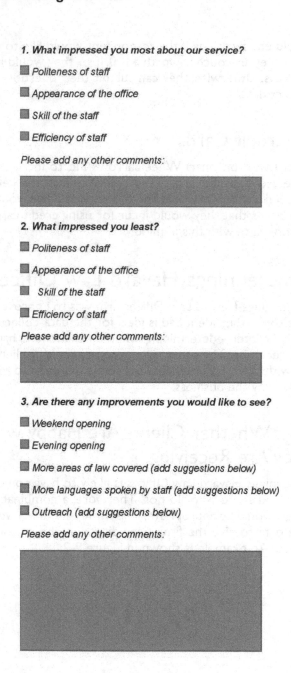

1. What impressed you most about our service?

- Politeness of staff
- Appearance of the office
- Skill of the staff
- Efficiency of staff

Please add any other comments:

2. What impressed you least?

- Politeness of staff
- Appearance of the office
- Skill of the staff
- Efficiency of staff

Please add any other comments:

3. Are there any improvements you would like to see?

- Weekend opening
- Evening opening
- More areas of law covered (add suggestions below)
- More languages spoken by staff (add suggestions below)
- Outreach (add suggestions below)

Please add any other comments:

Figure 9-2. Online survey form for Jennings-Havard Law Offices

A link to the survey could be included in all e-mail communications and a paper copy could be added to all outgoing mailings. Printed forms could also be available at the receptionist's desk.

Case Study: Connecting South Side

Connecting South Side has the potential to use many data-collection methods to meet its goals.

The organization conducts telephone assessments as part of its daily work, so it would be straightforward to ask enquirers if they would take part in a formal telephone interview. The purpose of the interview could be to gather feedback about Connecting South Side, with the aim of demonstrating to those who commissioned the grant that the service is being well-received. Online and paper questionnaires could also be used to gather comments about the service.

Connecting South Side could use the descriptions of the enquiries stored in the database to generate anonymized case studies, which would demonstrate the nature and depth of the work. They would need to be careful about data privacy and make sure that there were no identifying factors in those case studies, such as people living in unusual circumstances. An example is someone having an unusually large number of children at a very young age.

Connecting South Side gets involved in various local events. Usually this involves sending one or two employees to promote the service. These employees could collect data about problematic gaps in local services. They could collect this data on paper forms or using mobile devices and feed it back to the grant commissioners.

Summary

The data-collection methods that were introduced in this chapter are summarized in Table 9-1. The chapter explored the advantages and disadvantages of each method so you can make intelligent choices about which methods are best for your business. To provide real-life examples, the chapter also explored the data-collection methods that could be used by the three case studies introduced in Chapters 2–4.

Table 9-1. Summary of Data Collection Tools

Data-Collection Method	When to Use
Online survey tools	When cost is important, when time is of the essence, and when the client base has online access and know-how
Postal surveys	Suitable for those who are not confident using online surveys or do not have Internet access
Face-to-face interviews: using paper forms	Useful when unstructured interaction is required with the respondent and/or visual demonstrations would be helpful
Telephone interviews	Sit half way between (online and postal) surveys and face-to-face interviews: they are quicker and cheaper than face-to-face interviews and more in-depth than surveys
Collecting data using mobile technology by an interviewer	Useful when money is not an issue but time and quality of data are important

Data collection is closely connected to data cleansing, which is described in Chapter 10. Poor data collection can lead to data that's full of errors. It may be the case that data collection needs to improve to mitigate this situation.

Further Reading

Internet, Phone, Mail, and Mixed-Mode Surveys: The Tailored Design Method, by Don A. Dillman, Jolene D. Smyth, and Leah Melani Christian. John Wiley & Sons; 4th edition hardcover, 2014, ISBN-13: 978-1118456149.

Cleansing Your Data

Every set of data contains some errors. Detecting and removing these over-sights, known as data cleansing, can often be a lengthy process. However, efficient data cleansing is essential in order to be able to come to accurate conclusions from data analysis. In addition, one of the principles of the Data Protection Act (described in Chapter 8) is to ensure that your data is accurate and, when necessary, is up to date.

Overview

Data cleansing comprises three main steps:

1. Detecting the errors
2. Selecting and applying the most appropriate methods to correct the errors
3. If possible, preventing the errors from happening again

The process of data cleansing is usually open-ended, as some errors are hard to find and eliminate. In addition, databases are rarely static and are updated and appended on a regular basis. Therefore, the potential for unclean data is always present.

Depending on the intended application of the data, you must decide how much effort you want to expend on data cleansing. Your standard of accuracy is likely to vary in accordance with the data's intended use.

Large organizations often outsource the data-cleansing step. However, small businesses typically conduct their data cleansing in-house and need to acquire the appropriate skills. The following sections describe the types of errors that can arise and give advice about how to find, remedy, and prevent them.

Why Clean Data Is Important

The cleaner your data, the more useful and accurate your analysis and actions. Unclean data can be considerably costly. For example, these costs could take the form of failing to meet regulatory compliance or failing to address customer issues in a timely manner.

Data analysis may be used to determine further investments in a business. For example, if the rate of sales in a business has increased over the last couple of years, the existing stores may not be sufficient to handle the amount of expected sales. Thus, additional stores and staff will be needed. Clearly, if such investment is based on the analysis of unclean and erroneous data, money and time could be wasted. Clean data is essential when making such decisions.

Inaccurate data can lead to unnecessary costs and possible reputation loss when it's used to support advertising. For example, the list of customer addresses, buying habits, and preferences should be correct and free of duplicates if it is to be used to advertise a new product by direct mailing. Any incorrect addresses could cause letters to be returned as undeliverable, which wastes money; customers duplicated in the mailing list would receive more than one letter, again leading to unnecessary expense for the business and also to customer frustration. Inaccurate data about consumer buying habits and preferences could lead to poor customer profiling and the advertisement of products that do not correspond to people's interests.

Business data consists of much more than customer data, as has been shown in the case studies in Chapters 2–4. For example, Smart Wheelbarrows Inc. has a database table for Materials that standardizes codes for parts. It is essential that this data be accurate so that the correct parts are ordered and linked to their suppliers. If this is not the case then money and time could be wasted by ordering the wrong materials.

Causes of Unclean Data

Understanding the causes of unclean data can be useful for improving data-collection procedures (covered in Chapter 9) and for improving data-cleansing techniques. If, for example, you conclude that an erroneous data entry is the result of typing errors, the layout of the keyboard may lead you to the correct input.

The following sections identify a number of causes of unclean data.

Typing Errors on Data Entry

Data entry is often carried out by hand. The data can be the result of a phone conversation or can come from written or printed sources. In these circumstances, errors can occur at the time of typing data into the database due to misspellings or misunderstanding of the data source. Sometimes a data value can be entered in the wrong column, which makes the error difficult to detect.

Other problems include adding extra spaces at the beginning of words in columns, which causes problems during data processing, such as when data is sorted. For example, if Cats, Roses, Boats, Cars, and Castles are product names of cards from Cards for Everyone Inc. and they are sorted in alphabetical order, we would expect the order to be Boats, Cars, Castles, Cats, and Roses. However, if a space had been placed inadvertently in front of Cats, the order would change to Cats, Boats, Cars, Castles, and Roses. In a short list this does not present much of a problem. However, in a list of many hundred entries, sorting the list is hampered by data items appearing in unexpected places as such entries are effectively hidden.

Nonprinting Characters in Text

Nonprinting characters are instructions that are not intended to be seen in text: rather they are used to format text in the background. An example from HTML (used for writing web pages) is \n, which means "move to a new line". When text is transferred from one place to another, the nonprinting characters may become visible and can lead to confusion.

Text Inconsistency

Differences in case can lead to sorting errors and, at the very least, make the database look untidy. For example, "yoga class" and "Yoga Class" refer to the same thing. MS Access is not case sensitive but you need to check how the database package that you are using deals with upper- and lowercase.

Using singular and plural nouns can cause problems as well. For example, "Hinge" and "Hinges" might refer to the same thing. Having both in your database could lead to duplicate records (discussed later in this chapter).

Coding Errors

Coding errors occur when an incorrect code is entered. For example, if 1=Male and 2=Female and 1 is entered instead of 2 for a female in some instances by mistake then this forms a coding error. Such errors usually happen at the time of data collection, such as during a telephone or a face-to-face interview.

Sometimes columns can be set automatically to a default value. For example, a column representing gender may be set to male by default. If a data inputter passes over such a column by mistake, it will be left with the default value even in the case of a female customer.

Missing Data

Data can be missing for a number of reasons. For example, a client may have declined to answer a question, a data inputter may not have had the data to enter into the database, and so on. Useful data would be wasted if we ignored all rows with a missing value.

Missing values do not necessarily appear in databases in a consistent manner. For example, missing data can be coded with data that is out of range, such as 999, so that it is easy to see. However, sometimes values such as 0 may be used to code missing values that may not stand out. Other times, missing data are replaced by default values (for example, Gender=Male). Although such a value will appear correct and leave no obvious trace of an error, after a while the data will become meaningless or misleading.

Data Types

Numbers are sometimes not given a numerical type in the database and are stored with a textual type such as "short text". This means that mathematical operations required to make totals, averages, and so on cannot be applied to this value. In addition, the numbers cannot be sorted in a numerically accurate way. For example, if the numbers 5, 11, 4, 10, and 9 are saved with data type "short text" and sorted in ascending order, the result would be 10, 11, 4, 5, and 9 which is not numerically accurate.

Dates should be entered with a type such as "date/time". If not, operations such as filtering all the rows from a given month cannot be applied.

■ **Note** A *filter* enables you to concentrate on a subset of rows that interest you. For example, you can view or search only the rows that contain dates within a given time period; all rows that contain names beginning with s; or all rows that contain quantities fewer than 5. Figure 10-1 shows the types of filters available in Access.

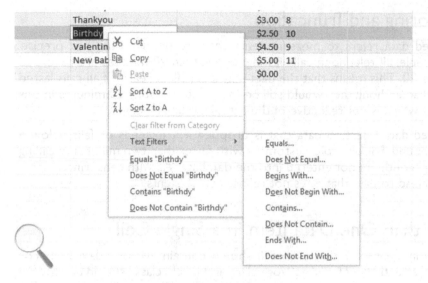

Figure 10-1. The filter function in MS Access

Data Integration Errors

Your database may contain data acquired from a number of sources using a variety of methods. This can mean using different data representations and inconsistently using units and abbreviations, to name a few. For example, alternative formats could be used to represent the customer address: one format with the whole address except the ZIP code in a single column, the other with each part of the address separated into different columns.

Here are some examples of varying formats of currency data:

- US$5 million
- $30-35 million
- 1,500 million
- US$ 2 billion
- 1,000,000
- 1000.00

Thus there is no consistent unit or data type.

Censoring and Truncation

Censored data refers to measurements that are bounded but not precise. For example, all telephone calls lasting longer than 20 minutes are recorded as lasting 20. This means that the data may not reflect reality: if all calls lasted longer than an hour, they would still be recorded as lasting 20 minutes in this scenario, which is not reflective of the actual circumstances.

Truncated data refers to data that is dropped if it exceeds or falls below a certain bound. For example, customers with fewer than two minutes of calling time per month are not entered into the database. As with censoring, truncation can lead to data that does not reflect actual events.

More than One Data Item in a Single Cell

We saw in Chapter 7 that each cell should contain just one data item. For example, an activity entered as "yoga class and tai chi class" should be entered on two separate rows as "yoga class" and "tai chi class".

Outliers

The term *outlier* refers to a significant departure from what is expected. For example, in the following sequence of numbers of monthly card sales per customer for Cards for Everyone Inc., the last value is unexpected as it is far higher than all the others:

2, 4, 9, 5, 10, 2, 7, 6, 8, 3, 104

Outliers are potentially legitimate and can be very useful. For example, if 104 is correct, it could represent a highly profitable customer. However, 104 could also represent a typing error.

Some outliers may only appear when two columns are compared, such as Age and Gender. For example, suppose you have a group of people of mixed gender, M=male and F=female, whose age is evenly distributed between 20 and 50, as shown in the Total column in Table 10-1. Suppose that one of the women is 10 years younger than all of the other women. This would be noticed only when the ages for genders are separated, as illustrated in Table 10-1.

Table 10-1. An Example of an Outlier Based on Two Columns

Age Range	Frequency (M)	Frequency (F)	Total
40 < age =< 50	11	9	20
30 < age =< 40	9	8	17
20 < age =< 30	18	1	19

Illogical Rows

Some errors occur because they do not correspond to the logical processes of your business. For example, it is illogical for invoice dates to fall before the date that your business started. Also, the quantity of any product should not be less than zero.

Duplicate Rows

Duplicate rows are two or more rows representing the same *thing*, such as a customer or product, when only one should exist. The values of these rows do not need to be identical: they can represent the same thing but with different values for all or some of their columns. For example, a customer for Cards for Everyone Inc. could have the same name in two rows but different contact data due to an erroneous update. The fact that duplicates can be made up of rows that are not identical increases the difficulty of their detection.

Duplicate rows can arise from different names being used for the same thing. For example, "Diabetes South Side" and "Diabetes S. Side" refer to the same organization and one needs to be removed.

The use of adjectives can also lead to duplicate rows. For example, "relaxing yoga class" is the same as "yoga class" and only "yoga class" need be used.

Names prefixed by "the" can also lead to duplicates. For example, "The Advice Center" is the same as "Advice Center".

Broken Links Between Database Tables

As time goes by, insertions, deletions, and updates will lead to rows that incur broken links. For example, in Cards for Everyone Inc., a supplier may stop trading. If you were to delete the supplier from the Suppliers' table but not delete the corresponding cards that they were supplying from the Products table, you could be offering cards to your customers that are no longer available.

In addition to links between tables, queries, forms, and reports may be based on tables that have been adjusted in an incompatible manner or that no longer exist.

Detecting, Correcting, and Preventing Errors

The following sections assume that your data is stored in a series of linked tables within a database as described in Chapter 7—all records are of equal length, all columns have the same data type, and each row has a unique identifier.

As with any data-processing exercise, it is essential to make a backup of your database before beginning. Having done this, use the following steps to detect, correct, and ultimately prevent errors. Your database should enable you to carry out many of these operations automatically. The examples in this chapter use MS Access 2013.

The background to error detection, correction, and prevention will often come from your own awareness of your business. For example, knowing that the entry for missing values for quantity is '999'. Such information is often only in people's heads, so it is essential to document it to ensure it can be passed on.

Detection and Correction of Typing Errors

You should start by detecting and correcting typing errors, because they can exacerbate other errors.

Some typing errors may come from a subgroup of employees and, if everyone attaches their initials to any rows they insert, additional training can be given where it is required.

Spellchecker

Most databases have a spellchecker facility that enables you to find and correct misspelled words. A spellchecker can also find values that are not used consistently, such as product or company names.

Frequency Distributions

When you're looking for typing errors, consider whether the distribution of frequencies matches what you are expecting. In a column such as Gender, you would expect to see two categories—male and female. The *frequency distribution* will help show any bias in the frequencies.

A frequency distribution provides the number of times each value occurs in the data. You have already seen an example of a frequency distribution for the categories of cards for Cards for Everyone Inc. in Chapter 1; this is shown in Figure 10-2.

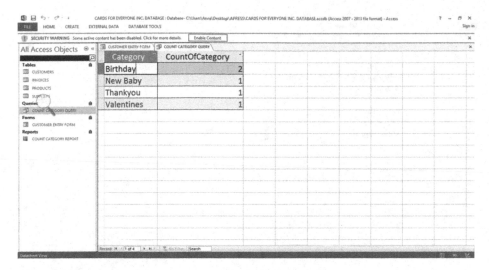

Figure 10-2. Sample query for Cards for Everyone Inc.

You can see that there are two cards with category "Birthday" in the database and one of each of the other three categories. Frequency distributions can be applied to data made up of names (such as in Figure 10-2) and numerical data.

If, for example, you notice that there are a large number of men compared to women, you might consider whether this could be an input error.

A frequency distribution will also show spelling mistakes: for example, if one of the categories of "Birthday" for Cards for Everyone Inc. was spelled "Birthdy" then the frequency distribution would have one occurrence for "Birthday" and one for "Birthdy". Figure 10-3 shows the query in Figure 10-2 with the spelling mistake in birthday. Frequency distributions are covered in more detail in Chapter 13.

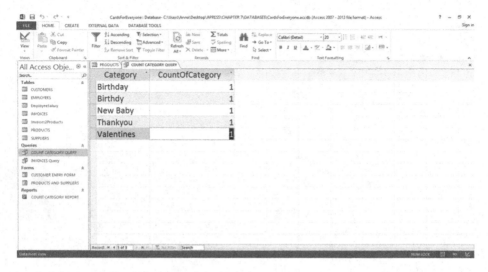

Figure 10-3. Sample query with spelling mistake in the Cards for Everyone Inc. database

Removing Unwanted Spaces from Text

To remove unwanted spaces, you can apply the following functions to a given column: LTrim (to remove spaces from the left), RTrim (to remove spaces from the right), and Trim (to remove space from both sides).

Using Mobile Technology

Entering data directly into a mobile device, such as a smartphone or tablet, prevents handwriting issues and can help cut down on input errors. Mobile technology is covered in Chapter 9.

Nonprinting Characters in Text

Correcting nonprinting characters is usually a matter of finding and deleting them. It may be possible to correct these errors in your database by finding the characters using the built-in find and replace function. The most difficult step is to identify the type of nonprinting characters that are likely to occur. It makes sense to build a list. Some possibilities for your list could be:

- \n (new line)
- \b (bold)
- \ul (underline)

As many nonprinting characters contain \, you could begin by searching your text for \ and using the results to identify your nonprinting characters. Ideally, it would be useful to write a macro that could automatically find and replace a list of nonprinting characters.

■ **Note** A *macro* is a single instruction that, when it runs, sets in motion one or more instructions to carry out a task. Macros are applicable to spreadsheets, word processor files, and databases. Macros are usually written to carry out a group of tasks that you will need frequently, such as creating a table with a fixed set of headings.

As a preventative step, if your nonprinting characters appear to be coming from a given source, you could try to identify an alternative method for obtaining the data.

Inconsistencies in Text

Inconsistencies in a short column of text, such as the first letter of a name (i.e. Pat as opposed to pat) can be detected by sorting the column in alphabetical order and scanning down for anything that is incorrect.

Some databases have functions that can correct case inconstancies. For example:

> LOWER: Converts all uppercase letters in a text string to lowercase.

> UPPER: Converts text to uppercase letters.

Singular/plural mistakes can be hard to detect and correct. It may help to create a list of checks to apply during each data cleanse. For example, your list may include checking for:

- Class vs. Classes
- Session vs. Sessions
- Church vs. Churches

If you choose to replace every instance of Classes with Class, you could use find and replace.

Coding Errors

To avoid default values such as male for gender, it's possible to use a lookup table with Not Known as the default. It may also help to have clear lookup tables with codes and corresponding descriptions together in a list so that there is no ambiguity.

A column can be set as type Lookup. This means that its values can be pre-determined in the form of a drop-down menu. These menus can be used for data entry in a table or form. Figure 10-4 shows a drop-down menu for the categories column for Cards for Everyone Inc. in the Products table. When filling in the column, the required value can be selected. The values will be consistent each time they are used, as they are determined by the drop-down menu. Typing errors aren't possible.

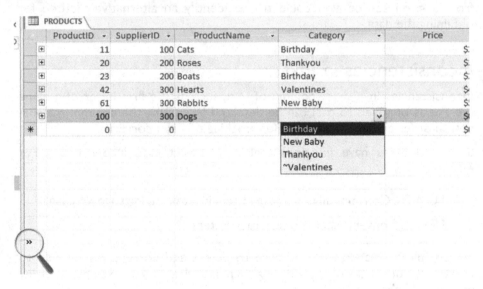

Figure 10-4. Lookup table for the PRODUCTS Table in Cards for Everyone Inc.

Missing Values and Outliers

Frequency distributions may help detect missing values. For example, with numerical data, missing values represented by an out-of-range number, such as 99, will be easy to spot as they often show an unusually high frequency. However, if missing values are represented by an in-range number, such as 0, they may be far less easy to find. If you have a distribution with an unexpect-edly high frequency of 0, some of these may represent missing values and could require closer attention.

A frequency distribution also shows if data is missing in a localized manner. For example, if all the surveys from a particular geographical area are missing, it will be clear that something has gone wrong in that area.

Bar charts are useful for detecting outliers. Bar charts display the frequency or other measure for distinct categories or groups, with the heights of the different bars being proportional to the size of the category they represent.

For example, the bar chart in Figure 10-5 shows the numbers of monthly card sales for the 11 Cards for Everyone Inc. customers described in the outliers section. These were:

2, 4, 9, 5, 10, 2, 7, 6, 8, 3, 104

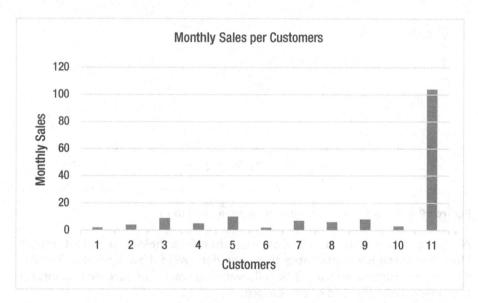

Figure 10-5. Outlier detection for Cards for Everyone Inc.

You can see immediately that the number of monthly sales for customer 11 is far higher than the others, reflecting the fact it is an outlier.

A particularly interesting case can occur when you're collecting what is known as *continuous ratio data*, which is numerical data that allows for infinitely fine sub-division. You'll learn more about this in Chapter 13. With such data, a pattern is often seen called a *normal distribution*. This is where the data is evenly distributed around the *mean* in a very regular way. The mean is:

$$Mean = \frac{Sum\ of\ data\ items}{Number\ of\ data\ items}$$

This is covered in Chapter 13.

If the frequency distribution of the data is plotted as a line graph, it will take the shape of a bell-shaped curve with the peak of the bell at the mean (Figure 10-6). The normal distribution, in very simple terms, tells us that most of the data will be close to the mean and that, if a large proportion do not, there may be a problem. The probabilities of some fictitious continuous ratio data in Figure 10-6 show how likely it is to observe any of the observed values.

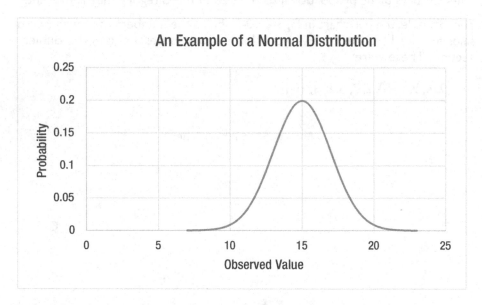

Figure 10-6. A normal distribuuion with the mean equal to 15

Analyzing the normal distribution may therefore help you detect errors. However, there is no guarantee that your data will follow a normal distribution, so this suggestion should be followed with care. For further reading, see the reference at the end of this chapter.

It is possible to substitute values in place of missing data such as the column mean. This procedure is known as "imputation". Simple imputation such as this does not take into account any relationships between columns and should be used sparingly, as it can introduce bias.

When you're inputting data it is important that you apply consistent and appropriate coding to the missing values. For example, in the context of the value State, using the term None to signify missing data is confusing. This could signify that a customer lives abroad. An entry such as Not Known would be more appropriate. Chapter 20 covers the subject of reducing missing values through efficient staff training.

Like missing values, perhaps the best way to address outliers is to set them to the column mean. However, as with missing values, you must be careful not to apply this approach too often.

An efficient method for detecting outliers generated from a pair of columns is to use a scatter plot. Scatter plots show the relationship between pairs of numerical values: in this case, columns in the same database table. A point represents each individual or object and is located with reference to the measurements on the two axes. Figure 10-7 shows an example.

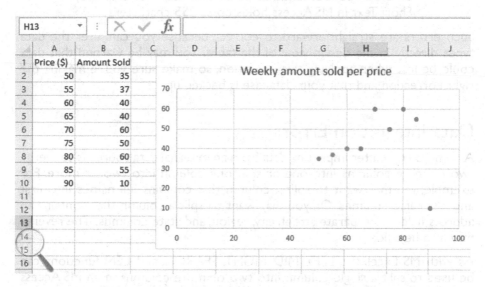

Figure 10-7. A scatter plot depicting the relationship between price and amount sold per week for Smart Wheelbarrows Inc.

Look for points that lie apart from the others. Figure 10-7 shows the weekly sales for varying prices of the small luxury wheelbarrow. You can see that when the price is set to $90 the drop in sales is disproportionate to the other levels of sales. Scatter plots are discussed in detail in Chapter 13.

Identifying the Data Type of Each Column

The data type of each column should be identified. In MS Access, data types are listed in the design view of the corresponding table, as shown in the appendix at the end of the book.

The data type of a given column should reflect the nature of the data in that column: a mismatch may be an indication of an error.

- Dates have a type such as Date/Time
- Dollars have a type such as Currency
- Columns taking just Yes or No answers have a type such as Yes/No

- Any column containing numbers that will need to have calculations and sorting applied to them should have a numerical type such as Number or Currency

- Text can appear in columns of differing types depending on the amount of text that will be inserted—for example, Short Text in MS Access holds up to 255 characters

Such errors are straightforward to correct because you can alter the data types directly in the design view of the table. You may be warned that data could be lost when applying this operation, so make sure you're making the right correction and that your database is backed up.

Data Integration Errors

A common task after importing data from an external data source is to merge two or more columns into one or split one column into two or more. For example, you may want to split a column that contains full names into first and last name columns. Or, you may want to split a column that contains an address field into separate street, city, region, and state columns. The reverse may also be true.

As with MS Excel, the LEFT, MID, RIGHT, SEARCH, and LEN functions can be used to split a single column into two or more columns in an MS Access query. The name will be split after searching for the space in the name.

Again, as with MS Excel, the & function can be used to merge columns.

■ **Note**   At this early stage, rather than learning how to apply these functions in your database, it may be easier to send your data to an MS Excel spreadsheet, apply the function in an environment that you are familiar with, and then send the data back into an adjusted table in your database.

Censoring and Truncation Errors

The frequency distribution may show both truncation and censoring errors. For example, if a frequency distribution showed a large number of telephone calls taking 20 minutes, but you know that many telephone calls had lasted longer than this, such analysis may indicate a truncation error.

Alternatively, if it appears that data at the left end of the frequency distribution is missing, indicating that calls below a certain time have not been recorded even when you know they have taken place, this may indicate a censoring error.

In general, detecting censoring and truncation errors rests on the knowledge of those who work in the business. It is important that any censoring and truncation methods are documented so that other employees are aware of them.

Splitting a Row Into Two or More Rows

Data items may have been combined and require separation. For example, an organization entered as "yoga class and tai chi class" should be entered on two separate rows as "yoga class" and "tai chi class".

Detecting such entries is not easy. You could search for separators such as commas. You could search for words such as "and". You may just notice these errors as you are progressing through your data cleanse or using your database in your daily work.

Unless such errors occur frequently, it is probably best to correct them by hand by adding a new row to the table in question and splitting the offending cell.

Checking for Illogical Errors

You can use constraint checking to identify column errors, where illogical errors can occur. For example, you can ensure that:

- The date in the Invoices table is always after the date the business started

- The quantity ordered is never less than 1

- Someone's title and gender are consistent—for example, if their title is Mrs., their gender should not be coded as male

Rather than searching for these errors by hand, it is possible in some databases to set up what is known as a *validation rule*. Such a rule restricts the entry of data that does not satisfy constraints. Validation rules have similar syntax to expressions used in spreadsheets such as MS Excel. Some illogical errors, such as those concerning name and gender, may be difficult to identify at the point of entry and some checking by hand could be necessary.

Eliminating Duplicate Rows

You should attempt to eliminate duplicate rows toward the end of your data-cleansing process. This is because the very process of error removal can make duplicate rows more apparent, so you need to do this last to make sure they are all corrected.

You need to decide how certain names should be treated—such as whether to remove "the" from the beginning of organizations' names used in Connecting South Side.

Some rows may represent the same thing but use a slightly different name.

Using alphabetical sort on a frequency distribution for a column containing many distinct entries can help identify names that are nearly the same. Once you identify them, you can give them consistent names.

Alternatively, it is possible to make sure that each customer at a given address is unique, assuming that this is a reasonable assumption to make. If names differ slightly, the rows can be merged.

As with any business, your local knowledge is of paramount importance. For example, at Connecting South Side, there might be many yoga classes that are listed in the Organizations table. These classes could be filtered on the word Yoga and their adjectives could be removed, such as changing relaxing yoga class to yoga class, in order to try to obtain consistency.

Once you have looked for inconsistencies, you can apply a duplicate detection technique, available with many databases, to identify matching or partially matching rows.

■ **Note**   Rather than applying a duplicate detection method, you may find it easier to apply a frequency distribution to a group of columns in your table. Any row that has a frequency of more than one is a potential duplicate.

Detecting Broken Links Between Tables

The best way to avoid broken links between tables and queries, forms, and reports is by instructing your database not to insert, update, or delete a row or a table if it will lead to broken links. This is a prevention step that you enforce when you are inserting links between tables.

■ **Note**   This process is known as *enforcing relationship integrity*.

If you did not set these measures in place when you were setting up your relationships, you may be able to download free database add-ins that can identify all the broken links.

Another way to locate broken links between two linked tables is to run a query using columns from both of them, effectively joining the tables via corresponding rows. This is known as a *join query*. If the resulting query has fewer rows than the "child" table, then the child table contains broken links. The appendix to this book shows you how to set up a simple query.

An example from Cards for Everyone Inc. involves the link between the Customers and Invoices tables. The relationship between these two tables is one-to-many, with Invoices being the child table and Customers being the parent table. If the joined Customers and Invoices table had fewer rows than the Invoices table, you would know that some invoices were not linked to customers. Figure 10-8 shows a query design for a possible join query between the Customers and Invoices tables and Figure 10-9 shows the output. Figure 10-9 shows five rows, i.e. the same as the Invoices table, so you can conclude that there are no missing links.

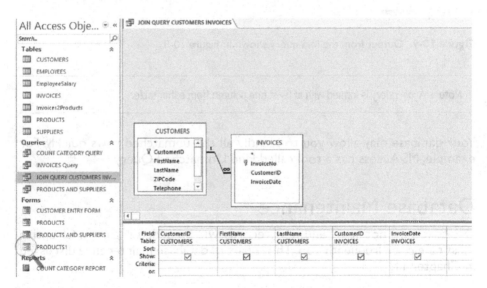

Figure 10-8. Query design of a join query between the Customers and Invoices tables of the Cards for Everyone Inc. database

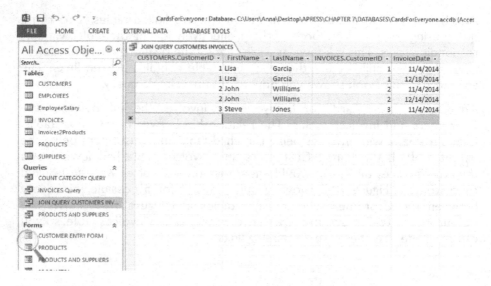

Figure 10-9. Output from the join query shown in Figure 10-8

▓ **Note**   A *join query* is formed with at least one column from either table.

Your database may allow you to identify all the unmatched rows quickly. For example, MS Access has a tool called Find Unmatched Query.

Database Maintenance

Databases are not static and new records will be added regularly. Cleansing must take place frequently too. This is part of database maintenance discussed in Chapter 11.

Summary

Clean data is fundamental to making effective business decisions. The process of cleansing data can be a lengthy one, involving detection, correction and, hopefully, prevention of errors. Errors can come from many sources, which means the cleansing process can be complex. In addition, data cleansing must be completed periodically to keep up with the development of your database.

Table 10-2 summarizes the correction and prevention of the errors discussed in this chapter.

Table 10-2. Summary of Error Correction and Prevention Techniques

Error Type	Cleansing Technique
Typing errors	Database spellchecker
	Frequency distributions
	Remove unwanted spaces from text
	Use mobile technology
Nonprinting characters	Identify and locate the offending characters and remove
Inconsistencies	Use built-in commands (to standardize cases)
	Choose singular or plural nouns and edit
Coding errors	Lookup tables that provide just the names or both the names and codes
Missing values	Frequency distribution
	Bar chart
	Normal distribution
Wrong data type	Alter data types directly in design view
Data integration errors	Use built-in commands (to split columns)
Censoring and truncation errors	Frequency distributions
	In-house knowledge
Multiple data items in a cell	Split a row into two or more rows
Illogical errors	Use validation rules
Duplicate rows	Frequency distribution and sort
	Use the built-in Duplicate Detection tool
Detecting broken links	Join query
	Run a Find Unmatched query

Further Reading

Statistics For Dummies, by Deborah J. Rumsey, John Wiley & Sons; 2nd edition, 2011, ISBN-13: 978-0470911082.

Maintaining Your Database

Database maintenance aims to keep a database running smoothly. Databases are not static; data is added, deleted, and moved around and, over time, such changes can cause the database to become sluggish. A poorly performing database can cost you money and waste users' time. Database maintenance includes backing up your database, compacting the database, and protecting the data. There are overlaps between this chapter and data cleansing, which is discussed in Chapter 10. This chapter discusses the jobs that you need to carry out on a regular basis.

Backing Up Your Database

One important aspect of maintaining a database is simply backing it up regularly. That way, if anything happens to it, there will be another copy available. Without a recent backup you have no chance of recovering your data after a catastrophe, such as a computer being lost or stolen or a hard disk ceasing to function.

It's not enough to back up your database whenever you can find the time. Backups should be scheduled regularly. Some database systems carry out backups automatically, sending a backup to another location periodically. The cloud also offers backup services, and this is covered in Chapter 18.

Ideally, you should run a number of backups over time as opposed to overwriting the same one repeatedly. This approach gives you the option of recovering from a problem that occurred at any given point in time. It's best that all backed up data be encrypted so that they cannot be stolen; you'll learn more about encrypting data later in this chapter.

Although onsite backups are important, it is critical to keep an encrypted copy of your database off-site as well. If a natural disaster or theft makes it impossible to access your onsite computers or servers, the off-site backup becomes critical. In general, back up any data that would hinder your business if it were lost.

The frequency of backups depends on your specific industry and business needs. For most businesses a nightly backup is sufficient. However, if your data changes dramatically during the day, it might make sense to back up your database throughout the day when critical information is changing.

After you have a good backup system in place, you need to test it regularly to make sure it works. You also need to decide who will be responsible for the backups.

Compacting Your Database

As you add and update data to your database and/or change its design, the file becomes larger. Some of this growth comes from new data, but some comes from other sources:

- When you delete a database row or object (table, query, form, etc.), the disk space that the row or object occupied is not automatically reclaimed. This is because the altered row or object cannot be deleted while it could still be connected to other rows and objects elsewhere.

- Your database creates temporary, hidden rows and objects to accomplish various tasks. An example is a query that requires your data to be sorted. Sometimes these temporary rows and objects remain in your database after the task is completed.

Database files can grow quickly, filling up with the remains of temporary and deleted rows, together with objects such as tables, forms, and queries. Performance can be affected: objects may open more slowly, queries may take longer than normal to run, and typical operations may be more time-consuming.

To address this performance issue, once such object and row versions are no longer needed, the space they occupy can be reclaimed for use by new objects and rows. The easiest way to avoid database growth and the corruption that sometimes accompanies it is to *compact* the database regularly. Many databases have a function that allows you to do this; for example, MS Access has a function called Compact and Repair. The compact process copies the database file, repairs its objects, deletes any temporary data, and rearranges the fragmented pieces.

Clearly, a table that receives frequent updates or deletes needs to be compacted more often than tables that are seldom updated. It may be useful to set up periodic tasks that compact only selected tables, skipping those that don't change often.

At the very least, it makes sense to compact your database once a day at a low-use time, with additional compacting of more heavily-updated tables when necessary. Keep in mind that you can't compact a shared database while it's open. You will therefore need to tell users how long they must avoid using the database. If you keep records of how long it takes to compact your database, you can make reasonably precise estimates about the time it will be unavailable and provide guidance accordingly.

Optimizing Your Hard Disk and Storage Devices

Optimizing your hard disk, sometimes known as *defragmentation*, can be viewed as compact and repair for your hard disk or a storage device. Fragmentation happens over time as you save, change, or delete files. The changes that you save to a file are often stored in a different place than the original file. Over time, your machine slows down because it has to look in different places to open a single file. Disk optimization or defragmentation is the process of consolidating fragmented data on, for example, a hard disk or a storage device, so it will work more efficiently.

A severely fragmented file (or drive) is slow. A busy database compounds the problem because all those transactions create even more fragmented pieces. For that reason, you should defragment your hard drive on a regular basis. A defragmentation tool, known as a *defragmenter*, is available with your operating system. By default, some defragmenters run automatically on a regular basis; for example, on Windows 8.1, the defragmenter runs every week. However, you can operate it manually if you wish.

Defragmentation can take a while, so schedule it for a time when the system won't be in use. Every program and file you have will benefit from this process, not just your database. However, due to its size, a database is particularly prone to poor performance due to fragmentation.

Splitting the Database

The databases we discuss in this book, such as MS Access or the LibreOffice and OpenOffice open source databases, exist on the desktop. This means that their file structure is different than larger databases such as SQL Server, because data and objects are stored in the same file. However, it is best to split your database into two separate files—a database that contains the data in the form of objects such as tables, queries, forms, and reports (backend) and a database that contains the entry point in the form of a user-friendly interface (front end).

An example of a front end is a web page that enables users to book an airline ticket while all the data processing takes place behind the scenes in the back-end of the database.

Such a setup can help prevent database files from being corrupted and limit data loss by keeping the data in a separate file that users do not access directly. When it comes time to upgrade the database, you simply replace the old front end file with the new version. If you store your data and front end in the same file, you must move data from the old file into the new one, which is inefficient.

Your database should contain a tool that enables you to split it using a few simple steps: MS Access uses a tool called Database Splitter.

Auditing Users

Authorized users should be checked periodically. For small businesses, this is likely to be every month or so. For example, some former employees of your business may still have access to your database and this will need to be resolved. Ideally it is best to update permissions at the time changes take place, but regular audits will help you find changes you forgot or missed.

Maintaining a Secure List of Passwords

If you password-protect your database files, it is important to keep a secure list of all passwords. The list and its location needs to be shared with someone you trust. If you become ill, have an accident, or are on vacation when a user forgets a password or a new employee needs training, the list will be essential.

Using Firewalls, Anti-Virus, and Spyware Protection Software

Your database needs constant and up-to-date protection from viruses and spyware, as is the case for all the files on your system.

■ **Note**   A computer virus is software that is loaded onto your computer without your knowledge, often carrying out undesirable actions. Even a simple virus can replicate itself and quickly bring a computer to a halt. Some viruses access private data or corrupt data.

Spyware is similar to viruses in that it arrives without warning and proceeds to do something undesirable. It is typically designed to spy on you or your computer, often tracking the web sites that you visit and recording your keystrokes in order to steal your account login information.

A *firewall* is a software or hardware block that sits between your computer and the network and only allows certain types of data to cross. For example, a firewall may allow checking e-mail and browsing the web, but may disallow actions such as file sharing. If you are connected to the Internet through a router, you already have a type of hardware firewall that prevents random network threats from reaching your system.

Sometimes viruses are able to cross the firewall and access your system. Therefore, it is essential that you use and update antiviral and antispyware software on all computers, including laptops and tablets. Keep in mind that new viruses are created daily and it takes the software designers a while to catch up with the hackers. For this reason, it is critical to keep your virus definitions up to date.

A virus scanner will locate and remove viruses from your hard disk. A real-time virus scanner will notice them as they arrive, even before they hit the disk, but these can be expensive and slow down your machine a little.

Keeping Your Hardware, Operating Systems, and Other Software Up to Date

Viruses can prosper on old equipment. To protect your database and other files, it is important to upgrade to new routers and computers when practically possible.

Operating systems should be reasonably new and should include the latest updates, including the most recent security fixes. This is also the case for other software running on your system.

As time moves on, older operating systems become unsupported. For example, as of April 2014 Microsoft stopped supporting Windows XP and updates are no longer available. Your computer will still work when using Windows XP but it might become more vulnerable to security risks and viruses. Internet Explorer 8 is also no longer supported.

Encrypting Your Database

Your database needs to be encrypted in order to protect the data within it from hackers. This is a data protection measure; data protection is covered in Chapter 8.

■ **Note** *Encryption* means to convert data in such a way that only someone with a specific code (known as a *key*) can read it.

You can activate full-disk encryption tools that come as standard on many operating systems. However, the standard version of Windows 8.1 does not include encryption. You need to upgrade to the PRO or Enterprise versions. Alternatively, there are free encryption tools you can use, such as TRUECRYPT and GnuPG.

Maintaining a Clean Database

Cleansing data is a time-consuming and expensive task and is described in Chapter 10. After you've cleansed your data, you will not want to repeat the whole process across the entire database again after a small proportion of the values change. Determining how to maintain the cleanliness of your database is challenging. Two possible approaches are:

- Clean any new data that is destined for the database before it is added.

- Clean any data that is amended within the database using tools such as the *Database Compare* function in Windows, which flags design changes to objects between two versions of a database. If you want to identify changes to the data itself, one approach is to move your data to a spreadsheet and use *Spreadsheet Compare*.

In addition to checking the accuracy of individual values, you need to identify duplicate rows. They can occur when amendments take place as well as when new rows are added to a table. Chapter 10 explains how to detect duplicate rows.

Summary

Database maintenance covers tasks that you will conduct on a regular basis. The goal is to keep your database running as smoothly as possible as well as to protect it from disasters and outside threats. Tasks such as backing up your database, compacting your database, and keeping the software and hardware up to date are all important.

Searching Your Database

There is little point in storing your data in a database if you cannot access it efficiently. For example, customers don't appreciate being kept on hold for a long time while you search the database for their details. In general, it is straightforward to find data quickly if you understand a few basic techniques.

To put this chapter into context, Chapter 13 covers data analysis, which is involved with the *examination* of data, whereas this chapter concerns *finding* data, the step prior to analysis. There is some overlap between this chapter and Chapter 19, which covers online searching. In addition, it is important that your staff can search the database efficiently; staff training is covered in Chapter 20.

As with all chapters in this book, the examples use MS Access 2013. The appendix to the book also has examples in LibreOffice 5 Base.

Types of Searches

You may wonder what type of searches you will want to carry out on your database and, indeed, which types are possible. Determining factors include:

- The number of tables of your database that the search will cover

- Whether you have full or partial search terms

- Whether you are searching for a single data item or a large section of data

Examples of searches include:

- Determining whether a customer is new or existing

- Identifying the supplier of a given product

- Finding the most regular customers

- Flagging up customers who do not pay their bills

Database searches are a useful precursor to your marketing efforts. For example, most businesses do not cater to just one type of customer, even if they do sell a single product or service. For example, Smart Wheelbarrows Inc. may sell to a large garden center as well as to the owner of a condominium. These are two very different types of customer, with diverse requirements. Therefore, targeting these customers with the same advertising e-mail would not be as effective as sending each tailored information. The garden center owner may be interested in deals for buying wheelbarrows in bulk, whereas the individual could be interested in discounts for single items. It is important to be able to divide the database into blocks of customers based on one or more columns such as address, age, and gender: this process is known as *segmentation*.

As is the case throughout the book, many of the examples in this chapter are based on the Cards for Everyone Inc. case study. Figure 12-1 restates the design of its database for reference.

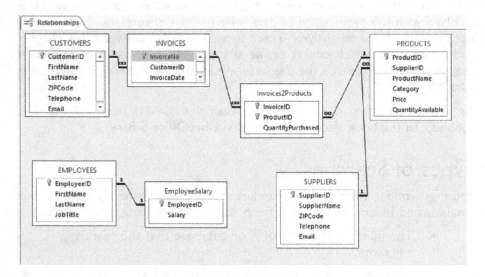

Figure 12-1. Database design for Cards for Everyone Inc.

Searching for One or More Rows Within a Table

Searches involving one or more rows in a given table can be divided into those based on a given column value and those based on more than one column value.

Searches Based on a Given Column Value

The following sections cover searches for either one row or several rows based on a given column value.

Searches for a Single Row

The simplest type of search involves looking for one row in a given table based on a given column value, such as searching for a client given their surname. This would be useful if you wanted to know whether someone buying from you was a new or existing customer.

The most obvious approach is to look at the table directly. You can make the search far easier by sorting the required column in alphabetical order. Figure 12-2 shows the Customers table in Cards for Everyone Inc. before sorting by last name and Figure 12-3 shows the table afterward. (Three additional names have been added to the table used in Chapter 1 to make the example more useful.)

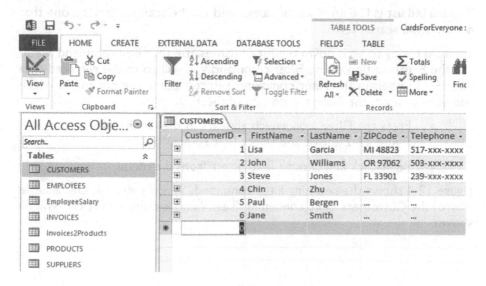

Figure 12-2. The Customers table from Cards from Everyone Inc.

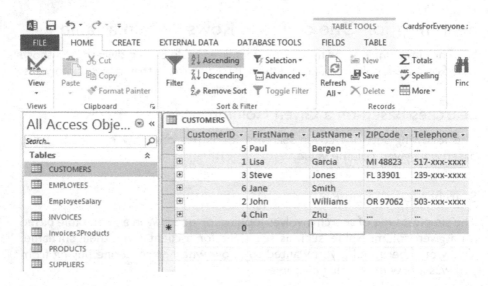

Figure 12-3. The Customers table from Cards from Everyone Inc. sorted on the LastName column

---

■ **Note** Sorting data in a database column is covered in the appendix at the end of the book.

The sorted list is like an index of names and can be scanned for the one that matches the search term.

To avoid having to scan down the list of names, use the *Filter* command. If you use the Equals option of the Filter command you will go to the required data directly. To operate the Filter command, select a cell in the column in which you wish to apply the filter and do one of these:

- Press the Filter icon, which appears in the top-middle of Figure 12-2 above, and select Text Filters.

- Right-click and choose Text Filters from the menu.

Figure 12-4 shows the resulting filter command. When you click OK, a single row of the Customers table containing "LastName is equal to Garcia" will be shown.

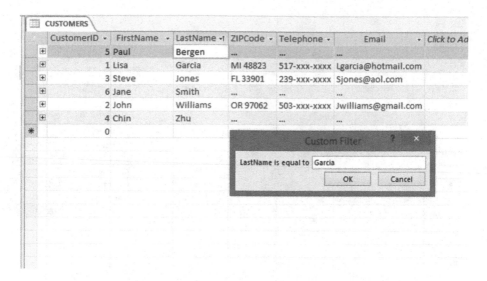

Figure 12-4. A text filter on the LastName field is applied to the Customers table of the Cards from Everyone Inc. database

This is a very simple example. In the real world, searches are likely to be far more complicated. Further searching would be required if:

- There was more than one customer with the last name of Garcia.

- Garcia were spelled incorrectly.

- Only Lisa's first name had been entered.

There are searches that can run to cover these eventualities; they are discussed later in the chapter.

Searches for Several Rows

Alternatively, you could be looking for several rows in a given table based on the value in one column, such as all products with Category = 'Birthday' in the case of the Cards for Everyone Inc. database.

Figure 12-5 shows the Products table for Cards for Everyone and Figure 12-6 shows the same table with just the birthday cards. In the latter case, a filter of Category = 'Birthday' has been applied.

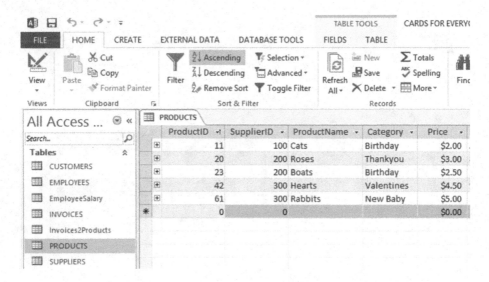

Figure 12-5. The Products table in the Cards for Everyone Inc. database

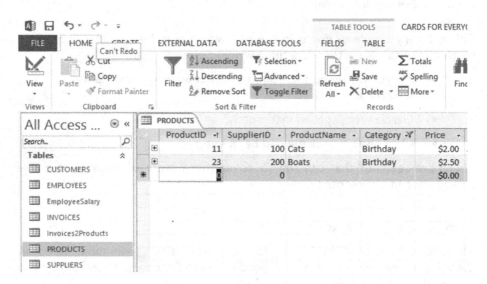

Figure 12-6. The Products table with the Category = 'Birthday' filter applied

A further type of search involves filters applied to numerical values. For example, in the case of the Products table, Figure 12-7 shows the case of rows filtered on a price that's less than or equal to $3.00.

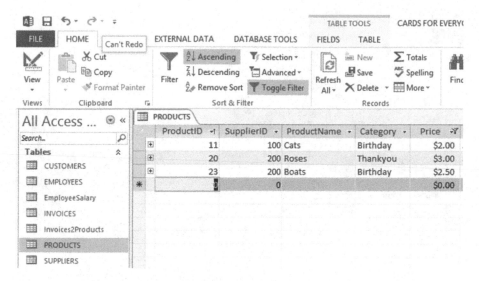

Figure 12-7. The Products table for the Cards for Everyone Inc. database filtered on Price ≤ '$3.00'

■ **Note**   Such a filter can be set in motion using the same method as for text explained previously, except that the options apply to numbers.

Searches Based on More Than One Column Value in a Given Table

You may be looking for one or more rows in a given table based on the values in more than one column, such as clients based on their first and last names. For example, assume that there is a customer named John Garcia in the Customers table for Cards for Everyone Inc., as shown in Figure 12-8.

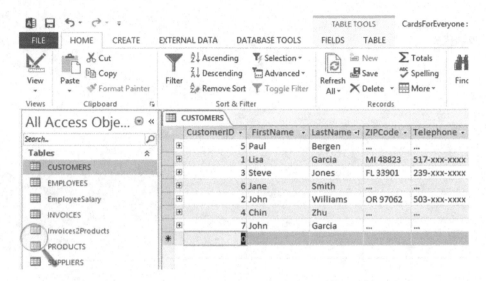

Figure 12-8. Updated Customers table in the Cards for Everyone Inc. database

Filtering on LastName = 'Garcia' gives the output shown in Figure 12-9.

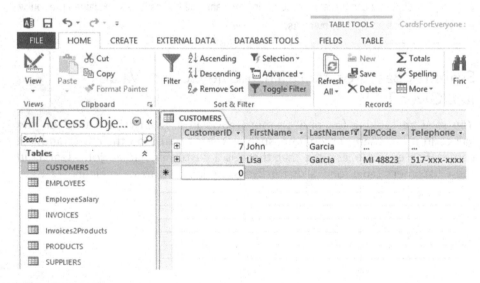

Figure 12-9. Filtering the Customers table from the Cards for Everyone Inc. database on LastName = 'Garcia'

If the filtered output was very long, you could apply a second filter using FirstName = 'Lisa' (assuming you were trying to locate Lisa Garcia only, of course).

Summary of Search Techniques on a Single Table

For this type of search, which seeks to find one or more rows within a given table, sorting and filtering are ideal methods for locating the relevant data. Working with a table fits in with your knowledge of spreadsheets, as you are using a method of viewing your data that you are already familiar with.

The previous examples provide an extremely simple portrayal of the possible situations you'll run into. As your business grows, your database tables may have many hundreds or thousands of rows, making the careful application of sorting and filtering essential.

This section assumes that you have complete information about the data you are looking for. The section on partial data later in the chapter will consider circumstances where this is not the case.

Searches Based on More Than One Table

In this section we are interested in searches involving more than one linked table. An example of such a search is all products that come from a given supplier in the database for Cards for Everyone Inc. In such a search, the concept of rows loses its relevance: the Products table has rows containing products and the Suppliers table has rows containing suppliers. However, to conduct the search you are interested in how these rows link together in the database.

It is no longer possible to open the Products or Suppliers table in isolation to carry out the search, because only part of the data that you require will be available. You need a method for bringing it all together. When your search involves more than one linked table, you'll begin to understand how powerful databases are and how they differ from spreadsheets.

The main considerations when conducting searches based on more than one table are how to bring the relevant data together and how to view it. There are two main options, both of which you have come across before. You can use a join query (introduced in Chapter 10) or a form (introduced in Chapter 1).

Using a Join Query

As a join query most resembles a spreadsheet, we will begin with this approach.

■ **Note** The appendix to the book describes how to set up a simple query.

Every time you design any query you have to first choose which table(s) you want to select the data from. To find which products come from a given supplier in the Cards for Everyone Inc. database, you need to select the Products and Suppliers tables. As explained in the appendix, you can either use the Query Wizard or the Query Design. Here I am using the Query Design as it shows a graphical representation of the tables. Figure 12-10 shows the linked Products and Suppliers tables for the Cards for Everyone Inc. database and two selected columns—ProductName and SupplierName. No other columns have been selected because, for this search, we are just interested in the name of the supplier and nothing more.

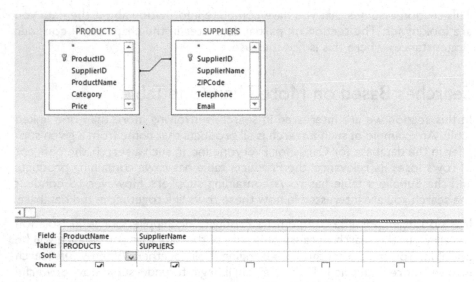

Figure 12-10. Query design over the Products and Suppliers tables in the Cards for Everyone Inc. database

Figure 12-11 shows the result of running the query in Figure 12-10. Note how the output of the query looks like a table or spreadsheet and reflects the presentation of data that you are used to. The tables have been "joined" on the basis of the SupplierID column, which links them together.

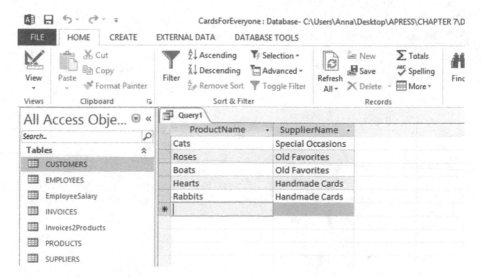

Figure 12-11. Output of the Products and Suppliers query on the Cards for Everyone Inc. database

With a small amount of output it is straightforward to identify the data you are looking for—for example, which products were supplied by which suppliers. However, as in previous sections, further work is required if you have a large number of rows. As with a table, a query can be sorted or filtered using the techniques described earlier in the chapter. If, for example, you want to know who supplied Boats, you could sort ProductName in alphabetical order, scan down the list for Boats, and read the supplier's name, Old Favorites, from the adjacent column. Or you could filter on ProductName = 'Boats', which would give you the result shown in Figure 12-12.

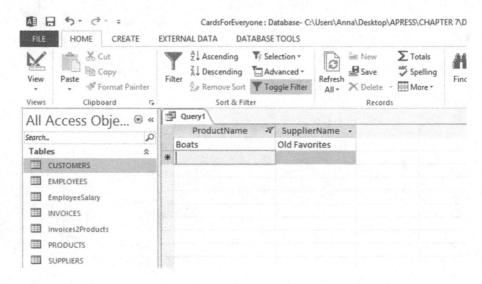

Figure 12-12. Query in Figure 12-11 for the Cards for Everyone Inc. database filtered on ProductName = 'Boats'

Using a Form

Figure 12-13 shows a form that covers the combined data for each product together with the associated data for its supplier.

■ **Note** The appendix at the end of the book explains how to create a simple form.

There are five forms in total, one for each product. The boxes on the form correspond to the columns of the Products and Suppliers tables in the database—as with a query, you can choose the columns that you include. Each box can be sorted and filtered, just as if it existed in a table. Figure 12-14 shows the form in Figure 12-13 filtered on ProductName = 'Boats'.

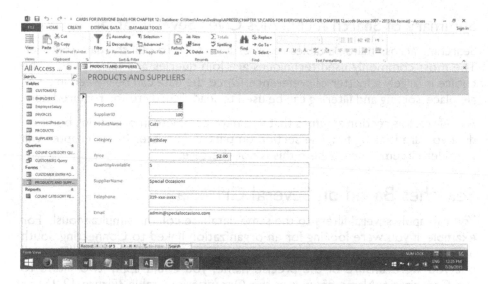

Figure 12-13. A form combining data from the Products and Suppliers tables of the Cards for Everyone Inc. database

ProductID	23
PRODUCTS_SupplierID	200
ProductName	Boats
Category	Birthday
Price	$2.50
QuantityAvailable	10
SUPPLIERS_SupplierID	200
SupplierName	Old Favorites
ZIPCode	CA 92591
Telephone	503-xxx-xxxx

Figure 12-14. A form combining the data from the Products and Suppliers tables of the Cards for Everyone Inc. database filtered on ProductName = 'Boats'

You can then identify the supplier of Boats, which is Old Favorites, directly from the form.

Summary of Search Techniques Over Several Tables

Searching across multiple tables requires a method to pull the data together. The most commonly used techniques are join queries and forms where the choice is largely a matter of preference. Once the data can be viewed in a single place, sorting and filtering can be used to lead directly to the required item.

As before, this section assumes that you have complete information about the data you are looking for. The section on partial data later in the chapter will consider circumstances where this is not the case.

Searches Based on Several Criteria

You can apply several filters to the same database column simultaneously. For example, if you were looking for an organization linked to Connecting South Side and you knew that the name contained the words "Yoga" and "Center" but you were unsure of the precise name, you could apply two filters to the OrganizationName column in the Organizations table (Figure 12-15) as follows:

- Apply one filter to the OrganizationName that contains the word "Center," giving you the output shown in Figure 12-16.

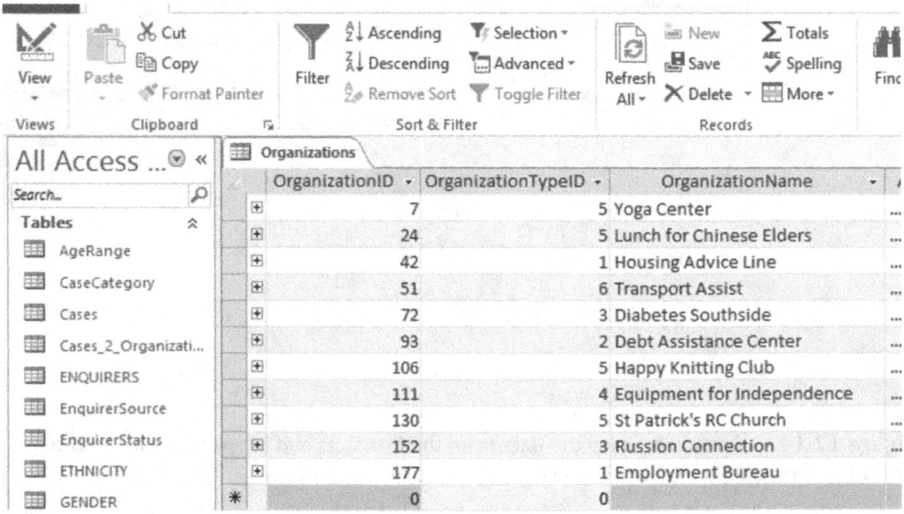

Figure 12-15. The first few columns of the Organizations table from Connecting South Side

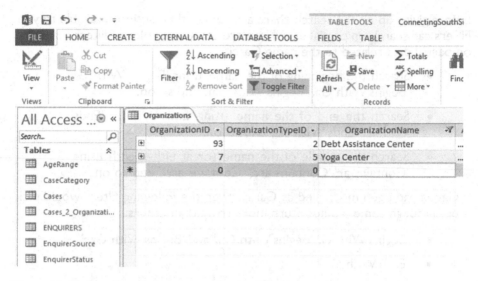

Figure 12-16. The OrganizationName column of the Organizations table filtered for the word "center"

- If there are a lot of rows returned from the first filter, apply a second filter on the OrganizationName, using the word "Yoga".

You can apply multiple filters to the same column, as well as apply filters to several columns simultaneously, whether in the same table or across several tables in a query or form. For example, if you're looking for Lisa Garcia in the Customers table in the Cards for Everyone Inc. database, you can apply two filters simultaneously: LastName = 'Garcia' and FirstName = 'Lisa'.

Searches Based on a Partial Column Value

Your search for Garcia in previous sections may not have been successful. It could be the case that Lisa's surname was not entered correctly, an error that was missed during the data-cleansing process. Lisa's surname may not have been entered at all or it could be the case that Lisa is not an existing customer.

Before giving up on the search, there are some other options available to you. Filters can search on partial data. Here are some examples of filters searching on partial data related to the name Garcia:

- Search the beginning of the name, using 'Begins With G,' 'Begins With Ga,' 'Begins With Gar,' and so on.

- Search the end of the name, using 'Ends With a,' 'Ends With ia,' 'Ends With cia,' and so on.

- Search the middle of the name (or at either end) using 'Contains ar,' 'Contains arc,' 'Contains arci,' and so on.

If Garcia had been misspelled as Garica, then the following filters would pick it up, although some would return more rows than others:

- 'Begins With G,' 'Begins With Ga,' and 'Begins With Gar'

- 'Ends With a'

- 'Contains ar' (as well as G, Ga, Gar, a, r, i)

It is advisable to find a feature of the name that is unusual so that the number of rows returned by the filter is as small as possible.

The following filters would not be successful in the case of Garica:

- 'Begins With Garc' or 'Begins With Garci'

- 'Ends With ia' (as well as cia, rcia, arcia)

- 'Contains arc' or 'Contains arci'

The search process can be repetitive and involves trial and error: don't expect to get the data you are looking for immediately. Revise your search as needed based on the number of hits and the relevancy of the results.

These types of searches can be time consuming and may not lead to anything. For example, if Lisa's surname was not entered into the database, you will be searching for something that doesn't exist. With this in mind, you may wish to filter on other columns to hone in on the correct data. You could filter on other columns as follows:

- FirstName Equals 'Lisa'

- Gender Equals 'Female' (if you know Lisa is female)

- State Contains 'MI' (if you know that Lisa lives in Michigan)

- InvoiceDate Equals 'Last Month' (if you know that Lisa's previous order from you was last month)

Each time you apply an additional filter, the number of rows returned will either be the same as before or less. The fewer there are, the easier it will be to identify Lisa's record (assuming that it exists).

There may come a point when you have made every reasonable attempt to find Lisa's details and you will need to stop and conclude that Lisa is a new customer.

You can make the searching process more efficient by adding keywords to some of your tables. For example, if Pat at Cards for Everyone Inc. was faced with very vague search criteria, such as "all cards with animals on them," it would not be efficient to trawl through all the cards to see if they matched this requirement. A more efficient method would be to add a keywords column to the Products table, with keywords reflecting the picture on the card, such as animals for cats and rabbits and flowers for roses. An example is shown for the Products table of the Cards for Everyone Inc. database in Figure 12-17.

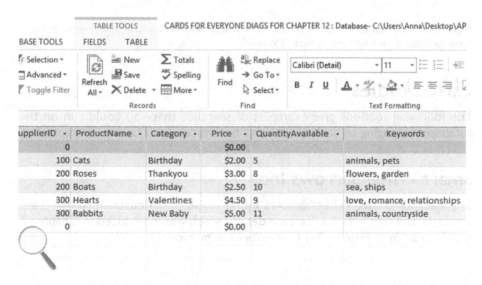

Figure 12-17. Adding a Keywords column to the Products table of the Cards for Everyone Inc. database

With the keywords in place, you could use a filter such as Keywords Contains 'Animals' to identify the animal cards. The result of such a filter from the Products table is shown in Figure 12-18.

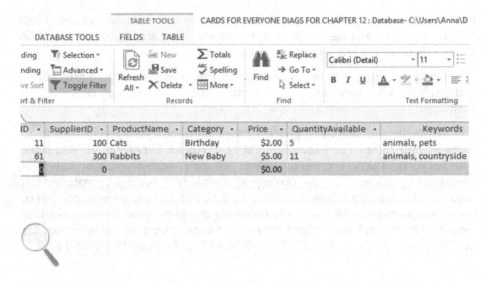

Figure 12-18. The Keywords column in the Products table for the Cards for Everyone Inc. database filtered on Keywords Contains 'Animals'

Case Studies

The following sections give examples of searches that you could run on the databases belonging to each of the small businesses described in Chapters 2–4.

Smart Wheelbarrows Inc.

The data for Smart Wheelbarrows Inc. is made up of customers, materials, products, and suppliers. Its database design, which was introduced in Chapter 7, is shown again in Figure 12-19 for reference purposes.

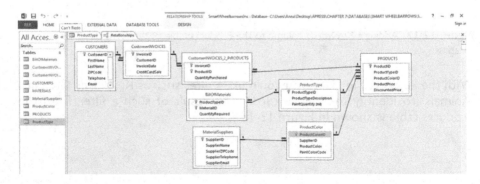

Figure 12-19. Overview of the complete database design for Smart Wheelbarrows Inc

The number of potential searches *is* large and varied. Here are a few examples:

- *A component or material is defective and the supplier needs to be identified*—A search is required to match the component or material with its supplier so that the situation can be resolved. In the section that covered searches spanning multiple tables, you saw an example where the Products and Suppliers tables in the Cards for Everyone Inc. database were merged using either a join query or a form. Either approach could be used in this instance.

- *To meet the requirements of a quality audit*—Chapter 5 discussed the possibility of Smart Wheelbarrows Inc. developing a children's wheelbarrow. To develop such a product, it is likely that a quality audit would be needed that would trace each component back to its source in order to make sure it is safe for children to use. Such an audit would involve identifying each of the components of the proposed product and linking them to their suppliers. This can be done the same way as for individuals components, with the help of the relevant Bill of Materials.

- *Identifying whether a customer has bought from the business before*—This should be a straightforward search (if the customer's name has been entered correctly) or a potentially lengthy process if there are input errors. Follow the steps for finding Lisa Garcia in the Cards for Everyone Inc. database described throughout this chapter for a systematic approach. If all these attempts to find the customer lead to nothing, the likelihood is that you have a new customer.

- *Identifying customers who do not pay their bills*—Many small businesses are affected by customers who do not pay their bills. A search to identify unpaid invoices and the customers who are responsible may be useful. This is an example of a search that cannot be conducted at the present time with the Smart Wheelbarrows Inc. database, as there is no column in the CustomerInvoices table that holds data about when the invoice has been paid. However, this is a straightforward addition—the column could be called DatePaid and be of data type Date/Time.

  Once the DatePaid column is in place, the Customers and CustomerInvoices tables can be joined using a join query or a form (see the section on searches based on more than one table) and the DatePaid column could be filtered for empty values. The customers appearing on this filtered query or form have not paid their bills (assuming that the database has been kept up to date).

Jennings-Havard Law Offices Inc.

The data for Jennings-Havard Law Offices covers clients, cases, and demographic particulars. The whole database design, which was introduced in Chapter 7, is shown again in Figure 12-20 for reference purposes.

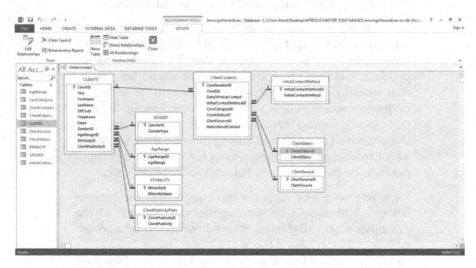

Figure 12-20. Overview of the database design for Jennings-Havard Law Offices

The following searches would be useful:

- *Identifying whether someone is a new or existing client*—As for Smart Wheelbarrows Inc. and for Lisa Garcia described in the previous sections.

- *Identifying repeat clients*—Customer loyalty is important to any business, but particularly to a law firm such as Jennings-Havard Law Offices, which could hold clients for many years.

One method for finding repeat clients is to set up a join query between Clients and ClientContacts, choosing the ClientID column from the ClientContacts table and the FirstName and LastName from the Clients table, as shown in Figure 12-21. This query places the names of clients against each of their contacts, enabling them to be counted. Upon running the query, the table in Figure 12-22 is displayed. You can see that Chin Zhu has contacted the firm twice.

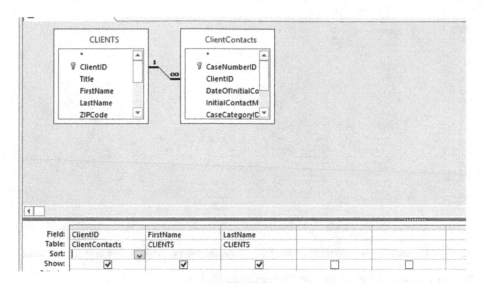

Figure 12-21. Query design for repeat clients of Jennings-Havard Law Offices

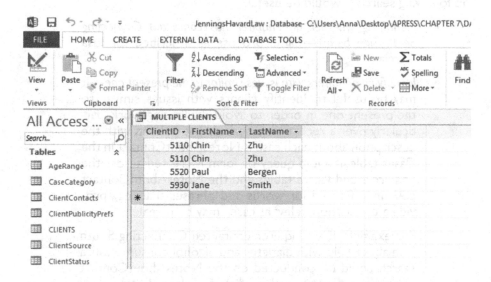

Figure 12-22. Query showing repeat clients for Jennings-Havard Law Offices

Connecting South Side

Connecting South Side holds data about their enquirers, the organizations the enquirers are signposted to, and demographic particulars about the enquirers. The whole database design, which was introduced in Chapter 7, is shown again in Figure 12-23 for reference purposes.

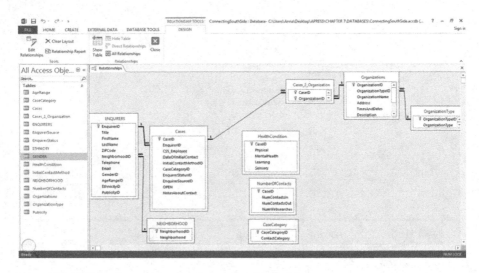

Figure 12-23. Database design for Connecting South Side

The following searches would be useful.

- *Identifying whether an enquirer has contacted Connecting South Side before*—Same process as described for Lisa Garcia.

- *Identifying enquirers with issues similar to the present one*—It may be useful to identify clients with issues similar to the present one in order to avoid duplicating work, particularly over a recent time period. The column with the description about each case is NotesAboutContact in the Cases table. If a join query or form is created across the Enquirers and Cases tables and the NotesAboutContact column is filtered for words and phrases that may provide a connection, relevant cases may be revealed.

  For example, if an enquirer contacted Connecting South Side about help with diabetes and alcohol consumption, a search could be conducted on the NotesAboutContact column using words such as diabetes, alcohol, and so on. With luck, this would identify a recent case in which an enquirer has been signposted for help with such a situation and fresh research would be unnecessary.

Summary

The number of different types of database searches is enormous. In this chapter we have considered those in a table, those across more than one table, and those involving multiple criteria. Searches can be based on complete or partial data. The process of searching for data is often repetitive. This chapter introduced many of the tools available for searching and, with experience, you will be able to apply them effectively.

Analyzing Your Data

You cannot press a button and expect all your data analysis to be conducted automatically. Data analysis involves detailed examination of the elements or structure of your data and can be fundamental to business decision-making.

The following sections introduce techniques for data analysis and describe the best circumstances in which to apply them. Even well-recognized data analytic techniques can be applied incorrectly and it is important to know what pitfalls to look for.

You must select techniques to meet the requirements of a given set of data and the goals of your small business. If you're just starting out, it's probably a good idea to experiment with several techniques to get a feel for how they work. Making a copy of your database or putting together a simple test database is wise. The tools considered here are available either in your database package or in a spreadsheet.

Overview

Data analysis can be divided into two main types—exploratory and confirmatory. Exploratory data analysis involves applying techniques that give you a "feel" for the data, enabling you to develop hunches (or hypotheses) about what may be going on. For example, you may be under the impression that more women than men respond well to a given marketing campaign. Confirmatory data analysis tests the hunches and produces estimates with a specified accuracy.

In statistics, a distinction is made between:

- A data sample from which you are predicting details about the population as a whole

- Data that is assumed to be the entire population

In this chapter, it is assumed that you have all the data that you are interested in unless mentioned otherwise. Details about working with samples can be obtained from the further reading listed at the end of the chapter.

Types of Data

Data analysis should always begin by assessing the characteristics of the data. As you have seen, data is not all the same and you have to conduct the analysis carefully, even with measurements that appear very straightforward. We will consider three types of data in this chapter, each one adding more properties to its predecessor:

- Nominal

- Ordinal

- Ratio

■ **Note**   The traditional scales for defining levels of measurement are nominal, ordinal, interval, and ratio. The distinction between interval and ratio data is that ratio data contains a meaningful and non-arbitrary zero.

Nominal Data

Nominal data includes items that are distinguished by a simple naming system such as the categories of the cards in the Cards for Everyone Inc. database, a list of the names of states in the address column of a customer table, and the names given to parts in the Smart Wheelbarrows Inc. database. Each item does not overlap any of the others. Nominal items may have numbers assigned to them in order to simplify collection and referencing, such as 1=Blue, 2=Red, 3=Yellow. These numbers do not have any mathematical meaning and, as such, could not be added together.

Ordinal Data

Ordinal data has a natural ordering, hence the name. Such data is frequently used in surveys that ask people to indicate their preference. They are also used to indicate pay bands in a business and in many other ways. The order of such items is often defined by assigning numbers to them to show their relative positions. Letters or other sequential symbols may also be used as appropriate. As with nominal numbers, you cannot perform arithmetic on ordinal numbers: they show sequence only. Also, the intervals ordinal numbers cannot be compared. For example, on a five-point question scale the difference between four and five cannot be compared to the difference between two and three.

Ratio Data

On a ratio scale, numbers can be added together. Multiples can also be compared. For example, one product can be twice as expensive as another product, as price is a ratio number.

Ratio data can be divided into continuous and discrete types. Continuous data is measured along a continuous scale that can be divided into fractions, such as height. Continuous data allows for infinitely fine subdivisions.

Discrete data is measured across a set of fixed values, such as age in years.

Frequency Distribution

Frequency distributions, introduced in Chapter 10, are useful for showing the "shape" of your data—that is, how the data values are distributed. Frequency is how often something occurs. For example, in a given week Cards for Everyone Inc. may sell one card on Saturday morning, one on Saturday afternoon, and one on Wednesday morning. The frequency is two on Saturday, one on Wednesday, and three for the whole week. Hopefully this is not indicative of normal sales! Frequency distributions can be applied to each type of data explored in the previous section, as illustrated in the following sections.

Discrete Ratio Data

By counting frequencies, we can make a frequency distribution table. For example, suppose the monthly card sales per customer for Cards for Everyone Inc. are as follows:

2, 3, 1, 2, 1, 3, 2, 3, 4, 5, 4, 2, 2, 3

A corresponding frequency distribution is shown in Table 13-1.

Table 13-1. Example of a Frequency Distribution for Cards for Everyone Inc.

Monthly Card Sales per Customer	Frequency
1	2
2	5
3	4
4	2
5	1

From Table 13-1, we can see interesting things such as:

- Customers buying two cards per month happens most often

- Only once did a customer buy five cards in a month

Next is an example from later in Cards for Everyone Inc.'s existence where some customers are putting in larger orders:

2, 8, 2, 5, 1, 6, 9, 3, 11, 5, 4, 12, 3, 15

To avoid a lengthy table with 15 rows, the values have been grouped into threes, as shown in Table 13-2.

Table 13-2. Example of a Frequency Distribution with Grouped Values for Cards for Everyone Inc.

Monthly Card Sales per Customer	Frequency
1 – 3	5
4 – 6	4
7 – 9	2
10 – 12	2
13 – 15	1

In general, the number of intervals should be limited to about 8 to 10. The labels should be clear and not overlap. For example, if you had 10-12 and 12-14, you would not know where to place customers buying 12 cards per month.

Nominal and Ordinal Data

Nominal and ordinal data can be represented in a frequency distribution such as the one shown in Table 13-1. However, it is incorrect to group nominal and ordinal data as shown in Table 13-2, because there is no mathematical relationship between them.

Table 13-3 shows the frequency distribution for the category of cards in the Products table for Cards for Everyone Inc. All categories should be included even where there is zero frequency.

Table 13-3. Frequency Distribution for the Card Category in the Products Table of Cards for Everyone Inc.

Category of Card	Frequency
Birthday	2
New Baby	1
Thankyou	1
Valentines	1

Continuous Ratio Data

It is not easy or accurate to express continuous ratio data as single values in a frequency distribution. This is because there can be very small intervals between the values (potentially, infinitely small). For example, values of price can be separated by a cent and a table detailing frequencies for all possible values of cents would be huge and unhelpful. Therefore, continuous data is expressed as intervals, such as $0 < Price \leq \$5, \$5 < Price \leq \$10$, etc. Such intervals must be written so that there is no ambiguity as to where any of the prices belong. For example, $5 belongs in the $0 < Price \leq \$5$ interval. Table 13-4 shows a frequency distribution for price from the Products table of the Cards for Everyone Inc. database.

Table 13-4. Example of a Frequency Distribution for Price Taken from the Products Table for Cards for Everyone Inc.

Price	Frequency
$0 < Price \leq \$1$	0
$1 < Price \leq \$2$	1
$2 < Price \leq \$3$	2
$3 < Price \leq \$4$	0
$4 < Price \leq \$5$	2

Charts

After creating a frequency distribution table, you can construct a bar or pie chart.

Bar Charts

Bar charts are one of the most commonly used types of chart. They are used to display and compare the frequency or other measure for nominal data, ordinal data, discrete ratio data, and grouped continuous ratio data. The heights of the different bars are proportional to the size of the data item they represent. As the horizontal axis represents the different categories, it has no scale. The scale of the vertical axis is the units of measurement. The bars can also be drawn horizontally, which is particularly useful for nominal data when the names of categories are long. Figure 13-1 shows a horizontal bar chart for the data listed in Table 13-3. A spreadsheet such as MS Excel will produce a bar chart directly from the frequency distribution table.

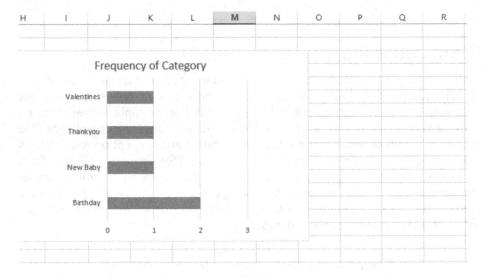

Figure 13-1. Horizontal bar chart for the Categories column in Cards for Everyone Inc.'s Products table

Pie Charts

Pie charts are used for visualizing nominal data. They can also be used for ordinal data, discrete ratio data, and grouped continuous ratio data, although this is less common. They display how the total data is distributed between different categories and are an effective way to relate the parts to the whole. They work best when the number of categories is small. Each segment of the pie reflects the proportion of the whole set of data accounted for by each category. The parts are often displayed in descending order of size.

The example in Figure 13-2 shows a pie chart corresponding to the frequency distribution of the categories of cards for Cards for Everyone Inc. shown in Table 13-3 above. As there are two cards with the Birthday category, these are allocated a slice of pie that is twice the size of the others. A spreadsheet such as MS Excel will produce a pie chart directly from the frequency distribution table.

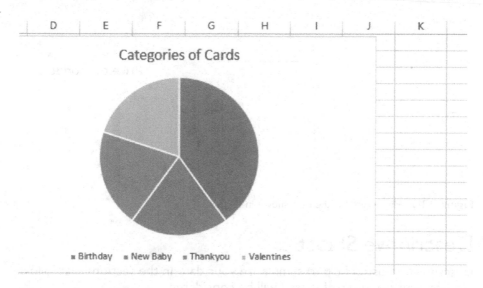

Figure 13-2. Pie chart for the Categories column in Cards for Everyone Inc.'s Products table

Histograms

Histograms are a special form of bar chart where the data represents continuous ratio data. Software packages will often partition your data for you without you needing to construct a frequency distribution. For example, Excel 2013 takes as its input to a histogram command a list of input data and a list of user-defined *bins*. It then places the data into these bins and produces a frequency distribution and a histogram. Figure 13-3 shows the input data and bins corresponding to the data in Table 13-4 above. Bin 2 corresponds to 1 < Price ≤ $2 so that the "bar" on the histogram represents this interval. Unlike a bar chart, in a histogram, both the axes have a scale. This means that the area of the bar is proportional to the size of the quantity represented and not just its height.

> ■ **Note** To construct a histogram in MS Excel 2013, you need to install the Analysis Toolpak that comes with the software.

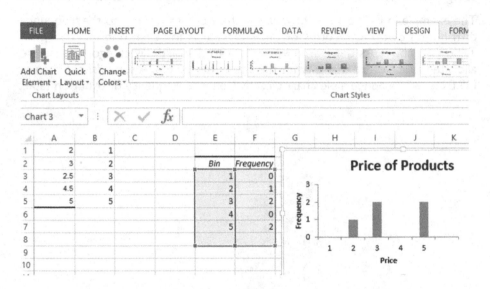

Figure 13-3. Histogram for the data shown in Table 13-4

Descriptive Statistics

Descriptive statistics help to summarize your data. In the sections that follow, averages and measures of spread will be considered.

Measures of Central Tendency

Measures of central tendency, or averages, are useful as they can summarize a lot of data with a single figure. For example, Cards for Everyone Inc. may discover that, on average, each customer buys two cards per transaction. It is unlikely that every customer buys exactly two cards per transaction; some will buy more and some will buy less. However, the figure of two cards per transaction is a good indicator of the amount of cards bought in general.

There are three alternative definitions of average, known as the mean, median, and mode. Each of these is calculated using different methods and can often result in different values when applied to the same set of data.

Choosing which definition to use will depend partly on the type of your data. It is important to understand what each statistic tells you about the data so that you can make an informed choice about which is most appropriate for the analysis you are conducting.

The Mean

By default, people usually refer to the mean when they talk about averages in everyday language. The mean of a set of data items is calculated by

1. Adding all the data items.

2. Dividing this total by the number of data items.

The mean is best applied when the data items are relatively evenly spread with no exceptionally high or low values. In addition, the mean is not an appropriate measure of average for nominal or ordinal data, as it is not possible to conduct mathematical operations on such data. The mean can be applied to discrete ratio data, although the result will need to be rounded to the nearest integer.

If a set of data items contains a small number of relatively high or low values, the mean will be less typical of the data items as a whole as these atypical values will have a relatively strong impact on the value of the mean.

In Chapter 10, the following example was used to define an outlier. The sequence of numbers shows monthly card sales per customer for Cards for Everyone Inc.:

2, 4, 9, 5, 10, 2, 7, 6, 8, 3, 104

The mean = 160/11 = 14.55 (or 15 to the nearest card). This average does not reflect the sequence of numbers very well as all but one are lower. The last number, which is unusually high, has a disproportionate impact on the calculation.

■ **Note**   In MS Access, the mean is calculated using the Avg command.

The Median

The most appropriate method of calculating the average for a set of ordinal data is to use the median or the mode. The median refers to the middle value in a set of data when the values are arranged in order of size from smallest to largest or vice versa. When there is an odd number of values in the set of data, the middle value is straightforward to find. When there is an even number of values, the midpoint between the two central values is the median.

The median is a good measure of the average value for ratio data when the data includes relatively high or low values because these have equal influence on the outcome, unlike with the mean.

For example, the sequence of numbers used in the last section to show monthly card sales per customer for Cards for Everyone Inc. was:

2, 4, 9, 5, 10, 2, 7, 6, 8, 3, 104

with a mean of 15. In contrast, the median can be found by first sorting the sequence (here in ascending order):

2, 2, 3, 4, 5, 6, 7, 8, 9, 10, 104

As there are 11 numbers, the median is in sixth position, which is number 6. Notice that the median of 6 is far more representative of the center of the sequence than the mean of 15.

The Mode

Unlike the mean and the median, the mode can be applied to nominal data. It can also be applied to ordinal and ratio data (both discrete and grouped continuous). The mode is the value that occurs with the greatest frequency in a set of data. It is representative or typical because it is the most common value. There may be more than one mode in a set of data if several values are equally common. In the frequency distribution for card categories for Cards for Everyone Inc. shown in Table 13-3, the mode (or modal class) is Birthday, as this category occurs most often.

Measures of Spread

A measure of spread is used to describe the variability in a set of data. The aim is to provide an idea of how well the chosen measure of central tendency (mean, median, or mode) represents the data. If the spread of values in the set of data is large, the measure of central tendency is not as representative of the data as when the spread of data is small. This is because a large spread indicates that there are probably large differences between individual data items.

The Range

The range is the difference between the highest and lowest values in a set of data and is suitable for ordinal data and for both discrete and continuous ratio data. For example, the sequence of numbers used in the last section to show monthly card sales per customer for Cards for Everyone Inc. was:

2, 4, 9, 5, 10, 2, 7, 6, 8, 3, 104

The maximum value is 104 and the minimum value is 2. This results in a range of 104 - 2 = 102. While using the range as a measure of spread is limited, it does set the boundaries of the values of the data items.

The Quartiles and Interquartile Range

Quartiles tell us about the spread of a set of data by breaking it into quarters, just like the median breaks it in half. Quartiles are the best measure of spread for ordinal data as well as being a useful measure of spread for discrete ratio data.

For example, the sequence of numbers used in the last section to show monthly card sales per customer for Cards for Everyone Inc. was:

2, 4, 9, 5, 10, 2, 7, 6, 8, 3, 104

Placed in ascending order, as for the median, this is:

2, 2, 3, 4, 5, 6, 7, 8, 9, 10, 104

The quartiles are as follows:

- The first quartile (Q1) is the data item that marks a quarter of the way along the sequence. In this example, that is the third data item, 3.

- The second quartile (Q2) is the data item that marks half way along the sequence (the median). In this example, it is the sixth data item, 6.

- The third quartile (Q3) is the data item that marks three quarters of the way along the sequence. In the example, that is the ninth data item, 9.

For an even number of data items, the quartiles are calculated by taking the sum of the two data items around each quartile and then halving them.

A common way of expressing quartiles is as an interquartile range. The *interquartile range* describes the difference between the third quartile (Q3) and the first quartile (Q1), telling us about the range of the middle half of the data items in the distribution. Hence, for the previous example, the interquartile range = Q3 - Q1 = 9 - 3 = 6

Variance and Standard Deviation

For ratio data, the measure of spread is either the variance or the standard deviation.

The variance is calculated by:

1. Adding the squared differences between each data item and the mean.

2. Dividing by the total number of data items.

Squaring the differences removes negative values and gives disproportionate weight to values far from the mean. Thus, if the values in the data set are spread out, the variance will be a large number. Conversely, if the scores are located closely around the mean, the variance will be a smaller number. However, the variance is not in the same units as the values in the set of data, which means that is not possible to interpret its value easily.

Calculating the standard deviation, which takes the square root of the variance, provides a result that has the same units as the set of data under consideration. Nevertheless, analyzing the variance is extremely important in some statistical analyses, discussed in the further reading at the end of the chapter.

■ **Note** MS Access provides functions for calculating the variance (Var) and for the standard deviation of a population (STDEV.P).

Cross-Tabulation and Segmentation

Cross-tabulation helps you understand the relationship between two or more columns of data. For example, suppose the manager at Cards for Everyone Inc., Pat, would like to answer the question, "Is there a difference between the intention to buy again between men and women?" Assuming that a survey has been conducted that asked participants whether they would buy from the business again (y or n) and their gender (m or f), a query could be set up as shown in Figure 13-4. The output is shown in Figure 13-5.

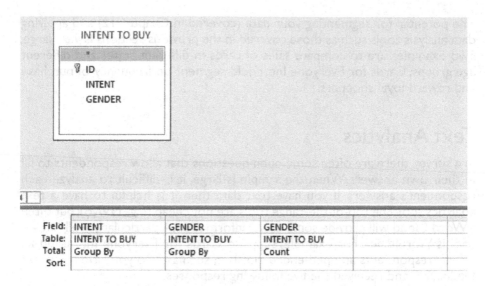

Figure 13-4. Query design for a cross-tabulation between Intent and Gender for Cards for Everyone Inc.

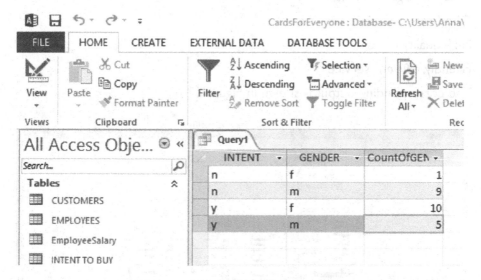

Figure 13-5. Query output for a cross-tabulation between Intent and Gender for Cards for Everyone Inc.

In Figure 13-5, you can see that 10 females responded positively, compared to only 5 males.

The potential for segmenting your data (covered in Chapter 12) and applying data analysis tools such as those covered in the previous sections is very large. Two examples are to compare sales of cards in different states and different age groups. Cards for Everyone Inc. could segment on frequency of purchase and reward loyal shoppers.

Text Analytics

In a survey, there are often some open questions that allow respondents to fill in their own answers. When the sample is large, it is difficult to analyze each respondent's answers. If you have text data then it is helpful to have a text analytics tool. The top-of-the-range tools are not cheap (e.g., NVivo), but often a Word Cloud will provide some useful information. A particularly well-known tool is Wordle.net. For example, suppose Cards for Everyone Inc. asked its survey respondents an open-ended question such as, "Do you have any other feedback?" and received the five following responses:

Service fast

Nice cards, good quality

Good response time, very fast

High quality cards

Friendly, efficient service

The corresponding output is shown in Figure 13-6.

Figure 13-6. Output from wordle.net for the Cards for Everyone Inc. survey

The emphasis given to each word is based on its occurrence and placement within the survey. Experimenting with such packages will help you analyze your text efficiently.

Correlations and Scatter Plots

Correlations are used when you want to know about the relationship between two columns of continuous ratio data. For example, Cards for Everyone Inc. may want to know the relationship between the sales of a card entitled "Paris by Moonlight" and changes in its price, because they suspect they have been selling it rather cheaply and would like to know the potential sales impact of raising its price.

- If the correlation is 1, the price of the card and its sales are completely positively correlated and rise and fall together.

- If the correlation is 0, there is no correlation between these two variables.

- If the correlation is -1, the price of the card and its sales are completely negatively correlated, meaning the higher the value of one, the lower the value of the other.

If the absolute value of the correlation is larger than 0.5, the correlation between the variables is usually regarded as "significant," which means the observed correlation is unlikely to have occurred by chance.

■ **Note**   It is straightforward to carry out an accurate significance test for correlated data based on a given probability. See the reference at the end of the chapter for further reading.

Imagine that Cards for Everyone Inc. keeps records of small changes in the price of the "Paris by Moonlight" card and the level of the corresponding sales on a weekly basis from April 6th, 2015. The following examples provide two possible outcomes. Figure 13-7 shows gradual increases in the price of "Paris by Moonlight" against a gradual falling off of sales.

■ **Note**   Price is the independent column; sales is the dependent column as it depends on the value of price.

The correlation, obtained by using the CORREL function in MS Excel (=CORREL (A2:A12,B2:B12) in this case), gives a very high negative correlation of -0.97 shown in cell A:13 of Figure 13-7. This correlation indicates that even a small rise in price has a negative impact on sales and that the impact on profits should be considered carefully.

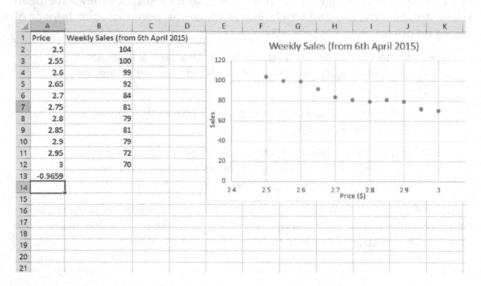

Figure 13-7. Example of a high negative correlation between Price and Sales from Cards for Everyone Inc.

The example shown in Figure 13-8, on the other hand, shows a very low correlation of 0.14 in cell A:13. This suggests that there is little evidence of rises in price producing a drop in demand. However, as this correlation is under 0.5, more investigation is needed before any firm conclusion can be made.

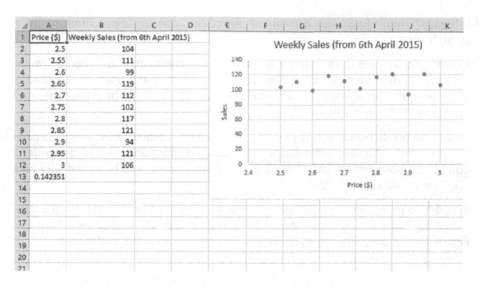

Figure 13-8. Example of a low positive correlation between Price and Sales from Cards for Everyone Inc.

You should use correlation with care. The correlation calculation only works well for relationships that follow a straight line. For this reason, correlations are best presented with a scatter plot. Scatter plots were introduced in Chapter 10 and are used to show the relationship between pairs of ratio data from the same object or individual. A point represents each individual or object (card in this case) and is located with reference to the measurements on the two axes (Price and Sales in this example).

By analyzing the pattern of points that make up a scatter plot, you can visualize whether there is a relationship between the two sets of measurements as indicated by the correlation calculation or whether the line of points is non-linear, thus rendering the correlation calculation unreliable. In addition, correlation does not mean that one thing causes the other (there could be other reasons why the data has a good correlation).

Linear Regression

Regression is a more accurate way to test the relationship between columns than correlation and is used to predict future values. For example, in the case of the sales of the "Paris by Moonlight" card, regression could be used to predict sales for changes of price of the card before they are actually observed, thus avoiding potential periods of low sales.

Price is not the only factor influencing the sales of "Paris by Moonlight"—the time of year, economic conditions, etc., may also have a bearing. However, if we are interested in predicting a small distance ahead (i.e. a slight price increase) then almost all non-linear functions can be approximated by a straight line.

When one independent column is used in a regression, it is called a *simple regression;* when two or more independent columns are used, it is called a *multiple regression.* A linear model assumes the relationships between columns are straight-line relationships.

To enable prediction, start by plotting the data on a scatter plot as in the previous section. The ideal correlation between the independent and dependent columns is somewhere between .5 and .99 or somewhere between -.99 and -.5. Our correlation is -0.97.

In order to make these predictions, a regression line must be drawn from the data appearing in the scatter plot. Figure 13-9 is the same as the scatter plot shown in Figure 13-7 above, with the addition of a regression line fitted to the data.

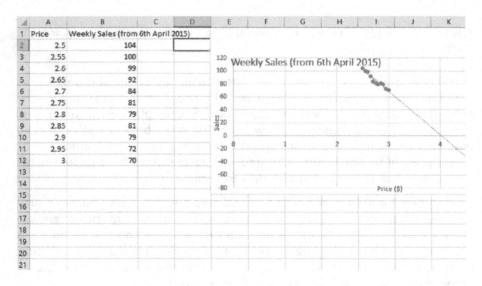

Figure 13-9. A regression line fitted to the data in Figure 13-7 covering price and sales from Cards for Everyone Inc.

From Figure 13-9, you can see that if the price were raised to $3.25, the expected value of sales would be about 60 cards.

The regression line is the line with the smallest possible set of distances between itself and each data point on the scatter plot. The distances of the data points from the regression line are called *residuals.* The typical procedure for finding the line of best fit, i.e. the line that minimizes the size of all of the residuals, is called the least-squares method.

This calculation is usually performed using computer software. For example, a regression line can be plotted directly onto a scatter plot in MS Excel 2013 using the Trendline facility. A regression line will almost always contain error terms, as the real world is not perfect.

The following assumptions are made in linear regression. If any of these do not hold for your data, you may want to consider a more sophisticated model:

- The relationship between the two columns is linear

- The variance around the regression line is the same for all values on the vertical axes (Sales in this example)

- Each of your observations is independent of each other (here, the number of sales in a day for a given price should not depend on previous results)

- The residuals should not show a pattern—if there is a pattern it suggests that the relationship between the two columns (Price and Sales in this case) is not linear and a more sophisticated form of regression is necessary

- The residuals should be reasonably symmetric with one modal class (i.e., they follow a normal distribution)

Confirmatory Data Analysis

Confirmatory data analysis uses the traditional statistical tool of inference to assess to what extent the observations of the exploratory analysis could have occurred by chance. The aim is to draw conclusions from a random data sample about the population as a whole. Examples of two approaches used are:

- *Confidence Intervals*—Estimate the precision of a summary statistic such as the mean, standard deviation, etc. For example, a 95% confidence interval provides the assurance that 95% of the time the true value of the summary statistic would be included.

- *Hypothesis Testing*—Assesses whether differences between groups of data (such as the mean, variance, etc.) are chance occurrences or statistically significant results (i.e. real differences). The process of inference starts from a neutral position—usually referred to as the "null hypothesis"—which is generally set to "there is no difference."

For details about confirmatory analysis, refer to the further reading provided at the end of the chapter.

Summary

In any data analysis exercise, it is important to begin by assessing the characteristics of your data. With this in mind, Table 13-5 lists each technique described in this chapter together with the type of data it can be applied to.

Table 13-5. Summary of Data Analysis Techniques and the Types of Data They Can Be Applied To

Technique	Data Type
Charts	
Bar chart	Nominal data, ordinal data, discrete ratio data, and grouped continuous ratio data
Pie chart	Nominal data, ordinal data, discrete ratio data, and grouped continuous ratio data
Histogram	Continuous ratio data
Measures of Central Tendency	
Mean	Continuous ratio data
Median	Ordinal data and ratio data
Mode	Nominal data, ordinal data, discrete ratio data, and grouped continuous ratio data
Measures of Spread	
Range	Nominal data, ordinal data, and ratio data
Quartiles and interquartile range	Ordinal and discrete ratio data
Variance and standard deviation	Continuous ratio data
Cross-Tabulation and Segmentation	Nominal data, ordinal data, discrete ratio data, and grouped continuous ratio data
Text Analytics	Text
Correlation	Continuous ratio data
Linear Regression	Continuous ratio data

Further Reading

Statistics for Business and Economics, by Paul Newbold, William Carlson, and Betty Thorne, Pearson Education; 8th edition, paperback, 2012, ISBN-13: 978-0273767060.

Reporting Your Small Business Data Analysis

Small businesses report the results of data analysis to internal decision makers, external consultants, funding bodies, and accountants and many others on a regular basis. Database reports contain useful information for decision-making, which should link directly to the business' goals.

The nature of a report will be guided largely by the purpose of the analysis and by the audience to which the results are targeted. Results of an analysis tend to be used to make decisions such as to:

- Repeat the analysis but with modifications
- Perform another analysis altogether
- Influence the levers of your small business

■ **Note** Goals, levers, and metrics are covered in Chapter 5.

The report should provide enough detail to enable the results to be repeated from the same set of data.

The Writing Style

The writing style should be as straightforward as possible so that the readers can focus on the analysis without distraction. On the one hand, very formal or flowery language is best avoided. On the other hand, overly relaxed or very brief language is also inappropriate. In addition, grammatical and spelling errors will detract from the main flow of the report, so take care to correct them. The use of highly technical language should also be avoided.

In a report, whole numbers are usually written as digits rather than spelled out in the text. For example, "Cards for Everyone Inc. had 85 new types of cards this year" as opposed to "Cards for Everyone has eighty-five new types of cards this year." Numbers should be kept simple, which may mean:

- Rounding them up to avoid using decimal places in circumstances where the exact number is not necessary; for example, 2 rather than 1.99

- Stating the units in words (e.g., $4 million rather than $4,000,000)

There should be a good balance between text and diagrams, as some readers respond better to images and others to text. A good balance will suit everyone.

The Structure of Your Report

Keep in mind that the people and organizations that you are reporting to may have different requirements than those suggested here. However, these basic elements should be included in most reports:

1. Introduction
2. Body
3. Conclusion(s)/Discussion
4. Appendix/Appendices

The Introduction

The Introduction should include the following information, using the order given:

- A brief summary of the analysis and data, as well as any relevant background issues

- The main questions addressed by the data analyses, and summaries of the conclusions

- A summary of the answers to these questions and the next course of action

- A brief outline of the remainder of the report

It is reasonable to report findings that you did not anticipate, which are otherwise known as *secondary findings*. However, the questions you set out to answer should take priority.

The Body of the Report

The body of the report can be approached in different ways.

It can be divided into several sections at the same level as the Introduction, with headings such as:

- Methods

- Analysis

- Results

Alternatively, the body of the report can form a separate section, sometimes called "Analysis," with a subsection for each question raised in the Introduction. Within each subsection, each question is analyzed and the conclusions presented.

Data and Methods

A report should be written in such a way that those reading it have a clear idea of where you started. You should also report the timescale of the analysis.

It is helpful to give clear details about the data used in the analysis. For example, clients who agreed to participate in a survey may differ in important ways than those who chose not to. For example:

- They may have a lifestyle where they have more time on their hands (perhaps skewed toward retired people)

- Those who take part may be on either end of the satisfaction spectrum—either very satisfied with the product or very unsatisfied

Either scenario could lead to bias in the results.

Also, it is best to describe the software used to analyze the data, as results may vary slightly from package to package.

Results

The Results section should be concise and focused. Avoid justifying the findings—this is left for the discussion section. A structure makes the information easier to absorb and can take a number of forms. For example, the results could be presented from the most general to the most specific, or from the most important to the least.

You should provide evidence from your analysis (e.g. via the use of tables or graphs) to support each point made, although detailed evidence, as well as other additional material, is best placed in the appendix.

A good way to begin the results section is with a table that numerically summarizes the underlying data. Such a table provides the reader with a clear idea of the data and how it compares to the wider population. This is typically the first table in your report. Table 14-2 illustrates a potential summary table for the data listed in Table 14-1, which has been restated from Chapter 1.

Table 14-1. Basic Product Table from Chapter 1

Product ID	Supplier ID	Product Name	Category	Price ($)	Quantity Available
11	100	Cats	Birthday	2.00	5
20	200	Roses	Thankyou	3.00	8
23	200	Boats	Birthday	2.50	10
42	300	Hearts	Valentines	4.50	9
61	300	Rabbits	New Baby	5.00	11

Table 14-2. Summary Products Table

Column Heading	Range	Mean
Price ($)	2.00 ≤ Price ≤ 5.00	3.4
Quantity Available	5 ≤ Quantity Available ≤ 11	9

■ **Note** In Table 14-1, Quantity Available is rounded to the nearest whole number.

It is essential that the wording in this section is accompanied by good quality tables and graphs, so that the reader can follow the arguments easily. See the last section in the chapter for further information about tables and graphs.

If your business goals were drafted carefully, your database designed with the goals in focus, and your data collected efficiently and cleansed well, your analysis should provide reliable results.

Discussion

The purpose of your analysis is to produce results that can be considered and acted on. The Discussion section is not a place where you put all the information that you couldn't fit in the previous three sections of the report. If you have presented your methods and results in a clear manner, the Discussion section enables you to present the results in such a way that the reader can make up his or her own mind.

Discuss the implications of the primary analysis first. Any results that came out during the analysis can be mentioned later so as not to shift focus from the goals of the business. In addition, you should mention any weaknesses or strengths with the data collection, analysis, or interpretation. Bringing these issues into the open provides you with the opportunity to defend them and/or recommend ways to overcome them.

The report should include a discussion about uncertainties associated with the results. Such uncertainties can arise in a number of ways and presenting them assures the reader that you've considered the limitations of the analysis. The types of uncertainties that can arise are:

- Uncertainty caused by the inability to account for all potential sources of variation in the data

- Uncertainty due to possible unidentified errors during data collection, coding, and analysis

- Uncertainty that findings from the data remain as they were at the time that the analysis was carried out

Where these or any other uncertainties occur, it is useful to provide discussion.

Conclusions

Limit your conclusions to those supported by your analysis. Important considerations are as follows:

- Give equal attention to positive and negative findings.

- Base your conclusions on fact and logic.

- Be careful when making causal links and correlations. For example, as mentioned in Chapter 13, correlation between two columns in a database table does not mean that one causes the other.

Tables and Charts

There are three main methods for presenting numerical data:

- Incorporate it into the main body of text

- Present it separately in a table

- Construct a graph or chart of it

Determining which of these methods is best depends on the amount of data you are dealing with and its complexity. The associated text should describe what the data reveals about the topic, but should not repeat what is described in the chart.

When there are only two numerical values to compare, numbers are best presented as part of the text. For example:

86% of the female customers at Cards for Everyone Inc. regularly bought cards, compared to 62% of the male customers

If you are discussing three or more numbers, it is often more appropriate to use a table. Tables are an effective way of presenting data:

- When you have a few numbers to present (as many numbers in a table can become confusing)

- When the precise value is crucial to your argument and a graph would not convey the same level of precision. For example, when it is important that the reader knows that the result was 2.48 and not 2.45

If you wish to draw attention to patterns in your data, these are best revealed in the columns of the table, rather than the rows, as it is easier to read down a column than across a row. Decide which column contains the most important trend and use this as a focus to structure the table. If more than one column is equally important, it is often better to include two or more simple tables rather than use a single more complex one.

It often helps to sort numerical data in a column according to its magnitude (e.g. from large to small) unless there is a particular pattern or trend in the data that you want to highlight. Further points for effective table presentation are as follows:

- All tables should include a descriptive title that contains enough detail that a reader can understand the content without needing to consult the accompanying text—units of measurements should be included in the title (e.g. percentages, total number, and frequency)

- Lines and/or bold text can be used to separate headings from the body of data

- Specific rows can be highlighted/shaded to draw attention to them

- Large gaps between columns should be avoided, as this makes it difficult to read along a row

Graphs and charts are a particularly effective way of presenting a large amount of data, but can also be used instead of a table to present smaller sets of data. Charts and graphs can be used to illustrate data quickly. Charts in two dimensions are generally easier to read than those in three. In general, charts and graphs should:

- Always show a title and axes labels and provide a key when necessary

- Show units of measurements (e.g. percentages, total number, and frequency)

- Use a scale whenever possible

- Use subtle gridlines that do not detract from the data

- Use colors or shading patterns in bar charts, histograms, and pie charts to reflect any natural sequences in the categories of the data being plotted so that the colors of adjacent areas grade from dark to light or vice versa

Presenting data by way of a graph may take some forethought in order to choose the best scales. For example, the best view of the data may come from starting either axis at a point other than zero. Figure 14-1 shows a graph of sales data from Cards for Everyone Inc. where the vertical axis begins at zero. Figure 14-2 shows the same data, but with the vertical axis beginning at 96.

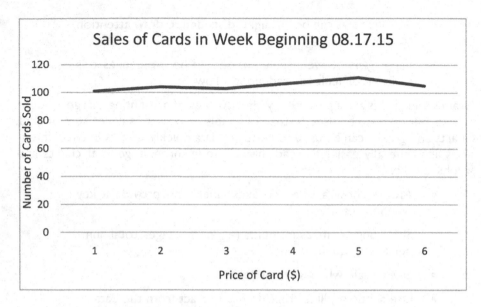

Figure 14-1. An example of sales data from Cards for Everyone Inc. presented on a graph with the vertical axes starting at zero

The trends in the data are far easier to see in Figure 14-2. In such cases, the starting value should be clearly labeled, with the readers' attention drawn to the non-zero start in the text.

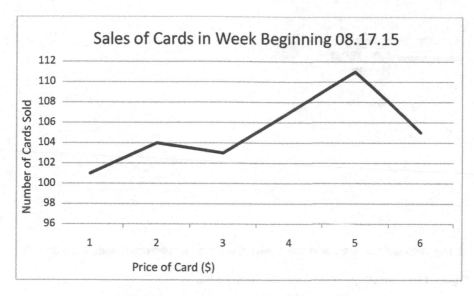

Figure 14-2. An example of sales data from Cards for Everyone Inc. presented on a graph with the vertical axes starting at 96

Producing Reports Directly from Your Database

Reports enable a document to be designed from database tables or queries that can be shared easily in electronic form or viewed away from a computer. As an example, reports can be used to summarize which products have been selling well and which customers have been buying them. Figure 14-3 shows a query that originally appeared in Chapter 1 and Figure 14-4 shows the corresponding report, which also appeared in Chapter 1.

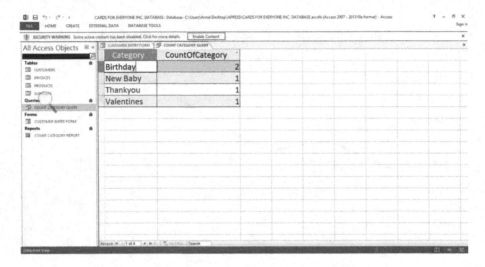

Figure 14-3. Sample query for Cards for Everyone Inc.

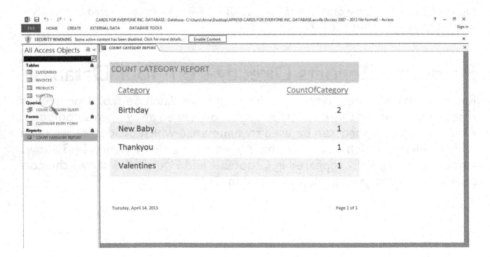

Figure 14-4. Sample report for Cards for Everyone Inc.

Details about producing a simple report from a database appear in the appendix at the end of the book.

Case Studies and Descriptive Reports

Not all data will involve analyzing numbers. Part of your report may describe events. For example, Connecting South Side may include some case studies in its reports that describe the issues faced by its enquirers and how the staff went about helping them. Such case studies will reveal the amount of effort the team is putting into each enquiry, effort that is difficult to capture with analysis of quantities such as the number of enquirers, the number of phone calls per enquirer, etc.

In order to protect the anonymity of the enquirers, any names and specific details should be carefully disguised. Often it is not enough to remove names and addresses. Someone's special circumstances may mean that they can be identified very easily—for example, someone with an unusual occupation. Each case study should be proofread by a number of people on the team to make sure any identifying features are masked.

Producing Reports as a Team

As with databases and some spreadsheets, team reports typically need to be accessed by several people simultaneously. The most efficient method for doing this is to use the cloud, which is covered in Chapter 18. In the past, the tendency was to exchange versions of the report via e-mail, which could lead to version confusion.

When several people contribute to the report, you need to make sure that each part is consistent. This covers language as well as font styles and font size. It is useful to ask at least one person who has not been involved in the writing to read the report through in order to identify inconsistencies.

When the report is ready, save it in a read-only format so that no unauthorized changes can be made to it. The PDF format is a good choice, as it can be viewed by anyone with a free PDF reader no matter what operating system they are using.

Summary

The report of your data analysis should be clear and concise, with a good mix of text and diagrams. The aim of your analysis, your results, and conclusions should all be clear. The main purpose of the report is to facilitate effective decision-making based on your business' goals.

Acting on Reports

Data analysis reports, if carried out efficiently, enable you to learn how well your business is meeting its goals. If changes are required, the quicker these can be carried out the better so that your business remains as competitive as possible. These actions can involve making permanent changes to the database. In contrast, Chapter 16 considers how to respond to one-off external requests for data without making any changes to the database.

Overview

In order to act on reports, your database design has to be flexible and you must be able to take the database offline for short periods of time. Employees need to be trained to use the adjusted database: training is covered in Chapter 20.

The following sections describe possible methods for altering your database in response to a report, using an example from Cards for Everyone Inc.

Example: Cards for Everyone Inc.

Figure 15-1, restated from Chapter 12, shows the design of Cards for Everyone Inc.'s database as a reminder. As described in Chapter 1, Cards for Everyone Inc. sells cards that it displays on its web site. The database has tables for its customers, invoices, products, and suppliers together with those for its employees and their salaries. The quantity purchased of each product by each customer is stored in the Invoices2Products table.

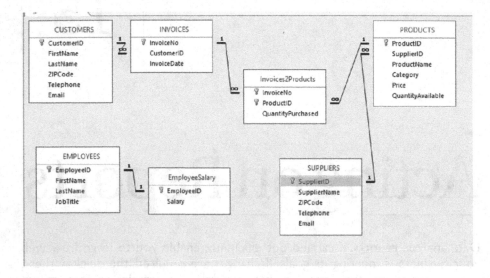

Figure 15-1. Database design for Cards for Everyone Inc.

Suppose that a report for Cards for Everyone Inc. provides evidence that sales of cards are flattening off after a year, suggesting that business growth is stagnating. The manager, Pat, wants to investigate and find out why sales have been sluggish.

Pat believes that the main attraction of Cards for Everyone Inc. is that customers can buy cards online quickly, from anywhere, and that the cards are easy to search through on the web site. She wants to review the data collection and data analysis, with the falling sales as the focal point, in order to find out what is going on.

Further Data Collection and Analysis

Pat organizes a customer satisfaction survey in order to gauge why sales are dropping off. The feedback from the survey reveals that customers find the selection of cards at Cards for Everyone Inc. rather limited compared to typical selections in highstreet stores or those offered by other Internet businesses. Customers also want to design their own cards—such as from a photo or from personal artwork. In addition, some customers have expressed irritation when cards have been out of stock and their orders have been delayed or cancelled.

Pat tries a few approaches to improve sales and retain customers:

- Increase the card selection by trying new suppliers

- Offer new services through suppliers who provide the ability to create your own card from photos and drawings

- Sell items related to cards, such as postage stamps, wrapping paper, gift tags, and small gifts

- Analyze sales across the year to determine when is the best time to increase stock and to make the business more responsive to orders

Data analysis is repeated on a regular basis to assess the impact these additional steps have on sales. A number of changes are made to the database in response to the new focus of Cards for Everyone Inc. These include:

- The addition of new columns

- The addition of new tables

- Splitting up an existing table

- Altering an existing query

- Altering an existing form

The procedures are illustrated in the sections that follow.

Adding a New Column

As the type of product will no longer be restricted to cards, it would be useful to have an additional column in the Products table to make this distinction. The column ProductType is added to the Products table, which can take these values—Card, Postage Stamp, Wrapping Paper, Gift Tag, Gift, and Personalized.

■ **Note** It is important to make sure that when you add new columns to a table, you follow the rules outlined in Chapter 7 in the "Further Checks" section.

New columns are added by going to the design of the table in question in your database. In MS Access, it's a matter of going into Design View and adding a column name and data type, as shown in Figure 15-2.

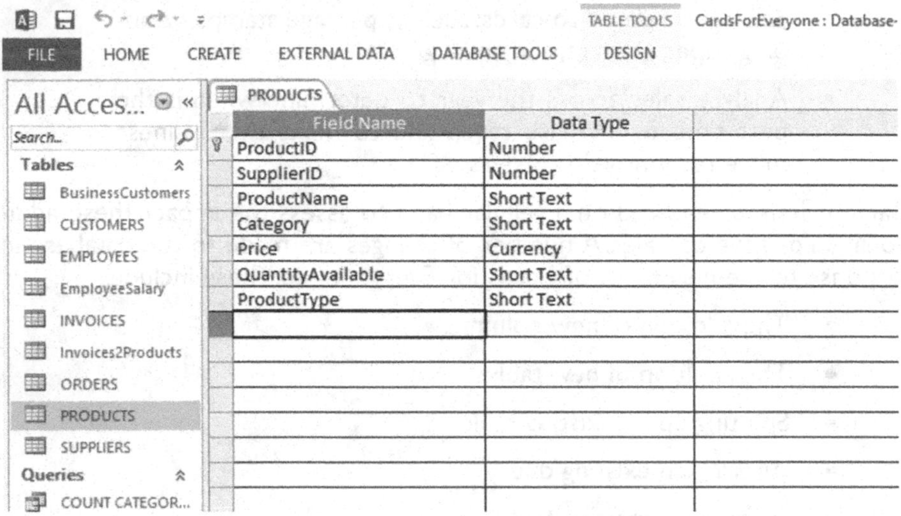

Figure 15-2. Adding a new column called ProductType to the Products table of the Cards for Everyone Inc. database

---

■ **Note** Specific details about creating and viewing tables are found in the appendix at the end of the book.

The data type for the ProductType column shown in the table in Figure 15-2 is Short Text. In order to keep the data as "clean" as possible, it may be better to set the data type for the ProductType column as Lookup and include each of the product types ready for selection, as discussed in Chapter 10.

At this stage, the ProductType column has been added to the Products table but it has not been populated with data. The ProductType column will remain unused if it is not brought into data entry forms, queries, reports, etc. It is important for Pat to explain to her team that the change has been made and to explain why the change was necessary.

Four actions are needed to add the ProductType column to the database in this example:

- The new suppliers need to be added to the Suppliers table

- The corresponding products need to be added to the Products table with their ProductID and SupplierID

- For each new product, the corresponding ProductType needs to be added

- The ProductType column needs to be populated for products in the Products table that existed before the ProductType column was added; these will each have ProductType = 'Card'

Suppose Cards for Everyone Inc. chooses three new suppliers—Art and Stuff (which sells cards and wrapping paper), Glittery Fun (which sells cards, wrapping paper, and small gifts), and My Designs (which produces cards from photos and drawings). The Suppliers table would be updated with three new suppliers, as shown in Figure 15-3.

	SupplierID ▾	SupplierName ▾	ZIPCode ▾	Telephone ▾	Email
⊞	100	Special Occasions	IA 52241	319-xxx-xxxx	admin@specialoccasions.com
⊞	200	Old Favorites	CA 92591	503-xxx-xxxx	office@oldfavorites.com
⊞	300	Handmade Cards	FL 33351	954-xxx-xxxx	enquiries@handmadecards.com
⊞	400	Art and Stuff	...	...	...
⊞	500	Glittery Fun	...	...	...
⊞	600	My Designs	...	...	...

Figure 15-3. Adding new suppliers to the Suppliers table of the Cards for Everyone Inc. database

Many of these new cards do not have a specific category and are blank inside: a new category is introduced to include such products, called All Occasions. This category can be applied to products other than cards, such as wrapping paper.

Cards for Everyone Inc. can order personalized cards on behalf of their customers in quantities of up to 100 at any given time: thus there is a maximum of 100 placed in the QuantityAvailable column.

The Products table would be updated, as shown in Figure 15-4, with the corresponding ProductType for each new product.

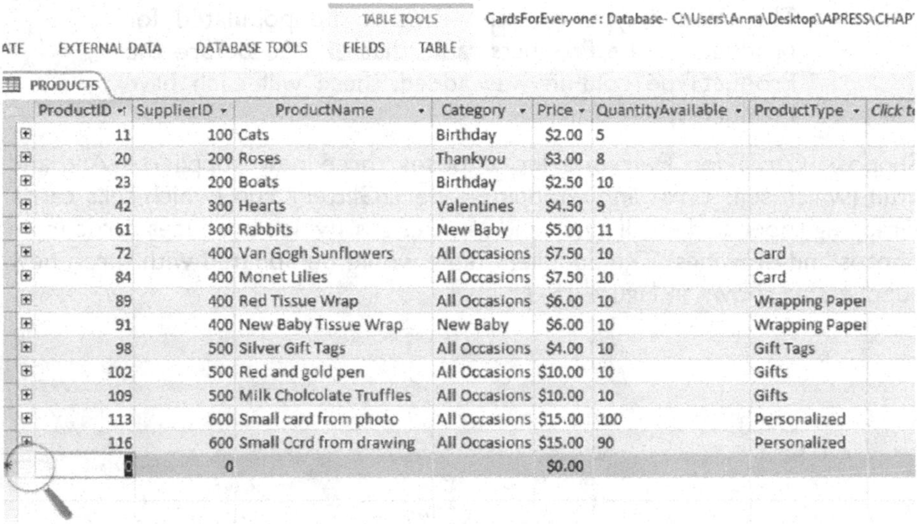

Figure 15-4. Populating the ProductType column with new entries in the Products table of the Cards for Everyone Inc. database

In Figure 15-4, you can see that there is no ProductType for products supplied prior to adding the ProductType column. This can be rectified by adding a ProductType = 'Card' to each of these rows, as shown in Figure 15-5.

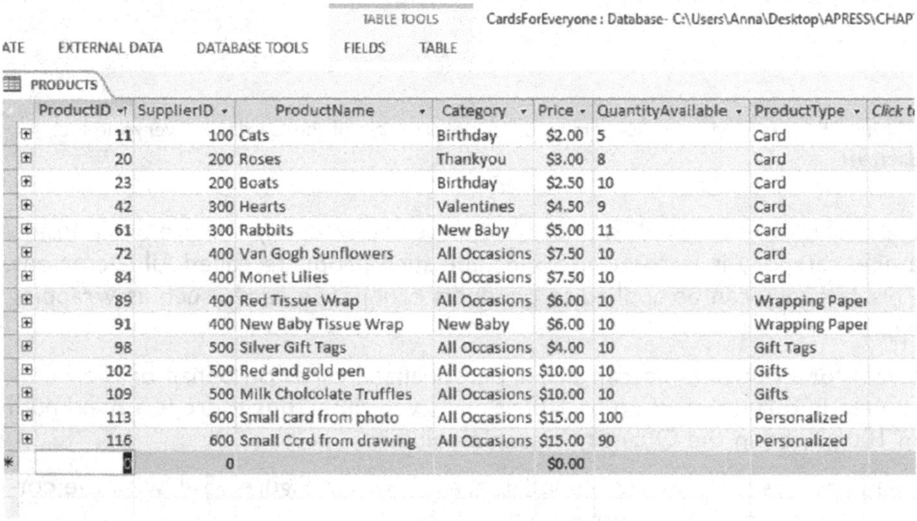

Figure 15-5. Completing the ProductType column for earlier entries in the Products table of the Cards for Everyone Inc. database

As your business grows, it is unlikely that changes such as those shown in Figure 15-5 can be made by hand. You will need to automate them. *Update queries* can be used to change several values in a column at once automatically. The procedure required for setting up a simple query is covered in detail in the appendix at the end of the book. A short example of an update query follows.

Before beginning this process, back up your database. There are then two steps.

The first step is to select the data in the column that you want to update. You can do this by specifying the required criteria. Figure 15-6 shows an example, which asks for all Null values of ProductType—that is, all values of ProductType that have not been filled. It also asks for ProductName so that each occurrence of ProductType can be identified. Check that the correct rows have been returned by the query. If not, you will need to adjust the criteria statement.

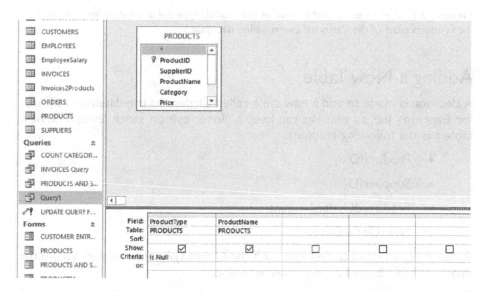

Figure 15-6. Query to select Null values in the ProductType column for the Products table of the Cards for Everyone Inc. database

Once you are sure you are selecting the correct values of the column in question, the second step is to apply an update query. In MS Access 2013, select UpdateQuery from the Design tab in the Query Type section. Figure 15-7 illustrates an update query that replaces all empty values in the ProductType column with the value 'Card'.

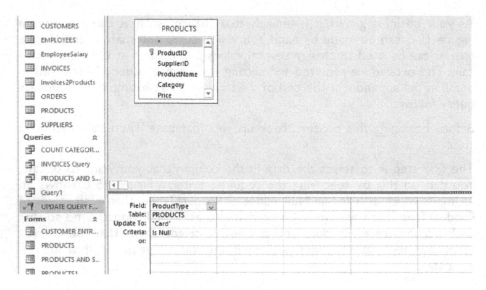

Figure 15-7. Update query that completes the ProductType column for earlier entries in the Products table of the Cards for Everyone Inc. database

Adding a New Table

A decision is made to add a new table called Orders to the database at Cards for Everyone Inc. so that Pat can keep a closer eye on stock levels. The new table has the following columns:

- ProductID
- SupplierID
- PredictedOrderAmount
- NextOrderDate

A check would need to be made with the QuantityAvailable column from the Products table before a new order was placed.

Creating a new table is straightforward. It requires taking the steps set out in Chapter 7 and inserting the required relationships shown in Figure 15-8. There are two relationships between the Orders table and the rest of the database:

- A one-to-one relationship between Orders and Products. The stock of each product is being considered individually. Whenever a new order is made, it applies to just one product. Conversely, when a product needs to be reordered, a single order is placed.

- A one-to-many relationship between Suppliers and Orders. Each order goes to a single supplier. However, one supplier can receive several orders.

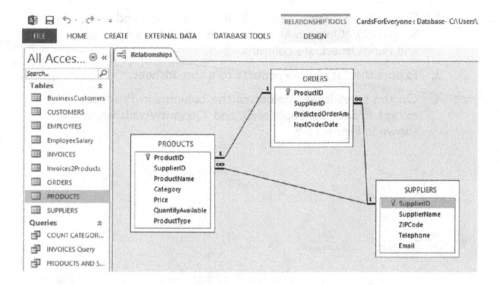

Figure 15-8. The relationships of the Orders table

■ **Note** Database relationships are covered in detail in Chapter 7.

As with the new column in the previous section, a new table will go unused if it is not populated and incorporated into forms and queries.

Splitting a Table

Pat decides that the QuantityAvailable column should be removed from the Products table and placed in the Orders table to avoid confusion. The reason for this decision is that the data in the QuantityAvailable column is directly relevant to orders but not directly relevant to products. Observations such as this are discussed in the "Further Checks" section of Chapter 7. Splitting a table has a number of steps and gets easier when you become more familiar with importing and exporting data.

■ **Note** Importing and exporting data is covered in the appendix at the end of this book.

There are a number of ways to move QuantityAvailable from the Products table to the newly created Orders table. Here is one suggestion:

1. Back up your database

2. Create a new table called Orders with the ProductID, SupplierID, QuantityAvailable, PredictedOrderAmount, and NextOrderDate columns.

3. Export the data from Products to a spreadsheet.

4. On the spreadsheet, delete all the columns in Products except ProductID, SupplierID, and QuantityAvailable, as shown in Figure 15-9.

	Clipboard	⌐		Font	⌐		Alignment	⌐	Number	⌐

| A1 | ▾ | : | ✕ ✓ ƒx | ProductID |

	A	B	C	D	E	F	G	H	I	J
1	ProductID	SupplierID	QuantityAvailable							
2	11	100	5							
3	20	200	8							
4	23	200	10							
5	42	300	9							
6	61	300	11							
7	72	400	10							
8	84	400	10							
9	89	400	10							
10	91	400	10							
11	98	500	10							
12	102	500	10							
13	109	500	10							
14	113	600	100							
15	116	600	90							

Figure 15-9. *Exported and cropped data from the Products table of the Cards for Everyone Inc. database*

5. Create two new columns on the spreadsheet entitled PredictedOrderAmount and NextOrderDate, as shown in Figure 15-10.

| | Clipboard | | 🗆 | | Font | | 🗆 | | Alignment | | 🗆 | Number | 🗆 |

| E3 | ▾ | : | ✕ | ✓ | *fx* | 8/24/2015 | | | | | | | |

◢	A	B	C	D	E	F	G	H
1	ProductID	SupplierID	QuantityAvailable	PredictedOrderAmount	NextOrderDate			
2	11	100	5	15	8/24/2015			
3	20	200	8	10	8/24/2015			
4	23	200	10	8	8/24/2015			
5	42	300	9	9	8/24/2015			
6	61	300	11	7	8/24/2015			
7	72	400	10	10	8/24/2015			
8	84	400	10	10	8/24/2015			
9	89	400	10	10	8/24/2015			
10	91	400	10	10	8/24/2015			
11	98	500	10	10	8/17/2015			
12	102	500	10	10	8/17/2015			
13	109	500	10	10	8/17/2015			
14	113	600	100	0				
15	116	600	90	0				
16								

Figure 15-10. The PredictedOrderAmount and NextOrderDate columns added to the Orders table

6. Add the data to the PredictedOrderAmount and NextOrderDate columns, as shown in Figure 15-10. (You can do this after the data has been imported to the Orders table in your database if you prefer.)

7. Import the data from the spreadsheet to the Orders table and ensure that it has moved successfully.

8. Delete the QuantityAvailable column from the Products table.

You need to be careful to investigate the impact of splitting the Products table on any query, form, or report that uses Products. Moving the QuantityAvailable column could lead to broken links and errors, and you might need to repair these at a later stage.

It's important to let everyone know that the change is coming so they can prepare for it. In addition, as mentioned earlier, the database should be taken offline when you're making the change.

Adding New Objects

The addition of new queries, forms, and reports follows the same steps as before. However, you must make sure that any table or query has not been corrupted by the changes made to the database. Check the links between tables, the values in the columns of the tables, and that queries run as you would expect them to. Once you are satisfied that everything is behaving as it should, you can add new objects taking the steps outlined in the appendix to the book.

Summary

After reading this chapter, you should have the confidence to assess when you need to make changes to your database and how to implement such changes. Databases can be very flexible and it is a myth that all of the design work needs to be carried out at the beginning of the project. Small businesses need to be able to respond to market conditions in order to stay competitive and grow.

Chapter 16 considers the response to external requests which, unlike this chapter, do not involve permanent changes to your database.

Acting on Outside Requests

Up until now databases have been designed with business goals in mind. But what happens if a request comes in from an external source with someone else's goal as its focus? How can you extract the appropriate data from the database?

The last chapter looked at making permanent changes to your database in response to results of reports and changes in business strategy. This chapter considers answering queries without making permanent changes. Responding to outside requests involves using tools that are familiar to you in as creative a way as possible, including:

- Searching
- Filtering
- Querying

You also need to be able to identify when you are unable to answer a query with your existing data. For example, suppose a legal regulator asks Jennings-Havard Law Offices to provide details of how many White British clients and White European clients they have. Their database contains data about clients' ethnicities, as shown in Figure 16-1.

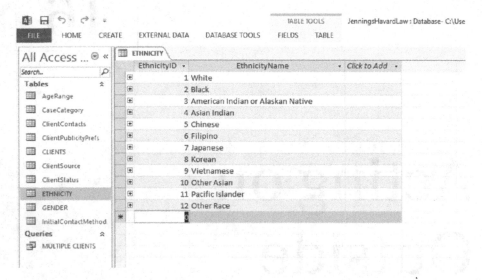

Figure 16-1. Ethnicity table from the Jennings-Havard Law Offices database

It can be seen that the White category isn't divided into sub-categories and it would not be possible to extrapolate the required data from the table in Figure 16-1. Guesses could be made, particularly about male clients and unmarried female clients (who have their family names), but inaccuracy would be high. Such a request is impossible to answer.

At the other end of the spectrum, you may anticipate that an external request will be made regularly and so your database should be adjusted accordingly. In that case, you need to revisit the techniques outlined in Chapter 15.

The following sections provide examples of outside requests made to Cards for Everyone Inc. and each of the small businesses in the case studies in Chapters 2–4 and demonstrate how they might be answered.

Cards for Everyone Inc.

Customers could contact Cards for Everyone Inc. with a variety of questions. For example, a customer who bought the Monet Lilies card might like to know about other products in the same product range. One method for extracting this data from the business database is to:

- Identify the supplier of Monet Lilies.

- Filter all products by the same supplier.

The Products table is shown again in Figure 16-2. Notice from the table that the supplier of the Monet Lilies card is SupplierID=400.

TABLE TOOLS   CardsForEveryone : Database- C:\Users\Anna\Desktop\APRESS\CHAP

ATE   EXTERNAL DATA   DATABASE TOOLS   FIELDS   TABLE

PRODUCTS

ProductID	SupplierID	ProductName	Category	Price	QuantityAvailable	ProductType	Click to
11	100	Cats	Birthday	$2.00	5	Card	
20	200	Roses	Thankyou	$3.00	8	Card	
23	200	Boats	Birthday	$2.50	10	Card	
42	300	Hearts	Valentines	$4.50	9	Card	
61	300	Rabbits	New Baby	$5.00	11	Card	
72	400	Van Gogh Sunflowers	All Occasions	$7.50	10	Card	
84	400	Monet Lilies	All Occasions	$7.50	10	Card	
89	400	Red Tissue Wrap	All Occasions	$6.00	10	Wrapping Paper	
91	400	New Baby Tissue Wrap	New Baby	$6.00	10	Wrapping Paper	
98	500	Silver Gift Tags	All Occasions	$4.00	10	Gift Tags	
102	500	Red and gold pen	All Occasions	$10.00	10	Gifts	
109	500	Milk Cholcolate Truffles	All Occasions	$10.00	10	Gifts	
113	600	Small card from photo	All Occasions	$15.00	100	Personalized	
116	600	Small Curd from drawing	All Occasions	$15.00	90	Personalized	
	0			$0.00			

Figure 16-2. The Products table of the Cards for Everyone Inc. database

---

Note   A search or filter may be needed to find this information from a large table. For example, a filter could be applied to the ProductName column for rows containing Monet or Lilies.

To find the other products (including Monet Lilies), filter on SupplierID=400. This filter returns the four products shown in Figure 16-3.

All Acces... ⊜ «

Search..

Tables ☆
- BusinessCustomers
- CUSTOMERS
- EMPLOYEES
- EmployeeSalary
- INVOICES
- Invoices2Products
- ORDERS
- PRODUCTS
- SUPPLIERS

Queries ☆
- COUNT CATEGOR...
- INVOICES Query
- PRODUCTS AND S...
- Query1
- Query2
- Query3

PRODUCTS

ProductID	SupplierID	ProductName	Category	Price	QuantityAvailable
72	400	Van Gogh Sunflowers	All Occasions	$7.50	10
84	400	Monet Lilies	All Occasions	$7.50	10
89	400	Red Tissue Wrap	All Occasions	$6.00	10
91	400	New Baby Tissue Wrap	New Baby	$6.00	10
0				$0.00	

Figure 16-3. Filtering the Products table of the Cards for Everyone Inc. database on SupplierID=400

You could then tell the customer about the three other products that SupplierID=400 sells.

■ **Note**   There is no need to know the actual name of the supplier in order to answer this request.

Many requests for information from customers follow a similar pattern and can be answered using queries. Three further examples are:

Example 1: A customer interested in all your blank cards. To produce a list, go to the Products table and then follow these steps:

- Release any existing filters.
- Filter on ProductType = 'Card'.
- Filter on Category = 'All Occasions'.

Example 2: A customer is interested in all your products that are under $4. To produce a list, go to the Products table and then follow these steps:

- Release any existing filters.
- Filter the Price column on 'less than' 4.

Example 3: A customer is interested in the range of wrapping paper that you sell. To produce a list, go to the Products table and then follow these steps:

- Release any existing filters.
- Filter the ProductType column on Equals 'Wrapping Paper'.

In general, if customers contact Cards for Everyone Inc. and make the same requests repeatedly, it would make sense to link the database to the web site where customers could run the queries themselves. Such features are often used on online shopping sites. In the case of Cards for Everyone Inc., a contractor was used to build the original web site. That contractor could also link the database to the web site and incorporate the queries.

Smart Wheelbarrows Inc.

Smart Wheelbarrows Inc. is looking for new investments. A potential investor asks for various efficiency ratios that measure how effectively the business uses its assets and manages its procedures.

For example, the inventory turnover ratio shows how efficiently a business is turning its inventory (stocks of materials in this case) into sales over a given period of time. It is calculated as:

Inventory Turnover ratio = Cost of Goods Sold / Inventory

where

- *Cost of Goods Sold* refers to the cost of goods sold over the given time period

- *Inventory* refers to the level of inventory, either at the end of the time period or an average of levels over the whole time period

The business will generally keep a record of the Cost of Goods Sold for accountancy purposes. In this example, we will consider how to calculate the inventory:

Inventory = Sum of (price × QuantityAvailable)

for each item of material in stock. A low ratio implies poor sales and excess inventory. High inventory levels represent an investment with a rate of return of zero. This can indicate that the business management should be more efficient. Also, if prices begin to fall, the business could be in financial difficulties. A high ratio implies either strong sales or ineffective buying.

Sometimes a very high inventory ratio results in lost sales, as there is not enough inventory to meet demand. It is always important to compare the inventory turnover ratio to the industry benchmark to determine if a company is successfully managing its inventory.

For Smart Wheelbarrows Inc.'s last year, suppose the cost of sales was $4,362. Figure 16-4 shows the query design needed to calculate the current inventory of Smart Wheelbarrows Inc., with the result shown in Figure 16-5. A new column, Inventory, is introduced which is the result of multiplying the Price and QuantityAvailable columns.

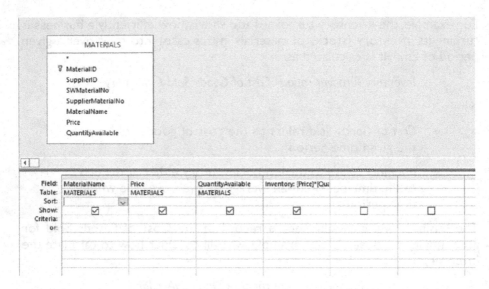

Figure 16-4. Query for finding the inventory on the Smart Wheelbarrows Inc. database

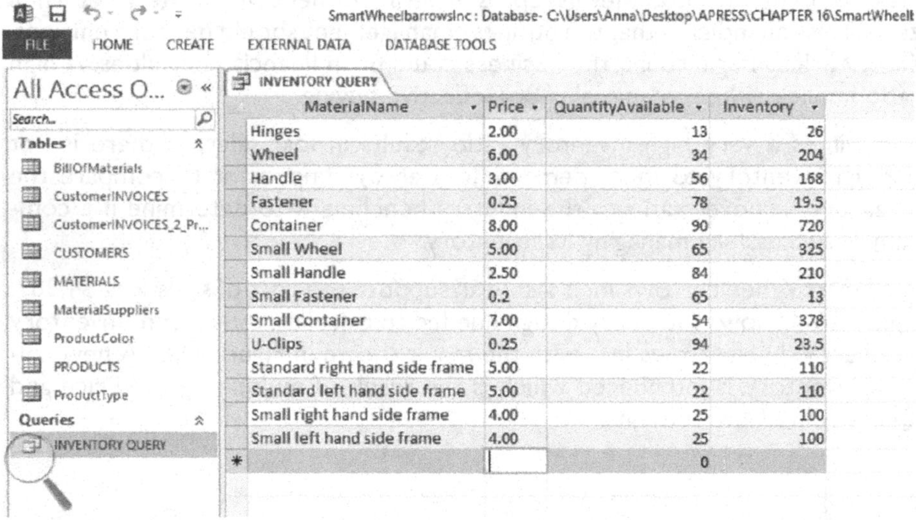

Figure 16-5. The output from the query in Figure 16-4

To find the total inventory for the given time period, you simply sum the Inventory column. You can create a query to carry out this calculation.

■ **Note** In the design of the database for Smart Wheelbarrows Inc. in Chapter 7, the details of the paint used for the wheelbarrows were stored in a separate table. These details are not included here in order to keep the example simple.

When the Inventory column is summed, there is a total inventory for the current period of $727. The inventory turnover ratio is 4362/727 = 6.

Jennings-Havard Law Offices

Jennings-Havard Law Offices wants to invest more money in its advertising and has been asked by a potential advertiser how useful social media has been for them. To find out, they set up a query to return the date of each contact and its source, as shown in Figure 16-6. Its output is shown in Figure 16-7.

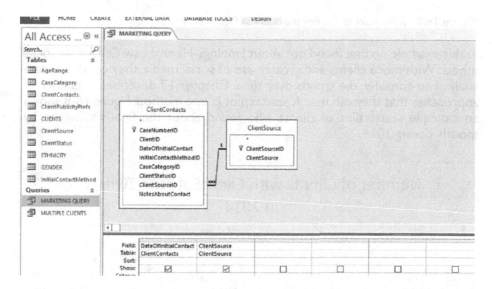

Figure 16-6. Query to find DateOfInitialContact and ClientSource for Jennings-Havard Law Offices

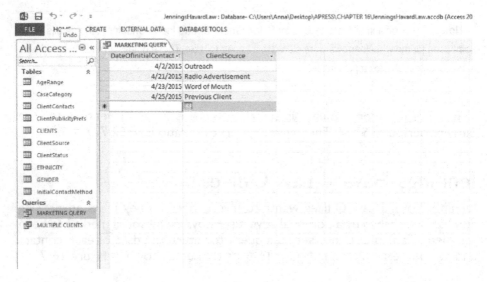

Figure 16-7. The Result of running the query in Figure 16-6

In this example no one found out about Jennings-Havard Law Offices via social media. With more clients and greater use of social media, they could use data analysis to consider the trends over time. Chapter 13 describes a number of approaches that they can use. A scatterplot is one method; Figure 16-8 shows an example scatterplot of clients who found about the firm via Twitter, by month, during 2014.

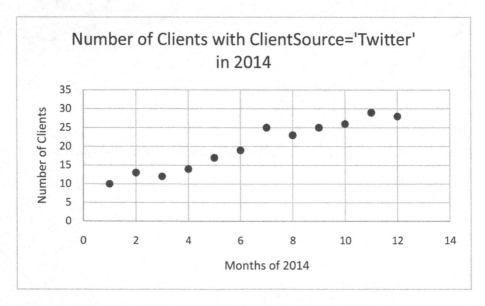

Figure 16-8. The number of clients per month with ClientStatus='Twitter'

From Figure 16-8, it can be seen that the number of clients finding out about Jennings-Havard Law Offices via Twitter is rising.

Connecting South Side

Connecting South Side would like to be in a position to use its database to answer unforeseen questions coming from its grant commissioners. Two examples follow.

Example 1: To which services does Connecting South Side signpost enquirers with a debt problem? Such a question can be answered in two steps:

- Identify the enquirers calling about a debt problem.

- Find the organizations that they were referred to.

Figure 16-9 shows the Cases table from Chapter 7 with an additional row so that two clients have a debt problem for the purposes of this example.

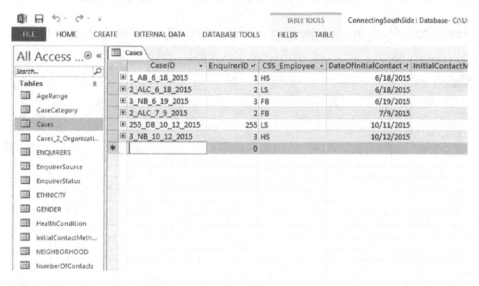

Figure 16-9. Cases Table from Connecting South Side

The query shown in Figure 16-10. selects all cases from the Cases table with CaseCategory = 'Debt' and, for each of these, displays the corresponding organizations from the Organizations table.

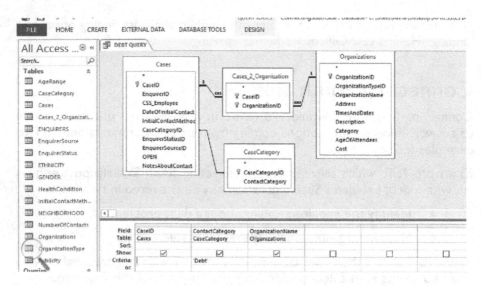

Figure 16-10. Query to output all organizations for cases with ContactCategory='Debt'

The output from running the query in Figure 16-10 is shown in Figure 16-11.

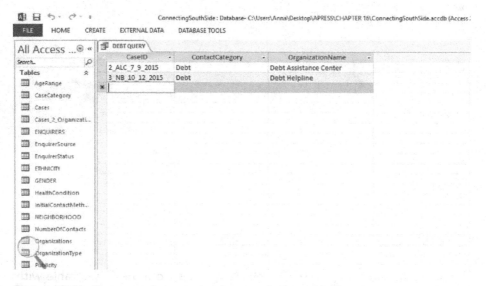

Figure 16-11. The output from running the query in Figure 16-10

Example 2: How many cases concern diabetes?

This can be answered by filtering on the NotesAboutContact column for the word "diabetes" in the Cases table. Figure 16-12 shows a simple form constructed for inputting data into the Cases table. A filter has been applied to the NotesAboutContact box. If the Contains option is used with "diabetes," all cases that mention diabetes in this box will come up.

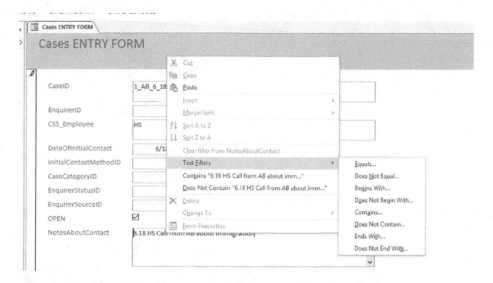

Figure 16-12. Input form for the cases table of the Connecting South Side database with a query applied to the NotesAboutContact column

Summary

This chapter demonstrated how flexible a database can be. When you're met with outside requests for data, you can use your database as a useful tool to answer questions. Sometimes it makes sense to incorporate such queries into the database permanently. Other times it will not be possible to answer requests for data as, no matter what queries and searches you try, the desired data cannot be extrapolated.

Archiving Your Database

Chapter 16 addressed how to meet outside requests for information, which often requires the storage of a lot of historical data, the amount of which becomes ever larger as your business expands. In addition, legislation such as the U.S. Sarbanes-Oxley Act of 2002, requires publicly traded companies, accountants, attorneys, and others to store business records for five years and financial data for seven years following an audit. This increases the burden of storing historical data even more.

Storing increasing amounts of data on computer systems can lead to poor performance, regardless of how much hardware is added or how much an application is fine-tuned. Therefore, businesses need an efficient method to manage this growth.

Data archiving refers to the process of separating inactive data from data that is in use and storing that inactive data for a defined period of time. *Database archiving* focuses on archiving data that is stored in a database. The primary goal of database archiving is to maintain access to inactive data in case it is later required to meet a particular business policy or government regulation and, at the same time, optimize performance of active databases. If and when the archived data is no longer required it can be destroyed. As discussed in Chapter 8, data protection laws often stipulate that data should not be kept longer than is needed.

Data archiving will take place after your database operations have settled into a routine and your data has been cleansed. The procedure is likely to be carried out on a regular basis. When you begin using a database, your archiving procedures are likely to be very straightforward—perhaps you're moving data between active and inactive tables in your current database or from your current database to a database set up especially for archiving purposes. However, as your business grows, you may need to look at more sophisticated methods.

The Difference Between Database Archiving and Database Backup

Database backup is intended to provide the ability to fully recover all, or major parts of, your current database in the event of a significant problem. In contrast, database archiving focuses on providing access to small amounts of data, such as a single row of a table, in response to a specific request for data.

Backups are secondary copies of constantly changing active databases and, as such, tend to be short-term focused and overwritten regularly. This can make them unsuitable for providing data in response to business policies and government regulations. In addition, retrieving specific data from backups can be time-consuming and expensive, especially if the storage media (such as magnetic tapes) is off-site. Unlike a typical backup, archives must be able to stand the test of time, which can be challenging given the constantly changing nature of technology.

Identifying Which Data Should Be Archived

Not all data is equally important. For example, as mentioned, some businesses will need to archive their financial records for at least seven years to meet government legislation, but other data, such as supplier contacts who are no longer used, will be less important. In light of these requirements, businesses can create data retention policies that specify criteria for retaining and archiving their various types of data. These archiving policies must take into account the data access patterns of the business in question.

The following examples from the case studies in Chapters 2–4 illustrate how archiving policies can evolve.

Smart Wheelbarrows Inc.

Suppose that Smart Wheelbarrows Inc. carries out a significant amount of data analysis on its customers' buying habits and its own purchasing patterns of materials. The analysis is used to formulate data retention policies as follows:

- It is found that customers who have not bought anything for over a year rarely buy from the business again. In light of this, a policy decision is made to archive all contact details and invoices of customers whose last invoice is more than a year old and store them for five years.

- The business rarely re-uses a supplier after a new one has been found for a component. However, if any components are faulty, previous suppliers may need to be contacted. That means their contact details and data about the products they supplied must be archived and kept indefinitely.

Jennings-Havard Law Offices Inc.

The data retention policies of cases at Jennings-Havard Law Offices focus on whether a will has been made as follows:

- Cases that **do not** contain a will are archived six months after they are closed and are kept for five years.

- Cases *concerning* wills are archived six months after they were closed and kept until the subject of the will dies or for five years if such a death occurs within five years.

Connecting South Side

Data retention policies are based on the patterns of the behavior of enquirers and the staff at Connecting South Sides

- Analysis shows that enquirers who do not come back to Connecting South Side after a year are unlikely to do so again. Given this, all cases that have been closed for a year or more are archived until the grant expires.

- Analysis also shows that organizations that have not been used by Connecting South Side for a year or more are unlikely to be used again. As a result, details of all organizations meeting these criteria are archived until the grant expires. When the grant expires and, if a new one replaces it, the archived organizations are audited: a grant with a different focus may mean that some of the archived organizations become relevant.

Practical Considerations

To begin, it is likely that you will archive your data in a small scale way, for example, on a flash or a hard disk drive. However, as time passes and the amount of data you need to archive grows, you will need to give more consideration to the storage medium you are using. Archives may be stored for a long time, so choose a type of media that will last as long as your retention policy dictates.

On a similar note, your archive policies as well as the storage mechanisms you use for archiving data will undoubtedly change over time. It is therefore wise to review your archives at least once a year to see if anything needs to be migrated to a different storage medium.

For businesses with large amounts of data, magnetic tape is often regarded as a good method for archiving data due to its longevity and cost effectiveness, particularly when compared with hard disk drives. For other businesses, cloud archiving is a viable solution. The cloud is covered in Chapter 18.

An Example of Using MS Access to Archive Tables for Cards for Everyone Inc.

The following example provides basic tools to archive your data which will be particularly useful in the early stages of your database. You can create tables for archiving the data in your existing database or in a separate database. The example uses tables in the current database using MS Access 2013.

Assume that the manager, Pat, wants to archive all invoices for Cards for Everyone Inc. that are older than December 2014 to a special archive table called Archived Invoices. The following procedure will move the required data from Invoices to Archived Invoices:

1. Back up your database.

2. Design a query that will select the required rows and columns from the Invoices table, as shown in Figure 17-1. Here you are backing up all the columns of the Invoices table and all the rows with InvoiceDate earlier than December 2014. Notice the criteria of the InvoiceDate column, which indicates that only invoices before December 2014 are selected.

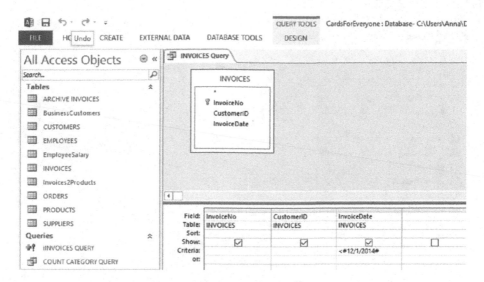

Figure 17-1. Query to select all rows from the Invoices table of the Cards for Everyone Inc. database with an InvoiceDate earlier than December 2014

■ **Note** There is much room for flexibility with the query in Figure 17-1. For example, you could select all the rows with dates in November 2014, all the rows from the year 2014, and so on.

You can use a filter on the InvoiceDate column if you prefer.

Simple queries are covered in detail in the appendix of the book.

---

3. Run the query (using !) and check that it returns the rows that you are expecting. Figure 17-2 shows the output after running the query in Figure 17-1.

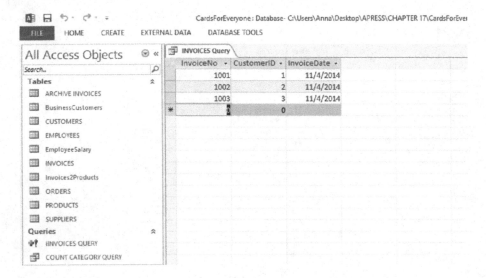

Figure 17-2. Output from running the query in Figure 17-1

4. If the output from the query is correct, you need to choose a destination table in which to archive the data. Here we are choosing a table called Archived Invoices, which has the same columns and data types as the Invoices table and resides in the same Cards for Everyone Inc. database.

5. Select the Append (Add) Query from the toolbar of the Design tab above the Query Design View. This will give you the options shown in Figure 17-3. You can see that you are given the choice of selecting destination tables either within your existing database or from another database.

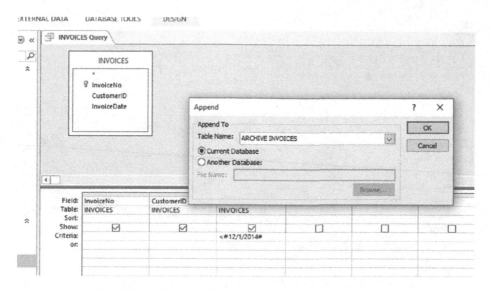

Figure 17-3. Append query design for the Invoices table for Cards for Everyone Inc.

6. Run the Append query just as you would any other query (using !).

7. Check the results of the Append query by opening the Archived Invoices table. You should find that the results in Figure 17-2 have been appended to the Archived Invoices table.

8. If all the rows that you are expecting have been appended to the Archived Invoices table, you can delete them from the Invoices table by running a Delete query. Such a query has the effect of selecting the rows from the table specified and removing them permanently. A Delete query is designed in the same way as an ordinary query, only with the Delete query option selected, as shown in Figure 17-4.

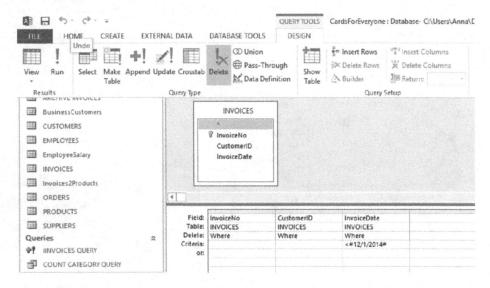

Figure 17-4. A Delete query to remove invoices with InvoiceDate before December 2014 from the Invoices table

This example does not take into account any relationships between tables which is particularly important when you are trying to avoid leaving rows without any "parents."

For example, Figure 17-5 shows that the Invoices table is linked to two other tables—the Customers and Products2Invoices tables.

- If a customer is left with no corresponding invoices, this does not present a problem as the customer may come back in the future and order more products. It is reasonable to keep their details in the Customer table in case this happens.

- Entries of the Invoices2Products table show which products have been bought for each invoice: an example of a populated Invoices2Products table is shown in Figure 17-6. If an entry of the Invoices2Products table is left with no link to an invoice, it is "orphaned." It serves no purpose and will never be used again, as it refers to a deleted invoice. If rows from the Invoices table are deleted, the rows with matching InvoiceNo in the Invoices2Products table will have broken links.

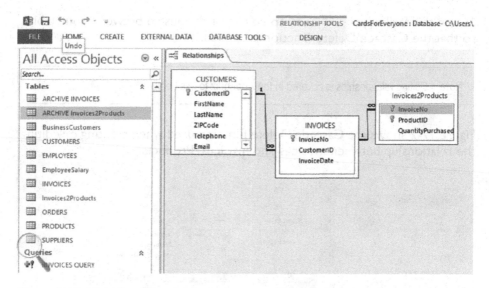

Figure 17-5. The relationships between the Invoices table and adjacent tables in the Cards for Everyone Inc. database

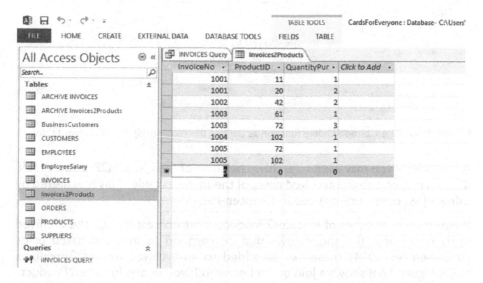

Figure 17-6. Populated Invoices2Products table in the Cards for Everyone Inc. database

The easiest way to solve the problem of "orphaned" rows is to use a Cascade Delete when you delete the rows from the Invoices table. This will not only delete the rows in the Invoices table, but will also delete all the rows linked to it in other tables with the same InvoiceNo.

To use this facility, you will need to edit the relationship between your tables so that the Cascade Delete function is applied.

■ **Note**   Editing relationships is covered in the Appendix to this book.

Figure 17-7 shows the Cascade Delete function used when creating or editing the relationship between Invoices and Invoices2Products.

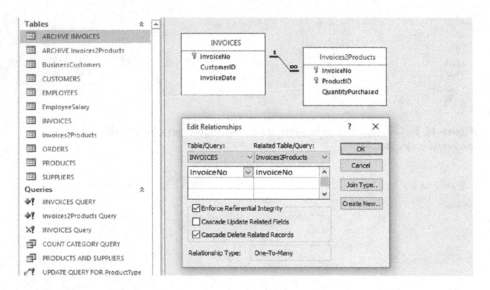

Figure 17-7. The Cascade Delete function as part of the relationship between two tables

Alternatively, you may want to archive the rows of the Invoices2Products table that correspond to the archived rows of the Invoices table. This is achieved by using a Join query (introduced in Chapter 10).

If you select the rows of Invoices2Products that correspond to the archived rows of invoices (i.e. those rows that correspond to invoiced dated prior to December 2014), these can be added to an archived Invoices2Products table. Figure 17-8 shows a Join query between Invoices and Invoices2Products that selects the InvoiceNo from the Invoices table and the corresponding ProductID and the QuantityPurchased from the Invoices2Products table.

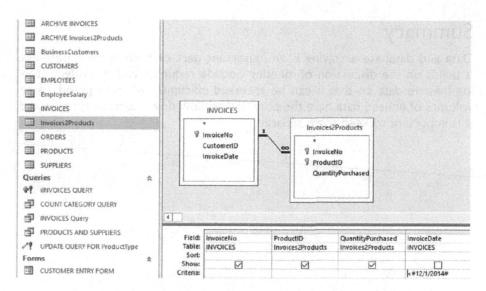

Figure 17-8. Join query between the Invoices and Products2Invoices tables on the Cards for Everyone Inc. database

Figure 17-9 shows the result of running the query in Figure 17-8. This data can then be appended to the archive of Invoices2Products using the method described previously.

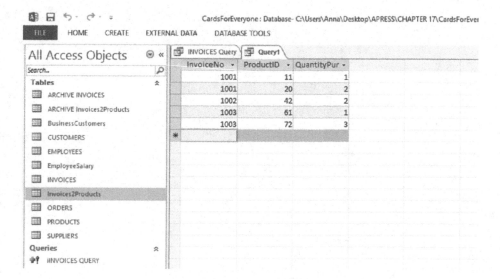

Figure 17-9. The output from running the query in Figure 17-8

Summary

Data and database archiving is an important part of running your business. It builds on the discussion of meeting outside requests, and it involves storing inactive data so that it can be accessed efficiently when required. Large volumes of unused data have the potential to slow down current systems and it is important to keep them separate.

Storing Your Database in the Cloud

Cloud computing refers to storing and accessing data and programs over the Internet rather than from your computer's hard drive. There are a number of key characteristics of the cloud:

- Services can be obtained directly without the need for the installation and configuration of any hardware or software up-front.

- Services are generally paid for as they are used, without a long-term contract or up-front payment. This is possible as providers can tell exactly how much of a given service users have consumed.

- The responsibility to administer software and hardware in the cloud falls solely on the provider.

- Resources in the cloud are scaled (up or down) by the provider in quick response to changes in demand from the users.

The three main "layers" of the cloud are as follows:

- *Software-as-a-Service (SaaS):* Access to software that offers network/web-based applications or services with examples being Dropbox, Google Docs, and Salesforce.com.

- *Platform-as-a-Service (PaaS):* A platform in the form of an operating system, computer language interpreter, or web server for software developers who can write their application and then upload their code into the cloud. Examples of PaaSs are Google AppEngine, MS Engine Yard, and OpenShift.

- *Infrastructure-as-a-Service (IaaS):* The provision of virtual servers and storage without the need for specific details. Examples of IaaSs include Apache CloudStack, Eucalyptus, OpenStack, Amazon Web Services EC2, and Google Compute.

Small businesses without an IT expert are likely to use SaaS only.

In addition, there is a difference between public and private clouds. Public clouds are based on shared physical hardware that's owned and operated by third-party providers. In contrast, private clouds are dedicated to and designed by a given business. Small businesses are generally concerned only with the public cloud.

The cloud has advantages and disadvantages for small businesses, both of which are explored in the following sections.

The Advantages of the Cloud to Small Business

The cloud has a number of potential advantages for small businesses.

- Your data can be accessed on any device with an Internet connection and compatible software. You can edit a file at home and then carry on where you left off when you get into work. Colleagues can also collaborate on the same document.

- The cloud enables you to free up the internal storage provision of your laptops and other devices.

- As the remote servers in the cloud handle much of the computing and storage, you don't need to buy expensive machines. Cloud computing services are typically pay-as-you-go, which means there is no need for capital expenditure. Cloud usage can therefore cut project start-up costs and lead to predictable ongoing operating expenses and potentially enable small businesses to compete with their larger peers.

- Cloud computing can provide quick and straightforward disaster-recovery plans compared to magnetic tape, which is often slow in comparison.

- Businesses using cloud computing only use the server space they need, which decreases their carbon footprint.

Disadvantages of the Cloud

Not everything about the cloud is positive. The main concerns are the reliability of the service (due to its reliance on the Internet) and its security.

Without a reliable Internet connection, you are unable to access your data and cloud-based applications. The same applies if there are any problems on the server side.

Some businesses use hybrid cloud solutions to mitigate this problem. Data that is stored in the cloud is replicated locally on a hard drive. Generally it is best not to rely completely on the cloud to safeguard a database in the event of a disaster.

Cloud security has been in the media recently. Cloud service providers have the money and motivation to make their services secure and are often blamed for breaches that are the responsibility of the consumer. Cloud-service providers are responsible for ensuring that their application and IT infrastructure is secure and in working order. However, it is the consumer's responsibility to manage passwords, protect against identity fraud, prevent loss or theft of devices, encrypt sensitive data, and provide access to devices via secure networks, to name but a few. Such facilities are often available as part of cloud packages, but it is up to you as a consumer to check that they exist and use them. Blaming the cloud for the loss of your data when you haven't secured it properly is like blaming a rental car company for the theft of the car after you have left the keys in the ignition.

It is important that you find a cloud service provider that uses state-of-the-art encryption to keep your data safe in transit as well as when it is at rest. All accounts should be password protected, and you should be able to set a personal encryption key that only you have access to.

In general, if you take the appropriate responsibility for your data, your database should be secure in the cloud.

Backing Up Your Database in the Cloud

Many cloud backup services offer a lot more than just storage space. In most cases, you'll get services such as the ability to schedule backups to run automatically so you don't have to remember. Other useful features can include deleted file recovery and file versioning, the latter gives you the power to revert to a previously saved copy of a file.

The amount of online storage you get with a single account varies. Many providers offer unlimited capacity.

Archiving Your Database in the Cloud

If you have a lot of data to archive, maintaining the archive on your own systems can be a costly and time-consuming exercise.

The aim of a cloud archive service is to provide a data storage environment as a service that is optimized for long-term data retention, security, and compliance with data regulation policies. Once in the cloud archive, data must be easy to search and be protected from overwrites or tampering. Automatically applied data retention policies should also be possible. You must make sure that you are confident that your data is in safe hands and protected by reliable disaster recovery systems.

With a cloud archive you will not need to buy, maintain, or upgrade any specific hardware in-house. You should be allocated an unlimited storage and unlimited retention for an affordable and predictable cost. The choice depends on how much data you have and how straightforward it is to store on your existing hardware.

Moving Your Database to the Cloud

Moving your database to the cloud gives you the freedom to work from anywhere with an Internet connection, the ability to collaborate with colleagues more easily, and access to greater storage and faster processing. The benefits can be achieved without having to invest in more hardware.

Cloud services are not generally free and it is up to you to decide whether the advantages justify the additional expense. You need to consider the security of your data carefully together with the reliability of the service you choose.

Moving an Access Database to the Cloud

The method for moving your Access database into the cloud depends on the version of Access you are using. The cloud version of MS Office is MS Office 365, which you may already be using.

If you do not already have one, create an MS Office 365 account.

■ **Note**   The services provided by MS Office 365 are hosted by MS SharePoint and you can publish your database to any SharePoint server that supports Access.

You can use Office 365 to provide a cloud location to store and operate your MS Access database. This is where the data and database objects will be stored in SQL Server or Microsoft Azure SQL. You will need to check that your version of Office 365 provides this feature—home versions do not cover it.

The ability to use a database stored in the cloud is particularly helpful when people are out of the office on a regular basis. For example, Howard, the CEO of Smart Wheelbarrows Inc., is often out of the office networking and marketing. With the business database accessible in the cloud, Howard can register a sale on the road and the customer's order will be instantly processed. Also, if Howard wants to take a large order from a prospective customer while he is away from the office, he can access the database and predict how long it will take to process the order, based on the amount of supplies of materials in stock and the number of other orders currently in the system.

Access 2010 and Before

It is straightforward to move MS Access (version 2010 and before) into the cloud using the following steps:

- Check that your database is compatible with SharePoint:
    - Select Save & Publish from the File menu.
    - Select the Publish to Access Services option in the Publish section of the menu that appears.
    - Click Run Compatibility Checker.

- If your database is compatible with SharePoint:

  - Select Save & Publish from the File menu.

  - Select the Publish to Access Services option in the Publish section of the menu that appears. You will need:

    a. The Server URL for your Office 365 site, which often takes the format http://yourname. sharepoint.com/teamsite.

    b. A name for your site, such as mysite.

  - After verifying these settings, click the Publish to Access Services button to continue. The URL of your database will take the form: http://yourname.sharepoint.com/ teamsite/mysite

Access 2013 and Later

For Access 2013 and later, you need to create an Access app. An Access app is a database that is used in a web browser and can be designed and edited in Access 2013 and later. With Access 2013 and later it may be easier to design your database in the cloud rather than design it on your desktop.

To create a custom Access app, follow these steps:

- Open Access 2013 or later and click Custom Web App.

- Enter a name and the server location for your app (you can also select a server location from the Locations list).

- Click Create.

- On the Add Tables page (the first thing you see when creating a new custom app), you can import data from various sources such as other Access databases, Excel, and SharePoint lists.

Summary

The cloud has the potential to provide many advantages for your small business. It can reduce start-up costs in terms of capital outlay, thus giving you the opportunity to compete with larger businesses. You can work flexibly due to the access to your data from a wider number of locations. Collaborating with colleagues is also straightforward. It is possible to publish your database to the cloud and take advantage of these benefits at the database level. As long as you are aware of your dependency on a good Internet connection and you are prepared to take responsibility for your role in your data's security, the cloud will be invaluable to your small business.

Searching Online Databases

Many small businesses search government and commercial online databases for information about areas such as law, grants, and research in their field. The key to searching online databases efficiently is to become familiar with the search techniques that you can apply to almost any database, including article databases and online library catalogs. Understanding such techniques is important, because searching online databases is a bit different from using web search engines.

There is no standardized format for an online database's appearance or user interface. For example, records in library databases are comprised of fields containing specific pieces of bibliographic information such as author, title, journal title, publisher, date/year of publication, subject, etc. A database of legal cases would be quite different. In addition, some simple characteristics, such as case sensitivity, can vary between databases.

Nevertheless, most databases offer similar search functionalities as well as help content and/or search tips. This chapter covers the features that are commonly available in online databases. You'll also learn how to structure your method of searching and see an example from the Cards for Everyone Inc. database.

Database Features

In order to search effectively, it is important to become familiar with the characteristics of the database. You can often do this from the help pages. The following sections summarize the key tools. Most databases also have a basic search function, which is used as our starting point, and an advanced search function.

Basic Searches

The basic search box usually searches one field. The basic search is useful to find out how many references are related to your keyword(s), giving you an idea of how much further work is required. It is also helpful when you're running a known item search, for example, when you know the exact title you're searching for.

Advanced Searches

The advanced search capabilities enable you to create a far more focused search when the number of potential references is large. You can search using several search terms in multiple fields simultaneously. Advanced search is also useful when information from more than one field would help you locate items of interest, such as combining a publisher's name with a subject.

Boolean Operators: AND, OR, NOT

When you want to combine search terms, you will need to use what are called Boolean operators or connectors. These are often used in the advanced search mode.

The AND Operator

The AND operator will retrieve results that mention all terms somewhere in their content. For example, the 'cats AND dogs' search would return all results that had both cats and dogs in their content. The use of AND generally will retrieve a smaller set of results. In other words, it narrows the search, as it eliminates the return of any results that mention only cats, only dogs, or neither cats nor dogs.

In many, but not all, databases, the AND is implied and is placed automatically between search terms.

The OR Operator

Using the OR operator between search terms will retrieve results that mention either term. For example, the 'cats OR dogs' search would return all results that:

- Contain both cats and dogs
- Contain just cats
- Contain just dogs

The use of OR generally will retrieve a larger set of results. In other words, it widens the search. OR is especially useful when you are searching for terms that deal with the same basic idea.

The NOT Operator

If you want to exclude terms, you use the Boolean NOT operator. For example, the 'cats NOT dogs' search would return all results containing cats but not dogs. This has the effect of narrowing the search.

Table 19-1 summarizes the Boolean search operators.

Table 19-1. Summary of Boolean Operators

Operator	Example	Impact on Search
AND	**"cats" AND "dogs":** All results containing both words "dogs" and "cats"	Narrows search
OR	**"cats" OR "dogs":** All results containing - Both "cats" and "dogs" - Just "cats" - Just "dogs"	Widens search
NOT	**"cats" NOT "dogs":** All results containing "cats" but not "dogs"	Narrows search

Combining Operators

Databases usually recognize AND as the primary operator and will connect concepts with AND together first. If you use a combination of AND and OR operators in a search, enclose the words to be "ORed" together in parentheses. For example, (dogs OR cats) AND (canine OR feline).

Truncation and Wildcards

Most online databases are not sophisticated enough to search for all variants of a word automatically. For example, a search containing "philanthropic" would miss results containing "philanthropist," "philanthropy," etc. Truncation serves to mitigate this problem. To use truncation, enter the root of a word and put the truncation symbol at the end. The database will return results that include any ending of that root word. Truncation symbols vary from database to database. Examples include: *, ?, !, %, and $.

For example, if you search for the term "philant?" in an online database, you would retrieve results that contain any words that begin with the letters philant, including: philanthropy, philanthropic, philanthropist, etc. Figure 19-1 shows the first three books in a search on the Library of Congress database (http://catalog.loc.gov/) for books published in the last five years and have the term "philant?" in their title or one of their subtitles. For the first two books, "philant?" appears in their titles and for book number three, "philant?" appears in one of the subtitles.

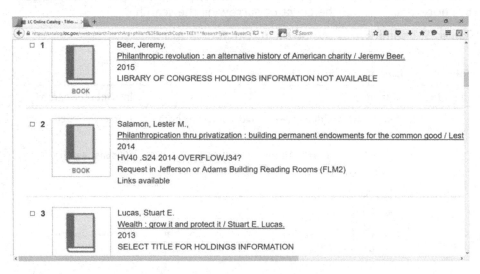

Figure 19-1. Keyword search based on "philant?" for books published in the last five years in the Library of Congress database

Truncating too early at the end of the word can broaden the search to unrelated topics. For example, truncating the word philanthropy to "phil?" would pick up many words (such as philistine, philosophy, and Philippines) that are unrelated to philanthropy. Figure 19-2 shows a repeat of the search in Figure 19-1 using "phil?" instead of "philant?". You can see that all of the books relate to philosophy and not to philanthropy.

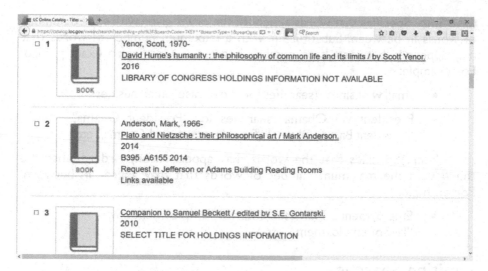

Figure 19-2. Keyword search based on "phil?" for books published in the last five years in the Library of Congress database

Wildcards are useful if a word is spelled in different ways but has the same meaning. For example, color and colour. Wildcards usually substitute a symbol for one letter of a word. For example, searching on colo*r will return all results containing color and colour.

Phrases and Proximity Operators

Though all your search terms are included in the results, they may not be connected in the way you would like. For example, the search "small businesses and databases" may be searched as a fixed phrase in some databases or translated to "small AND businesses AND and AND databases" in others, with the words appearing individually throughout the results.

Most databases allow you to specify that adjacent words be searched as phrases. Using parentheses or quotes around search words is a common way to instigate phrase searching. You will need to consult the help pages of the database you are using for specific instructions.

Proximity operators are another way to specify that the words you are searching are within a certain distance from each other. This makes your search more precise (and narrower). Proximity operators also vary by database, but some common ones include:

w# = *'with'*. Specifies that words appear in the order given with a fixed number of words in between. Substitute # with a maximum number of words that may appear in between. If no number is given, it specifies an exact phrase. For example:

- small w business (searches for the phrase "small business")

- President w3 Obama (searches for "President Obama," "President Barack Obama," "President Barack H. Obama," etc.)

n# = *'near'*. Specifies that the words may appear in any order. Substitute the # with the maximum number of words that may appear in between. For example:

- Employment n3 law (searches for "employment law," "law of employment," etc.)

Limiting Searches

Many databases have limits that control the returned results by specified parameters, for example, by date, format, material type, language, or location. This feature is helpful to eliminate results that are outside the selected limits, such as limiting the search to books published in the last five years.

Search Method

Finding the right information does not happen by chance. Creating a strategy is essential for successful search results. The next section presents a good strategy and includes an example from the Cards for Everyone Inc. database.

Identify Key Search Terms

Typically, the most difficult part of conducting a good search is not using the database itself, but identifying which search terms to use and in what combination.

Begin by writing down, in a sentence or a question, the information you are trying to find. This is unlikely to make a good database search by itself as there may be relevant information that you'll miss simply because it is phrased slightly differently or expressed in different words.

Your sentence may contain just one idea or, much more likely, several that you need to consider.

- Break your sentence into ideas and keywords of one to three words.

- Within each idea, determine the appropriate words or phrases, including words and phrases meaning the same thing, broader terms, related terms, narrower terms, and multiple spellings, as necessary.

- Try working backward from how you think the answer would be phrased using these words as part of your collection of search terms.

- Revise the list during the search process as related terms come to light.

Begin the Search

This section sets out the steps that will help you to begin your search.

Start with a general search. If you start with a complicated search, you will probably retrieve a very small number of results. It makes far more sense to start with a general search and then narrow it down as needed.

Ask yourself the following questions:

- Are there better terms that I could be using?

- Will I need to narrow or expand my search?

If you feel that there are better search terms that you could be using, consult the lists you made in the previous section.

If you need to *narrow* your search in order to retrieve fewer results, consider:

- Adding terms

- Applying limiting to particular fields

- Using Boolean operators such as AND and NOT

- Using truncation/wildcards with more restriction (e.g., "philant?" instead of "phil?")

- Using phrasing

- Using proximity operators with smaller numbers (e.g., w2 instead of w3)

If you need to **widen** your search in order to retrieve more results, consider:

- Removing terms
- Using the Boolean OR operator
- Using truncation/wildcards with less restriction (e.g., "charit?" instead of "charita?")
- Removing phrasing
- Using proximity operators with larger numbers (e.g., w3 instead of w2)

Above all, be flexible and persistent in your searching. If one term doesn't work, try a different one. There will never be one perfect search and it may take dozens of searches to retrieve all the necessary information.

If your search yields nothing useful, consider joining a relevant message board and asking your question, or even contacting an association of professionals. There will be many people with expertise in your subject who might be willing to point you in the right direction.

Asking for help from the reference staff at the public library can also be invaluable.

Cards for Everyone Inc.: Example

Suppose Pat from Cards for Everyone Inc. is interested in expanding the business. She wants to find out more about potential sources of funding.

She begins by writing down her research sentence:

"Small business funding"

She breaks this down into two main ideas:

- "Small business"
- "Funding"

To get started with identifying words of similar meaning, she enters Small Business Funding (with no quotes as she does not want to indicate a phrase) into a web search engine. This helps her to match each idea with the following words of similar meaning:

- "Small business"—start-up, startup, start up, sme, company
- "Funding"—investment, grant

She begins by going to the Library of Congress database at `http://catalog.loc.gov/`.

To get started she performs a simple keyword search on "small business" funding. An enlarged portion of the screen is shown in Figure 19-3.

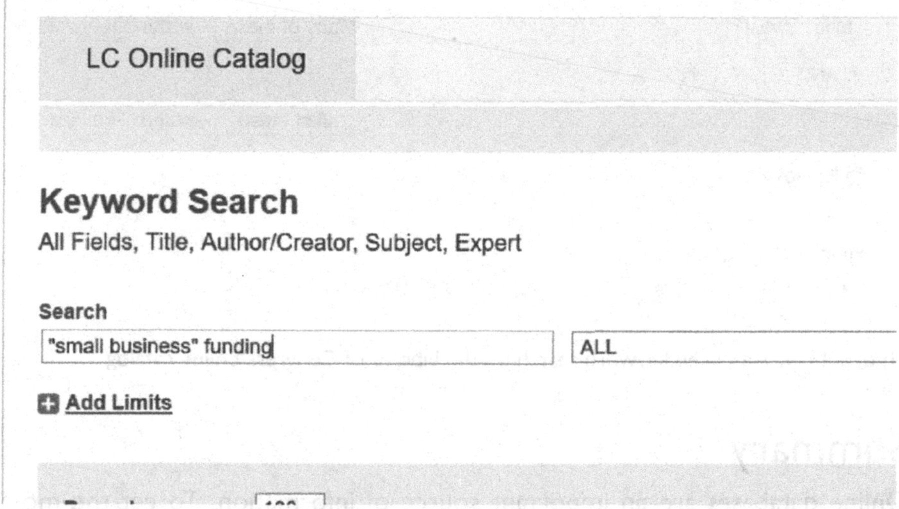

Figure 19-3. Keyword search on the Library of Congress online catalog

The search yields 59 results. Pat notices that some of these are very old and is concerned that the information may be too dated to be useful. She limits the search by using the sort facility to sort the results from newest to oldest. She finds a few useful books published recently on crowd-funding and writing successful bids.

However, she would like to widen her search to other terms with similar meanings to see if she has missed anything useful. She uses the Advanced Search, setting "small business" as a phrase and using the truncated "fund?" and the alterative truncated term "invest?" with the instruction "any of these" (as opposed to them both together). She also limits the search to results published or created within the last five years. The search design is shown in Figure 19-4. This search yields 187 results. Pat sorts them in date order from newest to oldest and finds more useful material. She feels she has more than enough to begin her investigation.

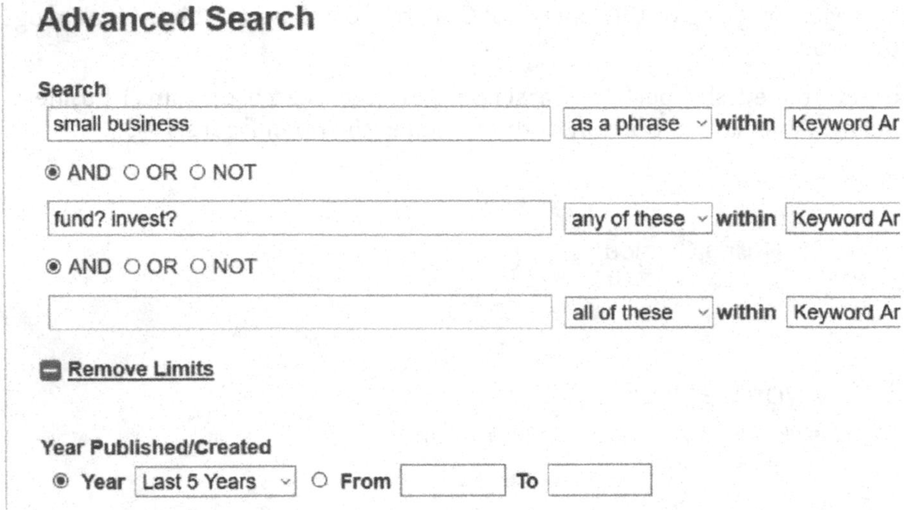

Advanced Search

Search

| small business | as a phrase ∨ | within | Keyword Ar |

◉ AND ○ OR ○ NOT

| fund? invest? | any of these ∨ | within | Keyword Ar |

◉ AND ○ OR ○ NOT

| | all of these ∨ | within | Keyword Ar |

▬ **Remove Limits**

Year Published/Created

◉ Year | Last 5 Years ∨ | ○ From | | To | |

Figure 19-4. Advanced keyword search on the Library of Congress online catalog

Summary

Online databases are an important source of information. To get the most out of them, it is worth taking a little time to become familiar with the generic search tools and to read the help pages of the database in question.

Searching the database is only part of the process of finding the required information. You need to take time to plan your search and to identify a number of similar search terms. Planning your search gives you the best chance of finding what you are looking for.

Training Your Staff

In order for your business to benefit from your database, your staff must be trained how to use it effectively. As you have seen, a complete understanding of databases goes much wider than operating the database itself. Data protection legislation, data cleansing procedures, data collection methods, database maintenance, and data analysis together with many other issues are also important. You need to consider all these aspects when designing a staff training program. Approaches to training are detailed in this chapter. Staff training should ensure that there is always someone available who is able to handle any issues that might arise: relying on just one person is not a safe policy.

How to Begin

You need to be patient from the start, as many staff will take time to learn the new techniques. Try to see the database from the viewpoint of someone who has just encountered it. Make sure to recognize successes in order to keep your team's enthusiasm high.

Perhaps start by explaining to all those who will be using the database why it has been adopted and how you hope it will help the business. Reassure your staff that they will all have the chance to become familiar with the database in a time period that suits their particular learning requirements. Further, one of the best ways to encourage adoption among staff who don't view the database as their responsibility is to focus on the direct advantages that they will incur. The benefits listed in Chapter 1 may help.

Consider providing a test database, such as a copy of the database you have designed, to the staff to use.

Actual Training Sessions

If you are performing training sessions, avoid explaining anything technical that is not directly relevant to operating the database. Try to split up your training sessions into short pieces that make it easy for the audience to absorb.

If you have only one training session available:

- Provide an overall description of the database
- Cover key concepts that need to be understood
- Cover one case study
- Reserve extra time for questions about how to solve various tasks

Everyone learns at different rates and it may be useful to record your training presentation and store it so that staff can watch it again if they need to. One way to do this is to use a site such as Slideshare, which lets you upload slides and record a voiceover to synchronize with them (you need to pay a subscription if you want to add privacy settings; otherwise, it is free). There are many other alternatives to Slideshare that enable you to create and share presentations, including MS PowerPoint Online, Office Sway, and Google Slides.

Your staff may be based in several locations, which makes it impractical to gather them together for training at one time. Rather than offering a prerecorded presentation, you could opt for an online conference. This is interactive and can therefore be tailored more closely to the needs of your staff. Online tools that share slides, documents, and so on, can be combined with an audio component across a telephone line for a low cost and straightforward way to bring staff together for "live" training. Tools such as WebHuddle, Yugma, and Adobe Connect offer free accounts if you are training only a few people. Others, such as GoToMeeting, WebEx, and ReadyTalk, offer a low-cost method for more substantial training programs. The only caveat is to make sure you are aware of how high the phone charges could be.

Hands-On Training

Training your staff from a distance may not capture their interest or provide them with the skills they need in order to learn how to use databases. Just listening to presentations and looking at online material might not provide the practical training they need. Consider providing a tutorial whereby your team completes tasks on a test database at their own pace. This is an ideal setting for learning. If they are sure that you will be there to answer questions when they arise they will be able to move forward at their own pace.

Documentation

A help guide with plenty of screenshots and other visuals is a useful tool to provide to your team as they learn about the new database. The documentation should contain details about all the processes and procedures used in your database.

Your team will need to learn three main sets of skills:

- Skills common to all databases
- Skills specific to the database package you are using
- Skills related to the database design you have implemented

Information about the first two skills is documented in detail elsewhere and you do not want to devote too much of your documentation to reiterating it: a summary of the main issues will suffice. Most database packages have help pages that cover their specific features. For example, when you open the help guide in MS Access 2013, you are presented with a list of Top Categories and a search facility enabling you to enter keywords to locate topics. You can make a list of suggested sections to look at. There are many tutorials available on the web. For example, AccessLearningZone.com provides a number of free tutorials on Access that may be useful. Your staff may also find various chapters of this book helpful when considering the broader subject of databases.

Try to split up your material to reflect how you think your team would use the system. Those looking for a single task should be able to find the required help without reading a lot of unrelated content. Explore the use of hyperlinks, content lists, etc.

As you have seen, your database is unlikely to be static. It makes sense, therefore, to hold the documentation in electronic form where it can be accessed and updated easily. Your team should be aware that the documentation is ever-changing and a date for the last update should be clear at the beginning of the guide.

No matter how extensive and carefully thought out your documentation is, you'll always encounter issues that you didn't cover. When you write the documentation, you will be doing your best to address the issues your team will need. As you have likely been involved with the database for a while and are not viewing it with fresh eyes any longer, there are bound to be important factors that you miss. It is therefore essential to collect feedback as soon as you can and adjust your guide accordingly. An editable comments document on the intranet may suffice. You could also provide a message at the beginning of the documentation asking your team to e-mail any comments directly to you with an automatic e-mail link.

You could ask a staff member to try the database without any guidance from you at all except for responses to questions that they ask. During this process you could take notes of questions as they come up and make sure that the documentation covers them.

Adopt the Database Step-by-Step

Your team is likely to be more receptive to the database if they can become familiar with it in small steps. For example, after they have been trained, you could move data from your spreadsheets to the database one or two tables at a time. Once everyone has had a chance to become comfortable with the existing tables, you can more other spreadsheets over. A logical place to begin is to move customer contact data into the database.

It is worth noting that a spreadsheet and a database can be used alongside each other until all staff are comfortable. The most obvious method to achieve this would be to allow staff to make changes to the spreadsheet and then you can use these to update the database at regular intervals. This process can be achieved with a few simple steps, as follows:

1. Back up your database.

2. Import the changes from the spreadsheet into your database into a table with identically named columns to that of the table you wish to update. Here, we use an example of a table named Update_Customers to update the FirstName and LastName columns of the Customers table in the Cards for Everyone Inc. case study.

■ **Note**   Importing data into a database table is covered in the appendix to the book.

---

3. Create a relationship between the Update_Customers table and the Customers table using the unique identifiers.

■ **Note**   The creation of relationships between tables is covered in the appendix to the book.

---

4. Use a query to select the rows from the table you wish to update. In this case, your query would look like Figure 20-1.

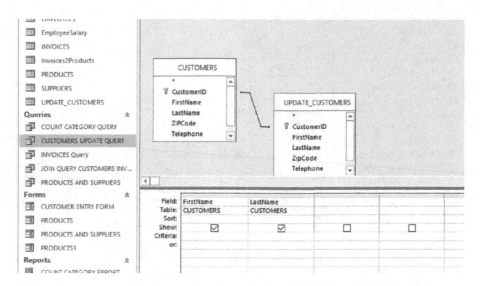

Figure 20-1. Query showing the FirstName and LastName columns of the Customers table in the Cards for Everyone Inc. database

---

■ **Note**   Creating a simple query is covered in the appendix to the book.

---

5. Run the query (using "!" on the Design tab) and make sure that the returned rows are the ones you want to update.

6. If all is well, you can convert your query to an Update query. To do this, select the Design tab and then select Update from the Query Type area of the top toolbar. You will see the Update To row appear in the grid at the bottom of your query design.

7. To update values in the FirstName and LastName columns of your Customers table to match those of the Update_Customers table, place the corresponding column references:

    [UPDATE_CUSTOMERS].[FirstName]

    [UPDATE_CUSTOMERS].[LastName]

    in the Update To part of the grid, as shown in Figure 20-2.

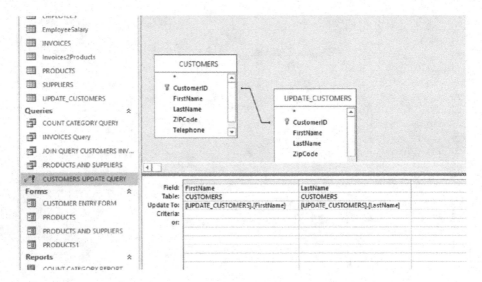

Figure 20-2. Update query renewing the FirstName and LastName columns of the Customers table with the corresponding columns of the Update_Customers table

8.   Run the query in the usual way. You will asked if you are sure you want to update the rows. Also, your database may have been "disabled" if you have not set up a safe area for it and, if so, you will need to "enable" it using the button that appears on the message bar.

This method allows your spreadsheets to keep operating as normal. At the same time, the staff can open the database to see how the data is stored and become familiar with how to access it. You can then set a deadline for the final switchover from the spreadsheets to the database.

The Bigger Picture

Staff training involves more than teaching the staff to operate the database directly. The subject of databases, as you have seen in this book, covers many aspects of data handling and database management: someone in your team must always be trained to take responsibility. However, most staff members will not need to be trained in all these skills. For example, there is no need to teach data analysis to a member of staff who will be collecting and entering data. As a recap, the basic areas covered in the book are:

- Data protection laws and data security

- Data collection

- Data cleansing

- Database maintenance
- Searching the database
- Analyzing your data
- Writing reports
- Acting on reports
- Acting on outside requests for data
- Archiving the database
- Searching online databases

You need to determine who requires which aspect of training. However, anyone handling personal data will need to be aware of data protection laws and will need to know how to set a strong password.

You also need to provide strong guidance about data entry. Where there is scope to make errors, you need to provide specific instructions so that everyone is behaving consistently. For example, everyone should be clear about how to handle issues such as missing values so that the data is unambiguous. For example, in the case of entering the State part of someone's address, using the term "None" to signify missing data is confusing, as it could signify that a customer lives abroad. An entry such as "Not Known" would be more appropriate.

When several members of staff are entering data, such as in the case study of Connecting South Side, it is useful to have a column that links the staff member's initials to the record. Everyone will then know which member of the team to contact in regard to the enquiry. Also, anyone tasked with cleansing the data will be able to spot where mistakes are being made frequently and by whom and will be able to provide feedback.

Case Study: Types of Staff Training for Connecting South Side

The following example shows how training requirements can be focused on different members of staff. The necessary training is assessed by each bullet point in the previous section in turn:

- ***Data protection laws and data security:*** Should be covered by everyone. This is particularly pertinent for Connecting South Side, which stores personal data about the lives of its enquirers.

- **Data collection:** Almost all team members are involved in data collection, as they take enquiries and create database records directly from them.

- **Data cleansing:** This should be covered by all staff who have contact with the database, as anyone inputting data must be aware that the quality of their work is highly important. Someone will need to be responsible for cleansing the database directly and will need training in the relevant techniques. Another member of staff will be required as a backup.

- **Database maintenance:** There must be one person in the office each day who carries out the necessary database maintenance, such as backing up the database. This means that one person should take the primary responsibility, with someone else able to step in if necessary, such as in cases of vacation, illness, or departure.

- **Searching the database:** All staff at Connecting South Side need to be able to search the enquirer database in order to find current cases. It is also important to identify previous cases that are similar to current ones so as to avoid redundant work. These skills could be acquired by one or two members of the team to begin with, but should ultimately become second nature to everyone.

- **Analyzing the data:** Usually only the manager needs to be able to analyze the data, as he or she will be writing the reports. However, in the case of an emergency, it is essential that another member of staff has enough training to step in. The reports are essential to the work of Connecting South Side, both to let relevant bodies know that the aims and objectives of current funding are being met and to help create bids for future grants.

- **Writing reports:** Again, in most circumstances, only the manager needs to be able to write reports. However, a backup person is needed if the manager becomes unavailable for any reason.

- *Acting on reports:* Chapter 15 showed that acting on reports requires making fundamental changes to the database. This needs far more skill than is necessary to operate the database on a daily basis. It would be unlikely that anyone other than the manager, who is assumed to have designed and implemented the database, would be trained highly enough to act on reports, although it would be prudent for another member of staff to learn the relevant skills.

- *Acting on outside requests:* Chapter 16 demonstrated that members of staff who are skilled at searching and designing queries could handle outside requests for information. It would not be necessary for everyone to have this degree of training but, as such requests will probably come in daily, at least one member of staff present in the office each day should have received the required training.

- *Archiving the database:* As with maintenance, one full-time (or equivalent) member of staff will need to be responsible for archiving the database as part of their duties and one full-time (or equivalent) backup member.

- *Searching online databases:* All members of staff need to be able to search online databases for information about organizations that can help the enquirers.

Summary

Tailored staff training is essential if your database is to be adopted successfully. Staff will vary in their responsibilities and their pace of learning. By providing a combination of presentations, hands-on tutorials, documentation, recorded material, and a test database, your staff will learn the necessary skills at a reasonable rate.

Appendix

The purpose of this appendix is to cover the first steps for:

- Creating a database
- Creating a table
- Sorting a column of data in a table
- Creating relationships between tables
- Creating a query
- Creating forms and reports
- Using external data

Two database packages will be used to demonstrate these operations: MS Access 2013 and LibreOffice 5 Base. Both packages are very straightforward for beginners, as almost no knowledge of programming is required. This is not the case for all databases: for example, MySQL is a popular database package but requires a solid understanding of the SQL programming language, which is not covered here.

MS Access 2013 has been used to provide examples throughout this book. It was chosen as it is well-used and therefore familiar. MS Access once came with MS Office, but this is no longer the case unless you buy the more expensive packages. LibreOffice is free and serves just as well.

This appendix is designed to introduce you to the basic functionality of a database. It is not intended to be comprehensive and should be regarded as filling in the steps that come before the database examples described in the book, and enable you to construct and use the databases. MS Access and LibreOffice both provide help guides that can take you beyond the basic information provided here.

The two packages have many similarities and in some sections will be considered side by side. You may be surprised at how similar the two packages are.

Creating a Database from Scratch

As with any word processor file or spreadsheet, you need to be able to create a new file. MS Access 2013 and LibreOffice 5 Base provide templates to help you. However, here we explain how to create a database from scratch.

MS Access 2013

To begin, double-click on the Access icon. Figure A-1 shows part of the output that will appear.

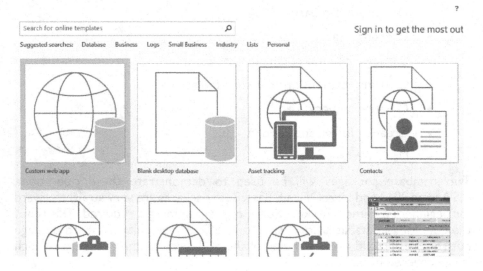

Figure A-1. Initial MS Access 2013 interface

Click on Blank Desktop Database (the second icon from the top left).

Type a name for your database in the File Name box that appears, as shown in Figure A-2.

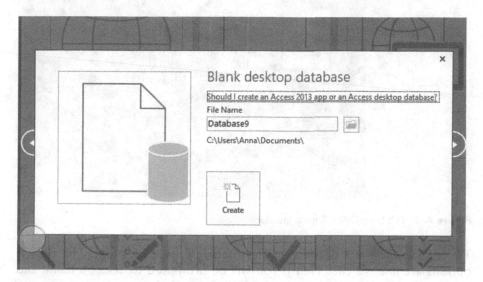

Figure A-2. The File Name box for your new database in MS Access 2013

You can use the default location that Access shows below the File Name box or click the folder icon to choose one.

Click Create. You will be presented with a new MS Access 2013 database with a new table. Note the tabs along the top: Home, Create, External Data, and Database Tools. These will be referred to throughout this chapter. Tables are discussed in the next main section.

LibreOffice 5 Base

Double-click the LibreOffice icon. Click the Base Database icon from the menu on the left, as shown in Figure A-3. The Database Wizard will open.

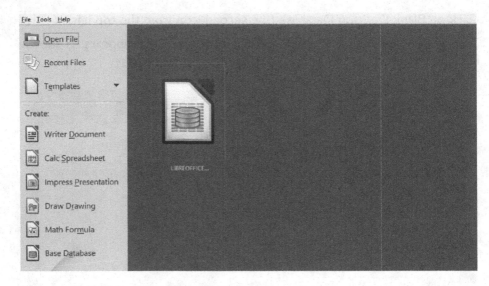

Figure A-3. The LibreOffice 5 main interface

The default option is to create a new database, so click Next. The default options are fine, so click Finish. You will be prompted to select a name and location for the new database, as shown in Figure A-4.

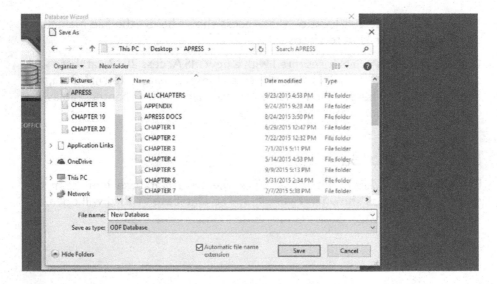

Figure A-4. Select a name and location for your new database in LibreOffice 5 Base

Click Save.

The database interface will open with three panels:

- **The Database Panel** is where you find the database objects
- **The Tasks Panel** is where you see the possible tasks for each object
- **The Main Work Area** changes according to the selection in the Database panel

Creating a Table

Tables were introduced in Chapter 7. Figure A-5, restated from Chapter 7, shows how to set the data types for the Customers table in the Cards for Everyone Inc. database. Figure A-6, also restated from Chapter 7, shows the Customers table populated with three items. This section covers how to create a table, which is the step prior to setting the data types and adding data.

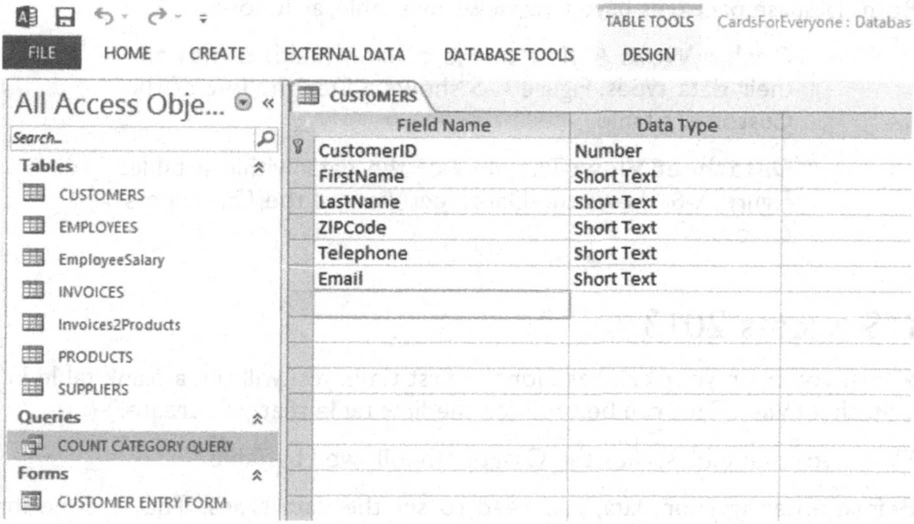

Figure A-5. Setting data types for a new table in MS Access 2013

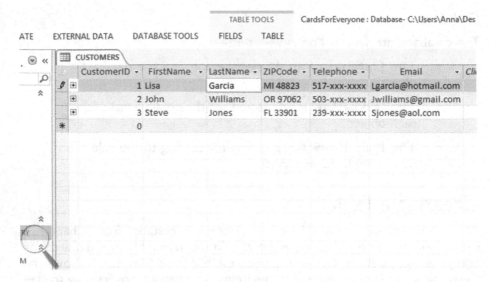

Figure A-6. Adding data to a new table in MS Access 2013

Both database packages have two views of a table, as follows:

- **Design View:** A view of the column (field) names and their data types. Figure A-5 shows a Design View of the Customers table.

- **Datasheet View:** The view of the data within a table. Figure A-6. shows the Datasheet View of the Customers table.

MS Access 2013

When you open your database for the first time, you will see a blank table in Datasheet View. This can be used for the first table that you create.

When you add tables, click the Create tab followed by Table.

Before entering your data, you need to set the data types. This is done in Design View, which you can access by clicking the Home tab and then choosing View and then Design View.

■ **Note** From now on, sequences of actions will take the following format: HOME ➤ View ➤ Design View.

Name the table in the Save As box.

You are now ready to set the types of your columns, as shown in Figure A-5.

The data types are selected by clicking in the relevant cell and using the drop-down menu. When you have chosen your data types, choose Home ➤ View ➤ Datasheet View and type in your data as shown in Figure A-6.

As you learned in Chapter 7, you need a unique identifier (also known as the primary key) for your table. Here, CustomerID has been chosen. You can see that CustomerID is the primary key by the key symbol beside it in Design View (shown in Figure A-5). You can set a different row as the unique identifier by:

1. Highlighting the row (by clicking on the area to the left of the Field Name column)

2. Right-clicking the highlighted area and selecting Primary Key from the drop-down menu that appears

3. Save your table when you have finished adding columns and data. You can do this by using Ctrl+S.

LibreOffice Base 5

Choose Table from the Database area.

From the Tasks panel, select Create Table in Design View. (You can use the Wizard to create the table if you prefer and follow the instructions.)

Use the Design View to type in the names of your columns and their data types. A drop-down menu of data types will appear in the Data Type column if you click on a cell. Choose the type that best fits your data.

You will now need to set a unique identifier (otherwise known as the primary key). To do this:

1. Highlight the row (or rows) that will make up the unique identifier by clicking in the area to the left of the Field Name column

2. Right-click the highlighted row and select Primary Key from the bottom of the menu that appears

3. Give the table a name and save the design using Ctrl+S.

When you close the Design View you will see your table toward the bottom of the Tasks panel. Double-click on the table to open it in Datasheet View. You can then add your data.

Relationships Between Tables

Relationships were introduced in Chapter 7. The simplest relationship is a one-to-one relationship. The example given in Chapter 7 was between Employees and EmployeeSalary, and is restated in Figure A-7. The type of relationship—whether it be one-to-one, one-to-many, or many-to-many—is created automatically by the database package. The following two sections explain a step-to-step procedure for creating relationships between tables in MS Access 2013 and LibreOffice 5 Base.

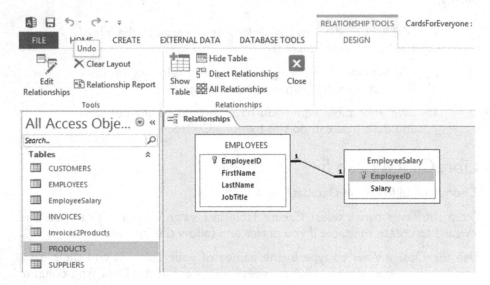

Figure A-7. A one-to-one relationship between tables

MS Access 2013

Click on the Database Tools tab. Click on Relationships.

To add new tables to the relationships area, right-click on any empty space, select Show Table from the menu that appears, and select a relevant table. Then click Add. Keep adding tables until you are finished. Then click Close.

If you want to remove any table from the relationships area, right-click on the top of it and choose Hide Table from the menu.

When creating a relationship, drag from a chosen column of one table (often the unique identifier) to a matching column in the related table. A dialog box will appear enabling you to set criteria such as Cascade Delete, as shown in Figure A-8.

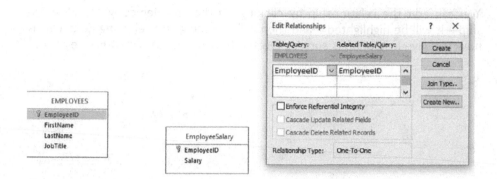

Figure A-8. Creating a relationship between two tables in MS Access 2013

You can remove the relationship by clicking on the line depicting the relationship—it will be highlighted—and then right-clicking and selecting Delete, as shown in Figure A-9.

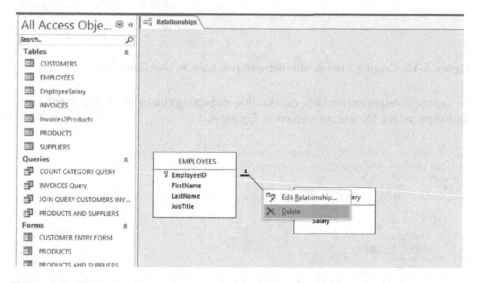

Figure A-9. Deleting a relationship between tables in MS Access 2013

LibreOffice 5 Base

Click on the Tools tab. Select Relationships from the menu that appears. From the Add Tables dialog box, double-click on each table of interest. Click the Close button.

When creating a relationship, you drag from on column (often the unique identifier) of one table to a matching column in the related table.

You can edit the relationship by clicking on the line depicting the relation-ship—it will be highlighted—and then right-clicking and selecting Edit. This is how you give instructions such as Delete Cascade, as shown in Figure A-10.

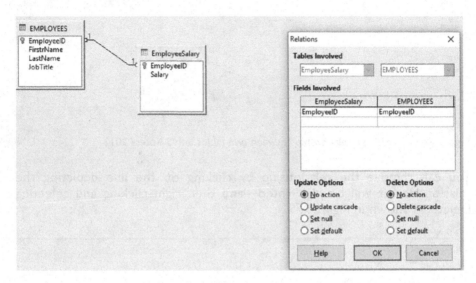

Figure A-10. Creating a relationship between two tables in LibreOffice 5 Base

To delete a relationship, click on the line depicting the relationship, right-click, and then select Delete, as shown in Figure A-11.

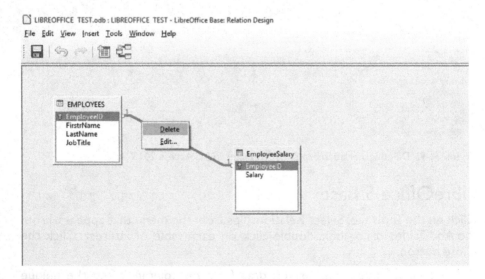

Figure A-11. Deleting a relationship between tables in Libre Office 5 Base

Sorting the Data in a Column

Sorting a column of data in a table was explained in Chapter 12. The most straightforward way to accomplish this in either database package is to open your table in Datasheet View and then follow these steps.

In MS Access 2013:

1. Right-click any cell in the column of data you wish to sort
2. Select Sort A to Z or Sort Z to A from the menu that appears

In LibreOffice 5 Base:

1. Highlight the whole column you wish to sort by clicking its name at the top
2. From the toolbar at the top, select one of the two sort options, either ascending sort (A above Z with a down-ward arrow alongside) or descending sort (Z above A with a downward arrow alongside)

Queries

The purpose of this section is to demonstrate how to set up and run a query in MS Access 2013 and LibreOffice 5 Base. Chapter 1 introduced a query that counted the number of cards of each category. This is shown again in Figure A-12. After reading this section, you will be able to set up this query and run it, producing the output shown in Figure A-12.

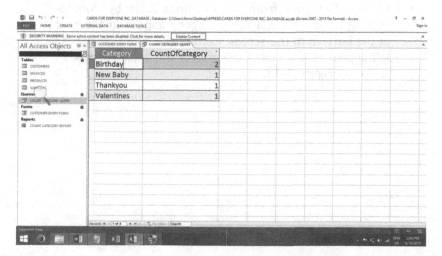

Figure A-12. Sample query from the Cards for Everyone Inc. database

This query involves two steps:

- Grouping the categories of the cards.

- Counting the number of cards in each group.

As with tables, queries can be viewed in Datasheet View (which is the output of a query, as shown in Figure A-12) and in Design View.

Examples of queries are introduced throughout the book. In each case, the design of the query is shown as well as the output. This means that if you know how to set up a query, you will be able to run all of the examples.

To learn about instructions that are not covered in the book, such as the range of instructions you can use as functions/criteria, go to the help pages of either MS Access 2013 or LibreOffice 5 Base and you will find a comprehensive list.

Queries are handled in a similar way by both database packages. In either package, you can save the query so that it is available for later use.

Designing and Running a Query in MS Access 2013

To open Design View for queries:

- Click the Create tab.

- From the Queries area, choose Query Design. (If you prefer, you can choose the Queries Wizard and follow the instructions.)

- Choose Products from the Show Table box by double-clicking on it and closing the box.

- Choose Category from the Products table by double-clicking on it. You will see Category appear in the grid at the bottom of the screen. Each of the labels on the far left applies to the cell in the grid of the adjacent row, as shown in Figure A-13.

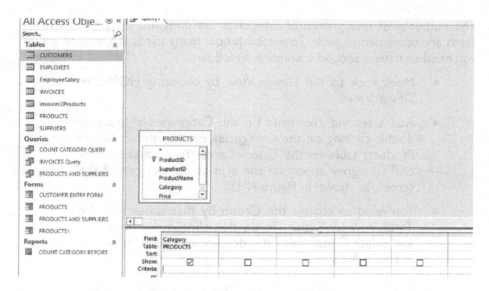

Figure A-13. The first step of query design in MS Access 2013 for the query shown in Figure A-12

To instruct the query to group the categories, select the Design tab followed by Σ (Totals). You will see a Totals section appear in the grid, which defaults to Group By. This is the command you are looking for.

To run the query, select the Design table followed by Run (depicted by a red exclamation point, "!"). This produces the output shown in Figure A-14.

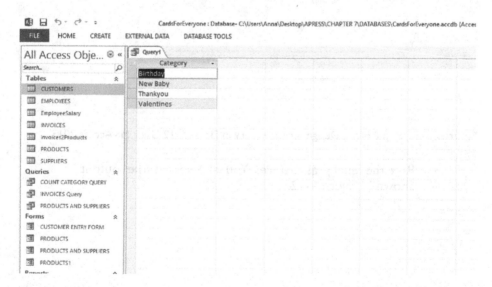

Figure A-14. Output from Step 1 of the query in Figure A-12 using MS Access 2013

The output gives four groups of categories but does not tell you how many cards are contained in each. To establish how many cards are in each group, you need to issue a second command, as follows:

- Move back to the Design View by choosing HOME ➤ Design View.

- Add a second command on the Categories column by double-clicking on the Categories column shown in the Products table on the Queries area. You will see a second Category appear in the grid at the bottom of the screen, as shown in Figure A-15.

- You need to change the Group By that appears in the Totals row to Count. To do this, click in the Totals cell and select Count from the drop-down menu, as shown in Figure A-15.

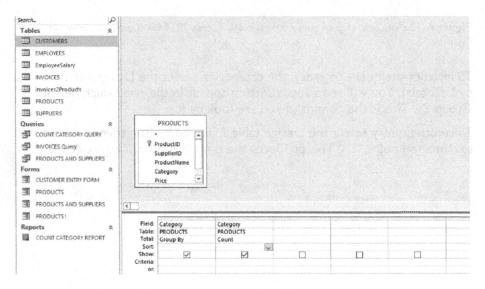

Figure A-15. Step 2 of the Design for the Query in Figure A-12 Using MS Access 2013

- Run the query as before. You should get the output shown in Figure A-12.

Designing and Running a Query in LibreOffice 5 Base

To open Design View for queries, follow these steps:

- From the main window, click on the Queries icon from the list on the left.

- Select Create Query in Design View. (You can also use the Query Wizard; it's self-explanatory. SQL View is beyond the scope of the book as the book doesn't cover the SQL language.)

- Choose Products from the Show Table box by double-clicking on it and closing the box.

- Select Category from the Products table by double-clicking on it. You will see Category appear in the grid at the bottom of the screen. Each of the labels on the far left applies to the cell in the grid of the adjacent row, as shown in Figure A-16.

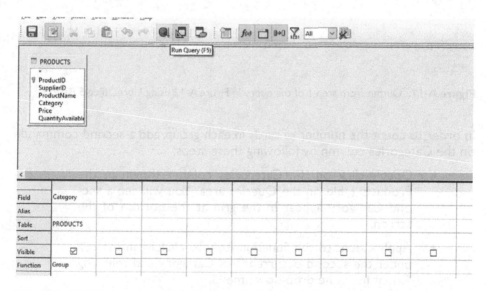

Figure A-16. The first step of query design in LibreOffice 5 Base for the query in Figure A-12

To instruct the query to group the categories, follow these steps:

- Click on the Function cell of the query grid.
- Select Group from the drop-down menu.

To run the query, click the icon shown in Figure A-16. You should get the output shown in Figure A-17.

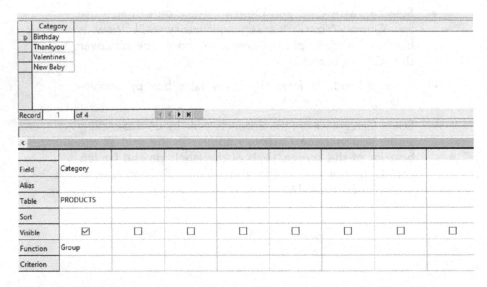

Figure A-17. Output from step 1 of the query in Figure A-12 using LibreOffice 5 Base

In order to count the number of cards in each group, add a second command on the Categories column by following these steps:

- Double-click on the Categories column shown in the Products table on the Queries area. You will see a second Category appear in the grid at the bottom of the screen.

- Apply Count to the Function Row by clicking in the cell under the second occurrence of Category and selecting Count from the drop-down menu.

Your Design View should look like the one shown in Figure A-18.

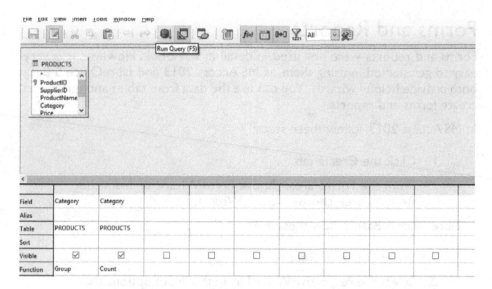

Figure A-18. Step 2 of the design for the query in Figure A-12 using LibreOffice 5 Base

When you run the Design View, you will get the output shown in Figure A-19, which corresponds to the output (from MS Access 2013) shown in Figure A-12.

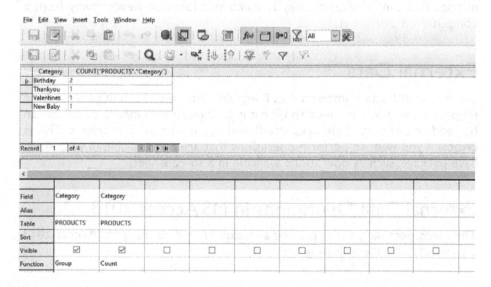

Figure A-19. Output in LibreOffice 5 Base from running the query in Figure A-18

Forms and Reports

Forms and reports were not used in detail in this book. However, it is very easy to get started in using them, as MS Access 2013 and LibreOffice 5 Base both provide helpful wizards. You can use the data from tables and queries to create forms and reports.

In MS Access 2013, follow these steps:

1. Click the Create tab.

2. From the Forms area, choose Form Wizard or from the Reports area, choose Report Wizard.

In LibreOffice 5 Base, follow these steps:

1. Select Forms or Reports.

2. Select the respective Wizard from the list of options that appears.

You can produce forms based on more than one table which can be useful both for inputting data into several tables and for searching data across the database. Reports enable a document to be designed from database tables or queries that can be shared easily in electronic form or viewed away from a computer on a printout.

External Data

Using external data is important as it enables data to be read in to a database (imported) without the need to type it in by hand. It also means that data can be read out of a database (exported) without the need to retype it. This is critical if you want to perform operations that are not available in your database package, such as operations available in a spreadsheet.

External Data Operations in MS Access 2013

The steps necessary for importing and exporting data using MS Access 2013 are discussed in the following sections.

Importing Data

To move data into your database (from another database or a spreadsheet for example), follow these steps:

- Click the External Data tab on the top toolbar.

- In the Import & Link section, click the data format you'll be importing from. If you don't see the right format, click More. You can import tables from other Access databases and data from Excel spreadsheets, among many others.

Follow the instructions in the Get External Data dialog box, as shown in Figure A-20. You can append data to an existing table or create an entirely new table. Your file must have the same column headings as the table that you are importing from. Also, you mustn't violate the unique identifier (primary key) by duplicating any values.

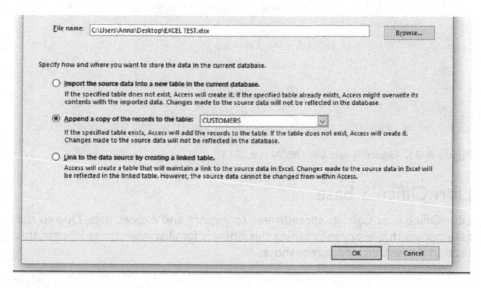

Figure A-20. Importing data into MS Access 2013

Exporting Data

To move data out of your database (to another database or a spreadsheet for example), follow these steps:

- Highlight the database object that you wish to export from the left side list by clicking on it once.

- Click the External Data tab on the top toolbar.

- Select the type of file you are exporting to from the Export part of the toolbar.

- Select your destination file.

- Follow the instructions.

Figure A-21 shows an example of exporting the Products table from the Cards for Everyone Inc. database to an MS Excel file.

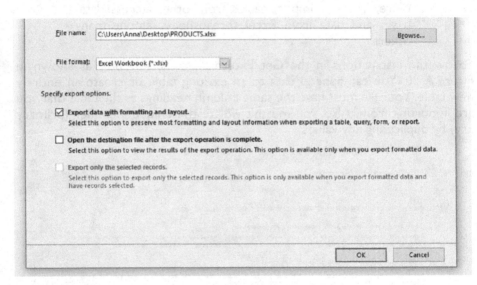

Figure A-21. Exporting data from MS Access 2013

LibreOffice 5 Base

LibreOffice uses Calc, its spreadsheet, to import and export data. Due to the assumption that everyone reading this book is familiar with spreadsheets, this section doesn't include screenshots.

Importing Data

To move data into your database (from another database or a spreadsheet for example), you must first import the data into Calc. Calc accepts text files such as comma-separated .CSV files. These can be opened in Calc by choosing File ➤ Open.

Make sure that the column headings of the file from which you are importing data match the column headings of the database object into which it is being moved.

- Open a Base file of the database type that you want.

- Either create a new Base file using the Database Wizard or open an existing Base file that is not read-only.

- Open the Calc file that contains the data to be imported to Base.

- Select the data to be copied to Base, including the column names on the first row.

- Select Edit ➤ Copy.

- In the Base window, click Tables to view the tables.

- In the Base window, select Edit ➤ Paste.

The Copy Table dialog appears. You will probably want to check the Create Primary Key box.

Exporting Data in Base

To move data out of your database (to another database or a spreadsheet for example), follow these steps:

- Open the database file that contains the database table or query to be exported.

- In Calc, choose File ➤ New ➤ Spreadsheet.

- In the Base window, right-click the name of the table to export and choose Copy.

- Click cell AI in the new Calc window then choose Edit ➤ Paste.

- Now save or export the data to the file type of your choice.

Summary

This appendix has filled the gap between the examples presented in the book and the steps needed to create a database, a table, and a query from scratch. The appendix also addressed table relationships, how to sort a column in a table, and how to import and export data. It also mentioned the creation of forms and reports using a wizard. Two database packages, MS Access 2013 and LibreOffice 5 Base, were used as examples.

Index

Get the eBook for only $5!

Why limit yourself?

Now you can take the weightless companion with you wherever you go and access your content on your PC, phone, tablet, or reader.

Since you've purchased this print book, we're happy to offer you the eBook in all 3 formats for just $5.

Convenient and fully searchable, the PDF version enables you to easily find and copy code—or perform examples by quickly toggling between instructions and applications. The MOBI format is ideal for your Kindle, while the ePUB can be utilized on a variety of mobile devices.

To learn more, go to www.apress.com/companion or contact support@apress.com.

Other Apress Titles You Will Find Useful

Beginning Database Design, 2ⁿᵈ Edition
Churcher
978-1-4302-4209-3

Oracle Core: Essential Internals for DBAs and Developers
Lewis
978-1-4302-3954-3

Database Systems
Foster / Godbole
978-1-4842-0878-6

Practical Oracle Database Appliance
Curtis/Arshad/Benner/Elsins/
Gallagher/Sharman/Velikanov
978-1-4302-6265-7

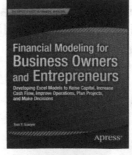

Financial Modeling for Business Owners and Entrepreneurs
Sawyer
978-1-4842-0371-2

Beginning Oracle Database 12c Administration
Fernandez
978-1-4842-0194-7

10 Don'ts on Your Digital Devices
Bachrach / Rzeszut
978-1-4842-0368-2

PeopleSoft for the Oracle DBA, 2ⁿᵈ Edition
Kurtz
978-1-4302-3707-5

Pro PowerShell for Database Developers
Cafferky
978-1-484205-42-6

Available at www.apress.com